Rhetorical Grammar

Grammatical Choices, Rhetorical Effects

FIFTH EDITION

Martha Kolln

The Pennsylvania State University

Pearson
Education

New York San Francisco Boston
London Toronto Sydney Tokyo Singapore Madrid
Mexico City Munich Paris Cape Town Hong Kong Montreal

Senior Sponsoring Editor: Virignia Blanford
Executive Marketing Manager: Megan Galvin
Production Manager: Ellen MacElree
Project Coordination, Text Design, and Electronic Page Makeup: Electronic
   Publishing Services Inc., NYC
Cover Design Manager: Wendy Ann Fredericks
Cover Designer: Kay Petronio
Cover Art: © Ryan McVay/Photodisc/Getty
Senior Manufacturing Buyer: Al Dorsey
Printer and Binder: Courier/Stoughton
Cover Printer: Phoenix Color Corp.

Library of Congress Cataloging-in-Publication Data

Kolln, Martha.
   Rhetorical grammar : grammatical choices, rhetorical effects / Martha Kolln.-- 5th ed.
      p. cm.
   Includes bibliographical references and index.
   ISBN 0-321-39723-1
   1. English language--Rhetoric. 2. English language--Grammar. I. Title.
   PE1408.K696 2006
   808'.042--dc22

                                             2006002721

Copyright © 2007 by Pearson Education, Inc.

Please visit our website at http://www.ablongman.com

ISBN 0–321–39723–1

1 2 3 4 5 6 7 8 9 10—CRS—09 08 07 06

Contents

PART II
Connecting with the Reader

Chapter 4
Cohesion   63

Chapter 5
Sentence Rhythm   89

Chapter 6
The Writer's Voice   107

PART III
Making Choices

Chapter 7
Choosing Verbs   129

Chapter 8
Choosing Adverbials   149

Chapter 9
Choosing Adjectivals **172**

Chapter 10
Choosing Stylistic Variations **210**

PART IV
Your Way with Words

Chapter 11
Word Classes   233

Chapter 12
Pronouns   250

PART V
Punctuation

Chapter 13
Punctuation: Its Purposes, Its Hierarchy, and Its Rhetorical Effects   270

Preface

Grammatical choices. Rhetorical effects. These two phrases tell the story of rhetorical grammar, the marriage of grammar and rhetoric for the composition classroom. Writers who recognize the choices available to them will be well-equipped for controlling the effects of their words. As I explain to students in the Introduction,

> To study grammar in this way—that is, to consider the conscious knowledge of sentence structure as your toolkit—is the essence of rhetorical grammar.

But is there really a place for the study of grammar in the composition class? Is there time for grammar in a syllabus already filled with prewriting, drafting, and revising and with reading what others have written? The answer is "yes." In fact you are already spending time on grammar—when you discuss cohesion and transition; when you explain in a conference why a structure is misplaced or awkward; when you help students understand the effects of certain words on the reader; when you point out redundancy; when you suggest sentence revision; when you praise gems of precision. These are principles of grammar and style and revision that are now part of your writing class. *Rhetorical Grammar: Grammatical Choices, Rhetorical Effects* will help you teach these and many more such principles—and it will do so in a systematic way.

And while the book is addressed to student writers in the composition classroom, I am gratified to know that it is also being used successfully in grammar courses for teacher preparation. In addition to the basics of grammar, those future language arts teachers will gain valuable insight into the teaching of writing.

You'll discover that the lessons in this book are not the definitions and categories and rules of traditional grammar that your students encountered back in middle school. Rather, *Rhetorical Grammar* brings together the insights of composition researchers and linguists; it makes the connection between writing and grammar that has been missing from our classrooms. It also avoids the prescriptive rules and error correction of handbooks, offering instead explanations of the rhetorical choices that are available. And, perhaps what is most important, it gives students confidence in their own language ability by helping them recognize the intuitive grammar expertise that all human beings share.

This difference in the purpose of *Rhetorical Grammar* is especially important. Too often the grammar lessons that manage to find their way into the writing classroom are introduced for remedial purposes: to fix comma splices and misplaced modifiers and agreement errors and such. As a consequence, the study of grammar has come to have strictly negative, remedial associations—a Band-Aid for weak and inexperienced writers, rather than a rhetorical tool that all writers should understand and control.

This book, then, substitutes for that negative association of grammar a positive and functional point of view—a rhetorical view: that an understanding of grammar is an important tool for the writer; that it can be taught and learned successfully if it is done in the right way and in the right place, in connection with composition. The book can also stimulate class discussion on such issues as sentence focus and rhythm, cohesion, reader expectation, paraphrase, diction, revision—discussions of rhetorical and stylistic issues that will be meaningful throughout the writing process. And the students will learn to apply these grammar concepts to their own writing. This is the kind of knowledge—this toolkit of conscious grammar understanding—that will support not only their academic career but their lifelong literacy as well.

For this new edition, I have tried to look at every topic, every explanation and description, through the eyes of the novice reader; and I have listened carefully to the suggestions of the reviewers. This scrutiny has resulted in refinements of the discussions and activities as well as major changes:

- A reordering of chapters, to group them in a more logical order.
- Added sections on Repetition, Metaphor, The Overuse of Metadiscourse, and Our Versatile Verbs.
- Enhanced explanations and practice on the passive voice.
- New examples from written sources.
- Added suggestions for class discussions.
- The transfer of the appositives and absolute phrases from their former chapter to the chapters covering adjectivals and stylistic variations respectively.

The reorganized chapters begin with three that cover the basics of sentence structure, including the use of the bare-bones patterns in prose and coordination, followed by three chapters that connect the writer and reader. Here, then, is the new arrangement with their section headings:

Part I: Understanding Basic Sentences

1. The Structure of Sentences
2. The Basic Sentences in Prose
3. Coordination

Part II: Connecting with the Reader

4. Cohesion
5. Sentence Rhythm
6. The Writer's Voice

Part III: Making Choices

7. Choosing Verbs
8. Choosing Adverbials
9. Choosing Adjectivals
10. Choosing Stylistic Variations

Part IV: Your Way with Words

11. Word Classes
12. Pronouns

Part V: Punctuation

13. Punctuation: Its Purposes, Its Hierarchy, and Its Rhetorical Effects

The opening Chapter Preview and the closing sections—Key Terms, Rhetorical Reminders, and Punctuation Reminders—help the students organize and review the material. The Glossary of Terms helps them with what is bound to be a new vocabulary; the Index directs them to other places where topics are mentioned or discussed. The self-instructional quality of the earlier editions has been retained, with the inclusion of answers to the odd-numbered items in the exercises in a section at the back of the book.

The primary focus throughout the book remains on revision and style, on the importance to students of understanding the writer's tools.

Depending on the goals of your course, you may find that *Rhetorical Grammar* is the only text your students need; on the other hand, it can certainly work well in conjunction with a reader or rhetoric. In either case, you'll discover that class time can be used much more efficiently when your students come to class with the shared background that the text provides. The *Instructors Manual* includes answers to the even-numbered items in the exercises, further explanations of grammatical principles, and suggestions for class activities.

ACKNOWLEDGMENTS

I am grateful to the following reviewers of the fifth edition of *Rhetorical Grammar,* who have helped me shape this new edition with their generous comments and valuable suggestions:

    Avon Crismore, Indiana University Purdue

    John Crow, University of South Florida

    Bonnnie Devet, College of Charleston

    David Flanagan, Ithaca College

    Sara Garnes, Ohio State University

    Joan Livingston-Weber, Western Illinois University

    Fridel Wiant, University of San Francisco

I extend sincere thanks and welcome to my new editor and friend, Ginny Blanford.

—*Martha Kolln*

Introduction

WHAT IS RHETORICAL GRAMMAR?

To understand the subject matter of a book with the title *Rhetorical Grammar,* you'll obviously have to understand not only the meaning of both *rhetoric* and *grammar* but also their relationship to each other. *Grammar* is undoubtedly familiar to you. You've probably been hearing about, if not actually studying, grammar in your English classes since middle school. *Rhetoric,* on the other hand—and its adjective version, *rhetorical*—may not be familiar at all. So, to figure out what rhetorical grammar is all about, we'll begin with the familiar *grammar.*

If you're like many students, you may associate the idea of grammar with rules—various do's and don'ts that apply to sentence structure and punctuation. You may remember studying certain rules to help you correct or prevent errors in your writing. You may remember the grammar handbook as the repository of such rules.

But now consider another possibility: that YOU are the repository of the rules. You—not a book. Consider that there is stored within you, in your computer-like brain, a system of rules, a system that enables you to create the sentences of your native language. The fact that you have such an internalized system means that when you study grammar *you are studying what you already "know."*

Linguistic researchers[1] now tell us that you began internalizing the rules of your language perhaps before you were born, when you began to differentiate the particular rhythms of the language you were hearing. In the

---

[1] See the section on Language Development in the Bibliography.

first year of life you began to create the rules that would eventually produce sentences.

You were little more than a year old when you began to demonstrate your grammar ability by naming things around you; a few months later you were putting together two- and three-word strings, and before long your language took on the features of adult sentences. No one taught you. You didn't have language lessons. You learned all by yourself, from hearing the language spoken around you—and you did so unconsciously.

This process of language development is universal—that is, it occurs across cultures, and it occurs in every child with normal physical and mental development. No matter what your native language is, you have internalized its grammar system. By the time you were five or six years old, you were an expert at narrating events, at asking questions, at describing people and places, probably at arguing. The internalized system of rules that accounts for this language ability of yours is our definition of *grammar.*

When you study grammar in school, then, you are actually studying what you already "know." Note that the verb *know* needs those quotation marks because we're not using it in the usual sense. Your grammar knowledge is largely subconscious: You don't know consciously what you "know." When you study grammar you are learning *about* those grammar rules that you use subconsciously every time you speak—as well as every time you listen and make sense of what you hear.

But as you know, studying grammar also means learning other rules, the conventions of writing—rules that have nothing to do with the internalized rules that enable us to speak. When you write, you must pay attention to rules about paragraphing and sentence completeness and capital letters and quotation marks and apostrophes and commas and, perhaps the trickiest of all, spelling.

To be effective, however, writing also requires attention to rhetoric—and here is where the adjective *rhetorical* comes into the picture. *Rhetoric* means that your audience—the reader—and your purpose make a difference in the way you write on any given topic. To a great extent, that rhetorical situation—the audience, purpose, and topic—determines the grammatical choices you make, choices about sentence structure and vocabulary, even punctuation. Rhetorical grammar is about those choices.

This meaning of *rhetoric* is easy to illustrate: Imagine writing a letter to your best friend describing your first week at school this semester; contrast that with the letter on the same subject to your great-aunt Millie. Think of the differences there might be in those two letters, those two different rhetorical situations. One obvious difference, of course, is vocabulary; you wouldn't use the same words with two such different audiences. The grammatical structures are also going to be different, determined in part by the tone or level of formality. For example, you might use longer sentences in the more formal version, the letter to Aunt Millie:

> My roommate, Peter Piper, is a very nice fellow from New York City.

> *or*

> My roommate, who grew up in New York City, is named Peter
> Piper.

In the letter to your buddy, you'd probably say,

> You'd like my roommate. He's a nice guy—from the Big Apple.
> And would you believe? His name is Peter Piper.

You would probably write this less formal version almost as easily as you speak; it sounds like something you'd say. The Aunt Millie letter, especially the sentence with the *who*-clause, would take a little more thought on your part. It doesn't sound as much like speech. In fact, a *who*-clause like that, set off by commas, is a modifier used almost exclusively in the written language.

Understanding rhetorical grammar, then, means understanding the grammatical choices available to you when you write and the rhetorical effects those choices will have on your reader. Aunt Millie will probably recognize—and approve of—your letter as evidence of a serious-minded, articulate student. She will feel assured that your twelve or more years of education have not been wasted. The good friend who gets your letter will hear your familiar voice and know that all is well.

You can think of the grammatical choices you have as tools in your writer's toolkit. You have a variety of tools for the differences in language that different rhetorical situations call for. To study grammar in this way— that is, to consider the conscious knowledge of sentence structure as your toolkit—is the essence of rhetorical grammar.

We begin this study of the tools by focusing, in Part I, on basic sentences, the structure of the sentence patterns, encouragement in using those simple sentences, and the system of coordinating sentences and their parts. In Part II you are encouraged to take the reader into account, with the connection of sentences in paragraphs, cohesion, sentence rhythm, and your writer's voice. Part III looks in more detail at sentence expansions.

In considering the words in Part IV, you will find yourself consulting— and appreciating—your subconscious language expertise in two chapters covering word classes and pronouns. The final chapter, in Part V, describes the purpose and hierarchy of punctuation. The Glossary of Punctuation that follows this chapter pulls together all of the punctuation rules you have studied in context throughout the book.

The Bibliography that follows the Glossary of Punctuation lists the works mentioned in the text, along with other books and articles on rhetoric and grammar. The future teachers among you will find them useful for research purposes and for your teaching preparation.

Throughout the book you will find exercises and issues for group discussion that you are encouraged to work on. Answers to the odd-numbered exercise items are included in the back of the book.

Be sure to use the Glossary of Terms and the Index if you are having problems understanding a concept. They are there to provide help.

CHAPTER 1

The Structure of Sentences

CHAPTER PREVIEW

In this chapter you will learn to think about a sentence as a series of slots, each of which has a particular role to play. Some of the slots are required and fairly stable, others optional and movable. Looking at sentence structure in this way should help you to appreciate both its systematic nature and its potential for variation. This grammar overview also gives you a vocabulary for thinking about sentences as you write and revise, a language for discussing language. The vocabulary will be useful throughout the book, where you will be learning about various tools for tinkering with the basic sentences you study in this chapter. And if your future plans include teaching, this overview of sentence structure, besides sharpening your own language skills, will help prepare you to help others understand and sharpen theirs.

THE TWO-PART SENTENCE

We begin this overview of grammar by looking at sentence structure in action, in the opening paragraph of an essay by Annie Dillard, a well-known essayist and observer of nature:

> A weasel is wild. Who knows what he thinks? He sleeps in his underground den, his tail draped over his nose. Sometimes he lives in his den for two days without leaving. Outside, he stalks rabbits, mice, muskrats, and birds, killing more bodies than he can eat warm, and often dragging the carcasses home. Obedient to instinct, he bites his prey at the neck, either splitting the

5

jugular vein at the throat or crunching the brain at the base of the skull, and he does not let go. One naturalist refused to kill a weasel who was socketed into his hand deeply as a rattlesnake. The man could in no way pry the tiny weasel off, and he had to walk half a mile to water, the weasel dangling from his palm, and soak him off like a stubborn label.

—Annie Dillard *(Teaching a Stone to Talk)*

Dillard's opening sentence couldn't be simpler. She has used a common **sentence pattern,**[1] "Something is something." You won't have to read far in most modern essays, or in this textbook, to find that use of *be* as a linking verb. (Notice the first sentence following the weasel quotation!)

Dillard could easily have come up with fancier words, certainly more scientific-sounding ones, if she had wanted to:

Scientists recognize the weasel, genus *Mustela,* as a wild creature. As with other wild animals, one can only speculate about the weasel's thinking process, if, indeed, animals do think in the accepted sense of the word.

Are you tempted to read on? (If you have to, maybe—if there's a weasel test coming up!) It's possible that some people might continue reading even if they didn't have to—weasel specialists, perhaps—but for the average reader, the effect of this stodgy rewrite is certainly different from the breezy

A weasel is wild. Who knows what he thinks?

Dillard's reader is likely to say, "Here comes an essay that promises a new glimpse of nature—one that I will understand and enjoy. It's written in my kind of language."

The linking-*be* sentence pattern provides a good illustration of both our subconscious grammar ability and the concept of rhetorical awareness, of recognizing the effect our sentences can have on readers. As native speakers, we learn to use *be,* including its irregular past forms *(was, were)* and its three present-tense forms *(am, are,* and *is),* perhaps without even realizing they are related to *be,* the form we call the **infinitive.**[2] If you are not a native speaker of English, you have probably spent a great deal of time learning the various forms of *be* and how they are used, just as native English speakers studying a foreign language must do when learning its equivalent of *be.*

---

[1]Words in boldface type are explained in the Glossary of Terms, beginning on page 293.

[2]The label *infinitive* describes the form of the verb that we use with *to: to be, to go, to have, to eat,* and so on. For verbs other than *be,* the infinitive form is identical to the present tense.

Before looking at all of the separate structures in the various patterns, we will examine the two major parts of every sentence: the **subject** and the **predicate.**

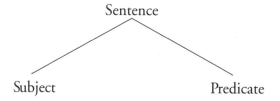

Sentence

Subject   Predicate

You probably know these labels from your study of grammar in middle school or high school. They name the functions of the two major slots of every sentence. The **subject,** as its name implies, is generally the topic of the sentence, the something or a someone that the sentence is about; the **predicate** is the point that is made about that topic. In the following sentences, you'll find a "something" or "someone" occupying the subject slot, so you will probably have no trouble recognizing the dividing line between the two basic parts:

1. A weasel is wild.
2. Tomatoes give me hives.
3. Jenny's sister graduated from nursing school.
4. Gino's father flew helicopters in Vietnam.
5. The gymnasium on our campus needs a new roof.

If you divided the sentences like this,

1. A weasel / is wild.
2. Tomatoes / give me hives.
3. Jenny's sister / graduated from nursing school.
4. Gino's father / flew helicopters in Vietnam.
5. The gymnasium on our campus / needs a new roof.

—and chances are good that you did—then you have recognized the two basic units of every sentence.

You were probably able to make the divisions between the subjects and predicates on the basis of meaning, by identifying what was being said about something or someone. But if you're not sure, you can use your grammar expertise to double check: Simply substitute a **pronoun** for the subject. That pronoun, you will discover, stands in for the entire subject slot:

He *(a weasel)* is wild. (*It* can also be used for animals.)
They *(tomatoes)* give me hives.

She *(Jenny's sister)* graduated from nursing school.

He *(Gino's father)* flew helicopters in Vietnam.

It *(the gymnasium on our campus)* needs a new roof.

Our automatic way of accessing pronouns provides a good illustration of our internalized system of grammar.

Another way to describe the two major sentence slots, the subject and the predicate, is according to the forms of the structures that fill them:

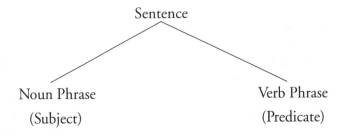

Sentence

Noun Phrase   Verb Phrase
(Subject)   (Predicate)

The term **phrase** refers to a word or group of words that acts as a unit. A **noun phrase** consists of a **headword** noun along with all of the words and phrases that modify—that describe or limit—it. In the following list of subject noun phrases from our five sample sentences, the headwords are underlined:

1. A <u>weasel</u>
2. <u>Tomatoes</u>
3. Jenny's <u>sister</u>
4. Gino's <u>father</u>
5. The <u>gymnasium</u> on our campus

The predicate in each of those five sentences is a **verb phrase** in form, as the predicate always is. Like the noun phase, the verb phrase is a unit with a headword—in this case, a verb. In the following list of verb phrases, the verb headword is underlined:

<u>is</u> wild

<u>give</u> me hives

<u>graduated</u> from nursing school

<u>flew</u> helicopters in Vietnam

<u>needs</u> a new roof

Remember that the term *predicate* refers to the whole verb phrase and the term *subject* to the whole noun phrase—not to just their headwords.

Note that we are using the word *phrase* even for a structure that consists of a single word, such as the subject "Tomatoes" in our second example. In the sentence "Babies cry," both the noun phrase and the verb phrase consist of single words.

Questions and Commands

This two-part structure—subject and predicate—underlies all of our sentences in English, even those in which the two parts may not be apparent at first glance. For example, in questions—also called **interrogative sentences**—the subject is sometimes located in the predicate half of the sentence; to discover the two parts, you have to recast the question in the form of a **declarative sentence,** or statement:

> *Question:* Which chapters will our test cover?
>
> *Statement:* Our test / will cover which chapters.

In the command, or **imperative sentence,** the subject—the "understood" *you*—generally doesn't show up at all; the form of the verb is always the infinitive, or base form:

(You)	Hold the onions!
(You)	Be a good sport.
(You)	Come with me to the concert.

Sometimes, for special emphasis, the *you* is included:

> You be nice to your sister.
>
> Don't you forget our date.

Questions and commands are certainly not structures to worry about: You've been an expert at asking questions and giving orders for many, many years.

THE EXPANDED VERB

In our five sample sentences, the underlined headword in each predicate is the complete verb, the simple **present** or simple **past tense:** *is, give, graduated, flew, needs.* As you probably know, however, many of the predicates we use in writing and speech include **auxiliary,** or **helping, verbs.** You'll find the auxiliary, sometimes more than one, in the position before the main verb. Here are some you have read in this chapter so far:

> In this chapter you *will* learn to think about …
>
> Note that we *are* using the word *phrase* …
>
> Here are some you *have* read in this chapter so far.

And in the following example, there are two auxiliaries, in this case separated by the adverb *easily:*

Dillard <u>*could*</u> easily <u>*have* come up</u> with fancier words ...

Here, then, are the primary auxiliaries we use to expand our verbs, providing variations in meaning related to tense (time) and such conditions as probability, possibility, obligation, and necessity (mood):

Forms of *be: be, am, is, are, was, were, been, being*

Forms of *have: have, has, had*

Modals: *can, could, may, might, will, would, shall, should, must, ought to*

Missing from this list is *do,* which is a special kind of auxiliary. We call on *do,* or one of its other two forms, *does* and *did,* when we need an auxiliary for converting a positive sentence into a negative or a statement into a question or for carrying the emphasis:

I don't like horseradish.

Do you like horseradish?

Joe does like horseradish.

Do sit down.

This auxiliary use of *do* is called **do-support;** in other words, *do* comes to the rescue when an auxiliary is needed. Like *be* and *have, do* can also serve as a main verb; all three are among our most common verbs.

EXERCISE 1

Draw a line to separate the subject and predicate in each of the following sentences. Remember the trick of substituting a pronoun to discover where the subject slot ends.

(Note: You will find answers to the odd-numbered items in the Answers section at the back of the book.)

1. My son's kindergarten teacher is teaching the children some simple French and Spanish songs.

2. The naturalist in Annie Dillard's story could not pry the tiny weasel off his hand.

3. The weasel simply dangled from his palm.

4. A friend of mine from Fort Wayne has been volunteering at the library for over twenty years.

5. My uncle from Laramie, my dad, and I are going to hike the Appalachian Trail next summer.

6. The long trail, extending from Maine to Georgia, is maintained by the Appalachian Trail Commission.

7. The name of the Mars Rover, *Sojourner,* was suggested by a schoolgirl in honor of Sojourner Truth.

8. The term *noun phrase* refers to a word or group of words that act as a unit.

SENTENCE PATTERNS

The linking-*be* pattern, which we looked at earlier, is one of seven basic **sentence patterns** we describe in this chapter. These seven represent the underlying skeletal structure of nearly all our sentences in English—perhaps 95 percent of them. As you study the patterns, you will find it useful to think of each one as a series of slots. You've already seen the two basic slots: the subject and the predicate. The next step is to differentiate among the seven patterns on the basis of the structures that fill their predicate slots. Here are the two slots in our earlier weasel sentence:

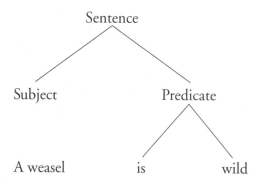

In this pattern the structure following the linking-*be* is called a **subject complement** because it says something about the subject: The adjective *wild* is a modifier of *weasel.*

There are four categories of verbs that produce our seven patterns: **be,** the **linking** verbs, the **intransitive** verbs, and the **transitive** verbs. They add up to seven patterns because *be* is subclassified into two groups and the transitive verbs into three.

The Be *Patterns*

Because *be* plays such an important part in sentence structure, not only as a main verb but also as an auxiliary, we put our *be* sentences into patterns separate from the linking verbs. And while most *be* sentences do have a subject complement, as we saw in the weasel sentence, some do not. The first pattern describes those sentences in which the second slot of the predicate contains an **adverbial** of time or place rather than a subject complement. Pattern 1 is not generally considered the linking use of *be*.

PATTERN 1	SUBJECT	*BE*	ADVERBIAL
	The weasel	*is*	*in his den.*
	The rehearsal	*will be*	*tomorrow.*

PATTERN 2	SUBJECT	*BE*	SUBJECT COMPLEMENT
	The students	*are*	*clever.* (Adjective)
	Gino's father	*was*	*a pilot.* (Noun phrase)

The subject complement describes or renames the subject. If it's a noun phrase, it has the same **referent** as the subject. *Referent* means the person or thing or event or concept that a noun or noun phrase stands for; in other words, *a pilot* and *Gino's father* refer to the same person.

When the subject complement is an adjective, as we have seen in two examples—*A weasel is wild; The students are clever*—that complement names a quality of the subject. An alternative way of modifying the subject is to shift the adjective to the position before the noun headword: *a wild weasel; the clever students.* That, of course, is precisely what the subject complement means; the difference between the two structures, the prenoun modifier and the subject complement, has to do with emphasis and purpose rather than meaning. The subject complement position puts greater emphasis on the adjective.

The Linking Verb Pattern

The term **linking verb** applies to all verbs other than *be* completed by a subject complement—the adjective or noun phrase that describes or identifies the subject. Among the common linking verbs are the verbs of the senses—*taste, smell, feel, sound,* and *look*—which often link an adjective to the subject. *Become* and *remain* are the two most common ones that connect a noun or noun phrase. Other common linking verbs are *seem, appear,* and *prove.*

PATTERN 3	SUBJECT	LINKING VERB	SUBJECT COMPLEMENT
	The pizza	*looks*	*delicious.*
	My sister	*became*	*a nurse.*

Here again, as with Pattern 2, the subject complement slot is in line for emphasis.

The Intransitive Verb Pattern

In the intransitive pattern, the predicate has only one required slot: the verb alone.

PATTERN 4	SUBJECT	INTRANSITIVE VERB
	The whole class	*laughed.*
	The baby	*cried.*

As you know, such skeletal sentences are fairly rare in actual writing. The point here is that they are grammatical: No further slots are required. In the section "The Optional Slot" later in this chapter, you will read about adverbial modifiers, structures that add information about time and place and manner and reason, which are commonly added to all the sentence patterns, including this one. However, adding a modifier does not change the basic pattern. The following variations of our samples remain Pattern 4 sentences:

The whole class laughed *at the teacher's jokes.*

The baby cried *for ten minutes.*

Other common intransitive verbs are *sit, stand, come, go, walk, run, work, play*—and literally thousands more. They are among the verbs known as *action verbs.* You've probably read or heard advice about using action verbs to enliven your prose. For example, instead of writing

Henry is a hard worker.

using *be* as your main verb, you could show action with

Henry works hard.

This is a simple example of what is called *paraphrase,* or finding an alternative way of saying the same thing—or almost the same thing (neither paraphrases nor synonyms are ever identical). One of the reasons for studying sentence structure, as you are doing here, is to develop your ability to paraphrase so as to expand the tools available to you as a writer.

EXERCISE 2

Identify the boundaries of the sentence slots in each of the following sentences. Then identify the pattern number. The adverbials are identified with italics. (Remember the trick of substituting a pronoun to find the boundaries of a noun phrase.)

Example: The world of computers / remains / a mystery / *to my mother.*
(Pattern ___3___)

1. The bus from Flagstaff arrived *at two o'clock.* (Pattern _____)

2. The public transportation in our area is not reliable. (Pattern _____)

3. The breeze from the neighbor's grill smells wonderful. (Pattern _____)

4. The weasel sleeps *in his underground den.* (Pattern _____)

5. Annie Dillard is a keen observer of nature. (Pattern _____)

6. Seemingly invisible bits of nature become visible *with her words.* (Pattern _____)

7. Our committee meeting is *in the library.* (Pattern _____)

8. Did you study *for the test?* (Pattern _____)

The Basic Transitive Verb Pattern

Transitive verbs are the other action verbs. Unlike intransitive verbs, all transitive sentences have one complement in common: the **direct object.** Pattern 5, which has only that one slot following the verb, can be thought of as the basic transitive verb pattern.

PATTERN 5	SUBJECT	TRANSITIVE VERB	DIRECT OBJECT
	Weasels	*stalk*	*rabbits.*
	My roommate	*borrowed*	*my laptop.*

Transitive verbs are traditionally defined as those verbs in which the action is directed to, or transmitted to, an object—in contrast to the intransitive verbs, which have no object. The direct objects tells "what" or "whom."

In Pattern 3 we also saw a noun phrase in the slot following the verb, and it too answers the question of "what":

> My roommate and I became *good friends.*

The distinction between the two patterns lies in the relationship of the complement noun phrase to the subject: In Pattern 3, the two have the same referent; they refer to the same people. We could, in fact, say

> My roommate and I *are* good friends,

using the linking *be,* turning the sentence into Pattern 2.

In Pattern 5, on the other hand, the two noun phrases, the subject and the direct object, have different referents. We obviously cannot say, with any degree of seriousness,

> Weasels are rabbits.

Later in this chapter, you will see another way of testing whether or not a verb is transitive. Can the sentence be turned into the **passive voice?** If the answer is yes, the verb is transitive.

Incidentally, the pronoun trick you learned for identifying the boundaries of the subject works for all noun phrase slots in the sentence, including direct objects. For example, in the right context the second sample sentence could be stated,

> My roommate borrowed it,

perhaps in answer to the question "Where's your laptop?" However, the use of the pronoun *it* changes the emphasis: When you say the sentence aloud, you'll notice that the main focus is now on the verb rather than on the direct object, as it is in the original sentence, the one with *my laptop.* You'll read about sentence focus again in Chapter 5 in the discussion of sentence rhythm.

Transitive Patterns with Two Complements

The last two patterns have two slots following the verb: In Pattern 6 an **indirect object** precedes the direct object; in Pattern 7 an **object complement** follows the direct object.

PATTERN 6	SUBJECT	TRANSITIVE VERB	INDIRECT OBJECT	DIRECT OBJECT
	Marie	*gave*	*Ramon*	*a birthday gift.*
	Annie Dillard	*gives*	*her readers*	*insights into nature.*

In this pattern, two noun phrases follow the verb, and here all three—the subject, the **indirect object,** and the direct object—have different referents. We traditionally define *indirect object* as the recipient of the direct object or the person to whom or for whom the action is performed. In most cases this definition applies accurately. A Pattern 6 verb—and this is a limited group—usually has a meaning like "give," and the indirect object usually names a person who is the receiver of whatever the subject gives.

Here are some other Pattern 6 sentences with *give*-like verbs:

My father bought my sister a new car.

The judges awarded our debate team the grand prize.

My boyfriend baked me a delicious carrot cake for my birthday.

An important characteristic of the Pattern 6 sentence is the option we have of shifting the indirect object to a position following the direct object, where it becomes the object of a preposition—in other words, switching the two object slots:

Marie gave a birthday gift to Ramon.

You might choose this order if, for example, you want to put the main emphasis, or focus, on Ramon, or if you want to add a modifier. A long modifier often fits the end of the sentence more smoothly than it would in the middle. Compare the two:

Marie gave a birthday gift to Ramon, *a friend from her old neighborhood in Northridge.*
Marie gave Ramon, *a friend from her old neighborhood in Northridge,* a birthday gift.

The original order will be more effective if it's the direct object you wish to emphasize or expand:

Marie gave Ramon a birthday gift, *a necktie she had made herself.*

PATTERN 7	SUBJECT	TRANSITIVE VERB	DIRECT OBJECT	OBJECT COMPLEMENT
	The teacher	*considers*	*the students*	*hard workers.*
	The teacher	*called*	*the students*	*brilliant.*

In this pattern the direct object is followed by a second complement, called an **object complement**—a noun phrase or an adjective that describes the direct object. Note that the relationship between these two complement slots is the same as the relationship between the subject and the subject complement in Patterns 2 and 3. In fact, we could easily turn these two complement slots into a Pattern 2 sentence:

The students are hard workers.

The students are brilliant.

It's obvious that this linking-*be* version of the relationship changes the meaning: To call the students brilliant does not mean that they really are brilliant.

With verbs like *consider*, we also have the alternative of using the infinitive *to be* to introduce the object complement:

The teacher considers the students *to be* hard workers.

This version has the identical meaning of the original; in fact, the *to be* is really "understood" in the first version. The only differences are in the length of the sentence and in its rhythm. Sometimes you may want the extra beat of rhythm that *to be* provides. If you read both versions aloud, you'll hear a slightly greater emphasis on *students* when the infinitive is included; in other words, both *students* and *hard workers* get emphasis.

Other verbs common to this pattern include *make, prefer, elect, appoint*, and *find:*

I prefer my coffee black.

Some students find grammar challenging.

The teacher made the test too easy.

California voters elected a movie star as their governor.

Sentence Pattern Summary

1. Subject	***Be***	**Adverbial**
The weasel	*is*	*in his den.*

2. Subject	*Be*	Subject Complement
The students	*are*	*clever.* (ADJ)
Gino's father	*was*	*a pilot.* (NP)

3. Subject	Linking Verb	Subject Complement
The pizza	*looks*	*delicious.* (ADJ)
My sister	*became*	*a nurse.* (NP)

4. Subject	Intransitive Verb
The baby	*cried.*

5. Subject	Transitive Verb	Direct Object
Weasels	*stalk*	*rabbits.*

6. Subject	Transitive Verb	Indirect Object	Direct Object
Marie	*gave*	*Ramon*	*a birthday gift.*

7. Subject	Transitive Verb	Direct Object	Object Complement
The teacher	*called*	*the students*	*brilliant.* (ADJ)
The teacher	*considers*	*the students*	*hard workers.* (NP)

THE OPTIONAL SLOT

The slots that make up the sentence pattern formulas can be thought of as the basic requirements for grammatical sentences. In other words, a linking verb requires a subject complement in order to be complete; a transitive verb requires a direct object. But there's another important slot that can be added to all the formulas, as mentioned in connection with the intransitive pattern: an optional slot filled by an **adverbial,** a structure that adds information about time, place, manner, reason, and the like.

Pattern 4, the intransitive pattern, rarely appears without at least one adverbial. Sentences as short as our two examples *(The whole class laughed; The baby cried)* are fairly rare in prose; and when they do appear, they nearly always call attention to themselves. The adverbials in the following sentences are underlined:

1. <u>During the Vietnam War,</u> Gino's dad was a pilot.
2. <u>Because a weasel is wild,</u> it should be approached <u>with great caution.</u>
3. <u>Yesterday</u> the teacher called the students lazy <u>when they complained about their assignment.</u>
4. <u>This morning</u> I got up <u>early</u> <u>to study for my Spanish test.</u>

The term *adverbial* refers to any grammatical structure that adds what we think of as "adverbial information." It adds the kind of information that **adverbs** add, and adverbs, you may recall from your grammar classes of old, are modifiers of verbs. In the first and second examples, you'll see **prepositional phrases:** *During the Vietnam War* tells "when"; *with great caution* tells "how." The second and third sentences include **subordinate clauses:** The *because* clause tells "why"; the *when* clause, of course, tells "when." The third and fourth include adverbs of time, *yesterday* and *early*. And sentence four also has a noun phrase, *this morning*, that tells "when," along with an **infinitive phrase**, *to study for my Spanish test*, that tells "why."

It's important to recognize that when we use the word *optional* we are referring only to grammaticality, not to the importance of the adverbial information. If you remove those underlined adverbials from the four sentences, you are left with grammatical, albeit skeletal, sentences. However, even though the sentence is grammatical in its skeletal form, many times the adverbial information is the very reason for the sentence—the main focus. For example, if you tell someone

I got up early to study for my Spanish test,

you're probably doing so in order to explain when or why about your morning schedule; the adverbials are the important information. The main clause—the fact that you got up—goes without saying!

The variety of structures available for adding information makes the adverbial a remarkably versatile tool for writers. You can add a detail about frequency, for example, by using a single word, a phrase, a whole clause—or a combination—depending on the writing situation:

My friends and I have pizza <u>regularly.</u>

My friends and I have pizza <u>with persistent regularity.</u>

My friends and I have pizza <u>for breakfast, lunch, and dinner nearly every day of the week.</u>

My friends and I have pizza <u>whenever the mood strikes.</u>

And it's not just their form that makes adverbials so versatile. Perhaps even more important is their movability: They can open the sentence or close it; they can even be inserted between the slots for special effect. Many of the discussions about cohesion and rhythm that you will read in the next few chapters are concerned with the placement of movable structures, including adverbials.

In Chapter 8 the various forms of adverbials are discussed in detail.

EXERCISE 3

A. Draw vertical lines between the sentence slots, paying special attention to the various adverbials.

Example: To save money / I / always /walk / to work / when the weather is nice.

1. Sometimes a weasel lives in his den for two days without leaving.

2. In 2000 campaign finance reform became a big issue during the primaries.

3. Very soon the issue simply disappeared from the Congressional agenda.

4. During warmups, before the game started, the basketball team looked exhausted.

5. Wash your hands thoroughly after handling chemicals.

6. My bicycle disappeared from the bike rack after I rode it to work on Saturday.

7. Jen worked steadily in the lab throughout the night to finish her project before the Monday deadline.

8. This morning my roommate gave me a bad time because I used her cell phone without permission yesterday.

9. Everyone smiles in the same language.

10. In Chapter 8 you will study adverbials in detail.

B. Rewrite the sentences in Part A in as many ways as you can by shifting the location of the adverbials. You'll discover that some are more movable than others.

THE PASSIVE VOICE

You're probably familiar with the definition of verbs as "action words," a description commonly applied to both intransitive and transitive verbs:

The baby cried. (Pattern 4)

My roommate borrowed my laptop. (Pattern 5)

In these sentences the subjects are performing the action; they are making something happen. Linguists use the term **agent** for this "doer" of the verbal action. Another term that describes this relationship of the subject to the verb is **active voice.**

What happens when we turn the Pattern 5 sentence around, when we remove the agent from the subject slot and give that role to the original direct object, *my laptop?*

My laptop was borrowed by my roommate.

This reversal has changed the sentence from active to **passive voice.** However, while *my roommate* is no longer the sentence subject, it is still the agent; and while *my laptop* is no longer the direct object, it is still the so-called receiver of the action. What has changed are their functions, their roles, in the sentence, not their relationship to each other.

The transformation from active to passive involves three steps:

1. The direct object becomes the subject.
2. A form of *be* is added as an auxiliary (in this case the past form *was*, because *borrowed* is past); it teams with the **past participle** form of the main verb.[3]
3. The original agent, if mentioned, becomes the object of the preposition *by* (or, in some cases, *for*).

If you think about the first step in the list, you'll understand why the other example of an action verb, *The baby cried,* is not being used to illustrate the passive voice: Intransitive verbs cannot be made passive because they have no direct object. That's why you read this statement in the discussion of Pattern 5, back on page 15.

> Later in this chapter, you will see another way of testing whether or not a verb is transitive. Can the sentence be turned into the passive voice? If the answer is yes, the verb is transitive.

We can add the following statement as well: If the answer is no, the verb is *probably* not transitive. A few transitive verbs generally don't appear in the passive voice, so we have to qualify the rule with "probably." The verb

---

[3]To figure out the past participle form of any verb, use the verb in a sentence with the auxiliary *have*—and you will automatically use the verb's past participle: I *have* already *eaten;* I *have walked* to work every day this week; I *have enjoyed* the party. In regular verbs, such as *borrow* and *walk* and *enjoy,* the past participle is identical to the past tense. In **irregular verbs,** such as *eat* and *go,* the two forms are often different: *ate/eaten; went/gone.*

have, for example, one of our most common transitive verbs, is rarely made passive—only in a few informal expressions:

> A good time was had by all.
>
> I've been had.

Most *have* sentences have no passive counterpart:

> Joe had the flu last week.
>
> *The flu was had by Joe.[4]

The passive voice has an important purpose: to shift the focus of the sentence, changing the topic under discussion. This shift is an important tool for sentence cohesion, a feature of writing you will explore in Chapter 4. You will also learn that the negative features of the passive voice that you may have been warned about are vastly overstated.

EXERCISE 4

A. Transform the following active sentences into the passive voice. (Note: If the active includes an auxiliary, be sure to retain it in the passive version.)

Example 1: *Active:*   Our waiter recommended the pasta special.

   Passive: The pasta special was recommended by our waiter.

Example 2: *Active:*   The teacher has assigned three chapters for Monday.

   Passive: Three chapters have been assigned for Monday.

1. Eero Saarinen designed the Memorial Arch in St. Louis.

2. The magnificent arch commemorates the pioneering spirit of the Westward movement.

3. The storm may delay our flight.

4. I should probably revise my opening paragraph.

5. The teacher could have given us clearer directions. (Use the indirect object as the subject of the passive.)

6. Our school district is now requiring achievement tests every year.

B. Now change these passive sentences into the active voice. Remember that the two versions will have different subjects. If the agent (the active subject) does not appear in the passive version, you will have to supply it.

---

[4]An asterisk marks the sentence as ungrammatical or of questionable usage.

Example: *Passive:*   Three finalists have been chosen for the science
award.

   Active: [The judges] have chosen three finalists for the science award.

1. Our garage roof was damaged by a falling tree.

2. Our garage roof is finally being repaired.

3. All of the lab experiments must be completed before the midterm
   exam.

4. Transitive verbs are often called action verbs.

5. Outer space has been called the last frontier.

6. Both defendants were found guilty of harassment.

"CLAUSE" AND "SENTENCE"

The sentence patterns you have just seen could also be called *clause patterns:*
The two words **clause** and **sentence** are close in meaning. First, we'll define
clause as a structure that contains a subject and a predicate. That definition,
of course, conforms precisely to the illustration of *sentence* shown earlier:

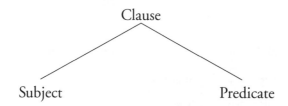

Clause

Subject   Predicate

When a clause functions independently—when it begins with a capital letter and ends with a period (or other terminal mark of punctuation)—we
call it a sentence:

   A weasel is wild.

But a clause need not be independent, an **independent clause** (also known
as the **main clause**): It can also function within another sentence, as a
dependent clause. For example, we could use our weasel clause as a direct
object following a transitive verb like *say:*

   Annie Dillard says *that a weasel is wild.*

This new structure, the one with *Annie Dillard* as subject, is also a sentence,
of course; it is an independent clause that has a dependent clause within it.

The weasel clause could function as another kind of dependent clause—a subordinate clause functioning adverbially, telling "why," as we saw in the discussion of the optional adverbial:

Because a weasel is wild, it should be approached with great caution.

In summary, then, we can say that all sentences are made up of one or more independent clauses. However, a clause need not be an independent, or complete, sentence; it doesn't always have sentence status. Understanding the status of clauses—whether independent or dependent—is basic to understanding punctuation. In fact, it is perhaps the most important concept overall for a writer to have under control.

As we have seen, the clauses that do not qualify as independent play other roles; they have other functions to perform. In later chapters you will read about those roles: in Chapter 8 as adverbials (modifiers of the verb), and in Chapter 9 as adjectivals (modifiers of nouns) and nominals (substitutes for noun phrases). Meanwhile, of course, you will see dependent clauses on every page of this text—in paragraphs such as this one—and in examples and exercises throughout the book. And of course you will use them yourself in both speaking and writing.

PUNCTUATION AND THE SENTENCE PATTERNS

There's an important punctuation lesson to be learned from the sentence patterns with their two or three or four slots:

Do not mark boundaries of the required slots with punctuation.

That is, never use a single comma to separate

- **the subject from the verb.**
- **the direct object from the object complement.**
- **the indirect object from the direct object.**
- **the verb from the subject complement.**

And, with one exception, never separate

- **the verb from the direct object.**

The one exception to this rule occurs when the direct object is a direct quotation following a verb like *say:*

He said, "I love you."

Here the punctuation convention calls for a comma before the quoted words.

Even though the structures that fill the slots in the following sentences may be long and require a pause for breath, there is simply no place for commas:

> The images and information sent back by *Voyager 2* / have given / our space scientists here on Earth / enough information about four of our distant planets to keep them busy for years to come. (Pattern 6)

> All of the discussion groups I took part in during Orientation Week / were / extremely helpful / for the incoming freshmen. (Pattern 2)

> Every sportswriter who saw the preseason contest between the Buckeyes and the Aggies / said / that it was a game that will be remembered for a long time to come. (Pattern 5)

In Chapter 9, in the discussion of noun phrases, we will encounter sentences in which punctuation is called for *within* a slot. We saw an example in the Introduction—the *who*-clause set off by two commas:

> My roommate, who grew up in New York City, is named Peter Piper.

And sometimes optional adverbial information can be inserted *between* slots, where it may call for two commas:

> Weasels, because they are wild, should be approached with great caution.

In both cases, the only reason for the commas is to set off the modifier; their purpose is not to mark the slot boundaries. Note that the rule, highlighted at the beginning of this section, refers to a *single* comma as a boundary marker.

EXERCISE 5

Draw vertical lines between the slots of the following sentences, and then identify their sentence patterns. You might want to begin by locating the verb. And don't forget the trick of discovering where a noun phrase slot begins and ends by substituting a pronoun. This trick will work for all of the noun phrase slots—not just the subject. Remember, too, that optional adverbial information can occupy the opening and/or closing slots in the sentence.

1. In 1747 a physician in the British navy conducted an experiment to discover a cure for scurvy.

2. Scurvy was a serious problem for men at sea.

3. Dr. James Lind fed six groups of scurvy victims six different remedies.

4. When the men were given oranges and lemons every day, they recovered miraculously.

5. Although it took fifty years for the British Admiralty Office to recognize Lind's findings, it finally ordered a daily dose of fresh lemon juice for every British seaman.

6. Interestingly, Lind's discovery also affected the English language.

7. The British called lemons "limes" in the eighteenth century.

8. Because of that navy diet, people call British sailors "limeys."

KEY TERMS

Active voice	Independent clause	Prepositional phrase
Adverb	Indirect object	Pronoun
Adverbial	Infinitive	Punctuation
Auxiliary verb	Intransitive verb	Referent
Be patterns	Irregular verb	Rhetoric
Clause	Linking verb	Sentence
Declarative sentence	Main clause	Sentence pattern
Dependent clause	Noun phrase	Sentence slots
Direct object	Object complement	Subject
Do-support	Passive voice	Subject complement
Grammar	Past participle	Subordinate clause
Headword	Phrase	Transitive verb
Helping verb	Predicate	Verb phrase

PUNCTUATION REMINDER

Have you made sure that a comma does not separate the required slots of your sentences?

The Basic Sentence Patterns in Prose

CHAPTER PREVIEW

In Chapter 1 you read that the sentence patterns you were studying are fairly unusual in their bare, unadorned form. Most of the sentences we read are expanded with noun modifiers or adverbials or compound structures of various kinds. You will read about these expansions in later chapters. When writers do use a bare pattern, it is often—if not usually—for one of two purposes: as a topic sentence or as an attention-getter. In this chapter we focus on the power of short sentences, their rhetorical effectiveness, in these two roles. You'll also have the chance to compare your own prose style, in terms of sentence length, with that of professional writers.

TOPIC SENTENCES

In this chapter you won't be getting instruction for writing or punctuating short sentences—as you have seen, most of them need no punctuation— but you may need instruction in using them. Or maybe *encouragement* is a better word: You may need encouragement in using short sentences. It's not unusual for inexperienced writers to believe that writing calls for long sentences rather than short ones, just as they may believe that writing calls for fancy words rather than plain ones. Both notions are wrong. In Chapter 6 we take up the topic of fancy words in the discussion of diction. Here we consider the effectiveness of short sentences, many of which are bare-bones sentence patterns.

Paragraph Openers

The bare sentence pattern as topic sentence is a common strategy, especially the "something is something" pattern discussed at the opening of Chapter 1 with the Annie Dillard sentence "A weasel is wild." Dillard uses many such sentences as paragraph openers—sometimes with a verb other than a form of *be,* sometimes with an added adverbial, but still very short sentences. These examples are from Dillard's *Pilgrim at Tinker Creek:*

> Today is the winter solstice.
>
> Bear with me one last time.
>
> In September the birds were quiet.
>
> I live in tranquility and trembling.

David McCullough, in his biography of Harry Truman, often opens a long paragraph with a "something is something." Here are examples from a chapter detailing Truman's early years in Missouri:

> He had been a big success as a soldier.
>
> The store had been a dismal failure.
>
> His real love, however, was politics.
>
> Politics was personal contact.

These two openers are from Stanley Coren's *The Intelligence of Dogs:*

> There are many folk tales about the first dog.
>
> The trail of the early dog is faint.

Most of these short topic sentences are Pattern 2, "Something is something," a sentence model you may have been warned about using. In Chapter 7, "Choosing Verbs," you'll read about the overuse of *be* along with revision possibilities. Certainly, sometimes you'll want to consider an alternative to *be,* especially if you find yourself using it to the exclusion of other verbs. But bear in mind that, given a particular context, *be* sentences can be just as effective as those of any other verb category. As these examples illustrate, they are commonly used by professional writers to introduce paragraph topics.

Internal Topic Sentences

All of the previous examples are opening topic sentences. But as you know, the topic sentence can also occupy other positions in the paragraph: in the middle or at the end. In the following paragraph, from an *Atlantic* article by James Fallows, the topic sentence is the short third one. It changes the focus from the preceding paragraph on the workplace to the following one about schools.

> In most Japanese offices people are busy-looking but are often engaged in busywork. Office ladies bustle back and forth carrying tea, groups of men sit through two-hour meetings to resolve a minor point, and of course there are the long evenings in the restaurants and bars. <u>Something similar is true of the schools.</u> The children are at school for more hours each week than American children, but in any given hour they may be horsing around, entertaining themselves while the teachers take one of their (surprisingly frequent) breaks, conducting "self-improvement" meetings, or scrubbing the floors during dai soji—literally, "big clean-up." (Most schools have no hired janitorial staff.)

The fifth sentence in the following eight-sentence paragraph from a *Smithsonian* article by Michael Parfit has that same gear-shifting purpose; again, it's actually the topic sentence. The four preceding sentences summarize the background and provide transition from the essay's previous paragraphs; the three sentences that follow explain and support this new focus.

> It is not surprising that ranchers continue to destroy forests wherever they can in spite of evidence that many Amazon soils don't support grass for long. Brazil's ranchers carry the moral scythe of manifest destiny. Once that energy belonged to the Soldiers of Rubber and their patraos [bosses]. Now the patraos live in dimly lit rooms among their thoughts of the past and wait for barges that don't come. <u>The momentum is in cattle.</u> In Brazil, where land-protection regulations and enforcement officers often fall off the truck between Brasilia and the forest, momentum is more important than law. Recent studies have shown that rain forest is far more valuable intact than burned, but that doesn't matter to momentum. In the United States in 1875 it would also have been more logical economically to have kept the cows and the alfalfa in Connecticut, and ranched bison on the plains.

The sentences in this paragraph, other than the five-word gear-shifting one, average twenty-four words each. In the paragraph about Japan, the two sentences on either side of the middle seven-word sentence have thirty-four and fifty-one words.

In the following example, from a *Time* article by J. Madeleine Nash on the movement to demolish dams, you'll see the same gear-shifting in the short third sentence. The sentence preceding it contains thirty-four words, the one following, thirty-seven.

> Shaping up as an important milestone is the demolition of two large dams in Washington State's Elwha River, which flows from the mountains of Olympic National Park into the Juan de Fuca Strait. Their removal, scheduled to begin in 2008, would occur in stages, and if it goes as planned, the Pacific Northwest will lose only a tiny amount of hydropower and regain a legendary salmon fishery. <u>But there could be problems.</u> Behind Elwha dams are some 18 million cubic yards of accumulated sediment, enough to fill four superdomes, and if a lot of that sediment starts to move downstream at once, the ecological consequences could be severe.

Short, focused sentences like this one and those in the preceding examples are bound to draw the attention of the reader.

◀   **FOR GROUP DISCUSSION**

The following paragraph opens a chapter of William W. Warner's *Beautiful Swimmers: Watermen, Crabs and the Chesapeake Bay.* The underlining has been added.

Winter

> It can come anytime from the last week in October to the first in December. There will be a fickle day, unseasonably warm, during which two or three minor rain squalls blow across the Bay. The sun appears fitfully in between; sometimes there is distant thunder. <u>A front is passing.</u> The first warning that it is more than an ordinary autumnal leaf-chaser comes near the end. The ragged trailing edge of a normal front is nowhere to be seen. Ominously absent is the steady procession of fleecy white puffball clouds that usually presages two or three days of fine weather. Rather, the front picks up speed and passes so rapidly that it is stormy at one moment and unbelievably clear and cloud-free the next. <u>Then it comes.</u> The wind rises in a few minutes from a placid five or ten knots to a sustained thirty or forty, veering quickly first to the west and then to the

northwest. <u>The dry gale has begun.</u> Short and steep seas, so characteristic of the Chesapeake, rise up from nowhere to trip small boats. Inattentive yachtsmen will lose sails and have the fright of their lives. Workboat captains not already home will make for any port.

1. Note that the title word *winter*—which is also the topic here—does not appear in the paragraph, represented only by the pronoun *it*. What effect does that omission have? In what way would *Winter* as the first word, instead of *It*, affect the drama?

2. You saw a three-word, a four-word, and a five-word sentence in this paragraph. What purpose do they serve? How did they affect your reading?

SPECIAL EFFECTS

Fiction writers also use short sentences to good advantage, often to evoke the disconnected nature of thoughts and feelings:

> Maybe she misses London. She feels caged, in this country, in this city, in this room. She could start with the room, she could open a window. It's too stuffy in here....
>
> Kat feels her own forehead. She wonders if she's running a temperature. Something ominous is going on behind her back. There haven't been enough phone calls from the magazine; they've been able to muddle on without her, which is bad news. Reigning queens should never go on vacation, or have operations, either. Uneasy lies the head....
>
> She isn't in good shape. She can hardly stand. She stands, despite his offer of a chair. She sees now what she's wanted, what she's been missing. Gerald is what she's been missing: the stable, unfashionable, previous, tight-assed Gerald. Not Ger, not the one she's made in her own image. The other one, before he got ruined.
>
> —Margaret Atwood ("Kat")

Here the short sentence signals a significant detail:

> Francis got home late from town, and Julia got the sitter while he dressed, and then hurried him out of the house. The party was small and pleasant, and Francis settled down to

enjoy himself. <u>A new maid passed the drinks.</u> Her hair was dark, and her face was round and pale and seemed familiar to Francis.

—John Cheever ("The Country Husband")

Sentences from all of the patterns are used for special effects and significant details like these. But when your teacher—or your handbook—recommends that you vary the length of sentences, do bear in mind that these short sentences, these bare-bones patterns, sometimes carry a message that goes beyond the words themselves, a message that tells the reader, "Pay attention! I'm special!"

FOR GROUP DISCUSSION

Sentences that we have been calling *linking*-be *sentences* are called *categorical propositions* (CPs) by logicians and rhetoricians. The CP makes an assertion—it states a proposition—about a particular subject. The following linking-*be* sentences illustrate the three basic kinds of CPs:

A. Chunky Monkey is Ben & Jerry's most delicious flavor.

B. New York City is the largest city in the United States.

C. Television is the cause of a great many social problems.

Although all three sentences look alike, in that all three conform to the "something is something" pattern, they are actually quite different. Only one has the potential for being an effective topic sentence. In other words, not all CPs can hold their own as topic sentences.

The CP that makes the best topic sentence is an arguable proposition. It calls up a response in the reader, a response that says "Prove it." And in so doing, it sets up expectations in the reader. Let's look at the responses the typical reader might make to the three sentences here:

A. Chunky Monkey is Ben & Jerry's most delicious flavor.

"How can you say that? It doesn't compare to either New York Super Fudge Chunky or Vanilla Caramel Fudge, if you ask me."

The categorical proposition in (A) is simply a matter of personal taste. It's not arguable: One person's opinion is as valid as the next one's.

B. New York City is the largest city in the United States.

"I know that. Doesn't everyone? Why are you telling me this?"

The CP in (B) is a fact, a statement that can be verified. Although it's fairly common to see facts as paragraph openers, they tend to be weak ones, especially well-known facts, because they give no clue as to their purpose. Try to predict where a paragraph with (B) as an opening sentence is going.

    C. Television is the cause of a great many social problems.

    "I disagree. What proof do you have?"

Like sentence (A), the third also states an opinion, but it's one that's open to debate—an arguable proposition. Because it deals with probability, you can bring evidence to support your side. The reader can infer where this paragraph is going.

Decide which of the following CPs would make good topic sentences. You'll want to think about the way in which a reader would respond:

1. Florida is the ideal place to retire.
2. It is wrong to use animals for testing cosmetics.
3. Jogging is boring.
4. Jogging is a popular sport.
5. Pearls are among nature's most amazing creations.
6. The lemur, a shrewlike creature, is at home both on the ground and in the trees.
7. Playing computer games is a complete waste of time.
8. Movie popcorn is always too salty.
9. History will probably rate Ronald Reagan as one of the great presidents.
10. The tsunami of December 2004 took the lives of over 200,000 people.

Now rewrite the weak topic sentences to improve them, if possible. Also try your hand at revising them to avoid using the linking *be*.

THE SHORT PARAGRAPH

Another attention-getter is the short paragraph that appears on a page of long, well-developed ones. In *Pilgrim at Tinker Creek* Annie Dillard adds drama with an occasional paragraph of one or two sentences, often used for transition from one topic to another. Each of these examples is a complete paragraph:

> The woods were restless as birds.

> The world has locusts, and the world has grasshoppers. I was up to my knees in the world.

In his book *Undaunted Courage,* the story of Lewis and Clark's journey to the Pacific, Stephen E. Ambrose often uses the short paragraph of transition:

> Thus armed with orders, guns, and goods, Lewis set out to meet the Indians of the Great Plains.

Like short sentences in a paragraph of long ones, these short paragraphs call attention to themselves. They, too, say, "Pay attention!" They, too, should be crafted carefully.

A SENTENCE SURVEY

In his textbook *Classical Rhetoric for the Modern Student* (Oxford, 1971), Professor Edward P. J. Corbett reports on a study of style he conducted in his Honors Freshman English class. His students compared the length of their own sentences and paragraphs with those of a professional writer, F. L. Lucas. They selected eight paragraphs from an essay by Lucas, avoiding short transitional paragraphs and any that contained two or more sentences of quoted material. Then they calculated the average number of words per sentence (20.8) and the average number of sentences per paragraph (7.6). In addition, they calculated the percentage of sentences that were ten words longer than the average (17 percent) and the percentage that were five words shorter than average (40 percent). Then they did the same with an expository theme of their own.

Here is Professor Corbett's summary of the findings:

> Most of the students found that their average sentence matched the length of Lucas's average sentence. Many of the students were surprised to learn, however, that they had a higher percentage of above-average sentences and a strikingly lower percentage of below-average sentences. Perhaps the most dramatic difference that the students noted was in paragraph development. At least half of the students found that they were averaging between three and four sentences in their paragraphs.

We cannot, of course, judge the effectiveness of a paragraph on the basis of statistics. However, these data certainly confirm the experience of many writing teachers: Their students need encouragement in writing short sentences; they also need encouragement in developing paragraphs.

EXERCISE 6

Do a contrastive study of your own writing style and that of a professional, following Professor Corbett's model. For the analysis, choose eight paragraphs from a magazine article (e.g., *Harper's, Atlantic, New Yorker, Smithsonian, Nature*) or from a professional journal in your major field. For purposes of this analysis, a sentence is defined as "a group of words beginning with a capital letter and ending with some mark of end punctuation." In some cases these sentences will be fragments; even so, you should include them in your analysis. However, among the eight do not include short transitional paragraphs or any paragraph that contains two or more sentences of quoted material. Do the same analysis with eight paragraphs from an expository essay of your own.

	Professional	Student
1. Total number of words	_____	_____
2. Total number of sentences	_____	_____
3. Longest sentence (in # of words)	_____	_____
4. Shortest sentence (in # of words)	_____	_____
5. Average sentence length	_____	_____
6. Number of sentences with more than ten words *over* the average length	_____	_____
7. Percentage of sentences with more than ten words *over* the average	_____	_____
8. Number of sentences with more than five words *below* the average	_____	_____
9. Percentage of sentences with more than five words *below* the average	_____	_____
10. Paragraph length		
longest paragraph (in # of sentences)	_____	_____
shortest paragraph (in # of sentences)	_____	_____
average paragraph (in # of sentences)	_____	_____

KEY TERMS

Categorical   Linking *be*   Topic sentence
proposition

RHETORICAL REMINDERS

Have I called the reader's attention to focusing ideas or shifted gears with short sentences?

Have I made use of short paragraphs where needed for transition or other special effects?

CHAPTER 3

Coordination

CHAPTER PREVIEW

In Chapter 1 we introduced basic sentence patterns, emphasizing their separate slots and the forms that fill them; here we examine the ways in which we expand both the slots and the sentence as a whole using **coordination.** The technique of coordination, of putting together compound structures in sentences, is old hat; you've been doing it all your life. Coordination is a natural part of language, one that develops early in speech. If you pay attention to sentence structure the next time you're within hearing distance of a small child, you'll hear the conjunction *and* used frequently between parts of sentences and between the sentences themselves:

> We built a snow fort <u>and</u> threw snowballs.
>
> Robbie is mean, <u>and</u> I'm not going to play with him anymore.

Compound structures also show up early and often in writing. Certainly in this book you can't read very far without coming to a conjunction—an *and* or a *but* or an *or.* Your own writing is probably filled with them, too.

So why do we need to study coordination? Because it's so easy!

Any structure or technique that we use as often as we do coordination needs to be under the writer's control. Remember, a written sentence is there to be looked at and pondered, to be read over and over again. We want to be sure that every one of those compounds is grammatical and logical. And, equally important, we want to use the most efficient and accurate conjunction for that compound structure.

This chapter is also about punctuation. Make no mistake, it is important to follow the conventions of punctuation; the effectiveness of your prose diminishes with every error the reader notices. As I'm sure you know, punctuation rules can get tricky in sentences with coordinate structures. You already know how to use *and* in your sentences; it's also important to know if and when that *and* requires a comma. Having punctuation under control will give you the confidence to construct long sentences. And, just as important, that control will send a message to your reader that you are a writer with authority.

COORDINATION WITHIN THE SENTENCE

In this chapter you'll find it useful to think again about the sentence slots you studied in Chapter 1. Most of the coordination that takes place within the sentence results from compounding one or more slots. Here we've compounded the subject:

> *Gino's father* **and** *my uncle* flew helicopters in Vietnam.

In the following sentence the complete predicate is compounded:

> The kids *played outdoors all morning* **but** *stayed inside all afternoon.*

In the following sentence, only the direct object slot is compounded:

> I will buy *wallpaper* **or** *paint* to spruce up the kitchen.

Now is a good time to review the important punctuation rule you learned in Chapter 1:

> **Do not mark boundaries of the required slots with punctuation.**

Here's another, a non-comma rule of sorts, that describes the sample sentences you have just seen:

> **Use no comma with the conjunction when it joins a two-part compound structure *within* the sentence.**

The connectors in the preceding examples—*and, but, or*—are the three primary **coordinating conjunctions** we use for connecting both full sentences and their parts; you can think of them as "the big three."

You may have had a teacher in elementary or middle school who taught you a list of six or seven conjunctions—and perhaps helped you remember them with an acronym: *fanboy* or *fanboys*. (The *a, b,* and *o* of *fanboy*, of course, stand for *and, but,* and *or.*) That list includes *for*, which, along with *so* or *so that*, includes features of both a coordinator and a subordinator (a word like *because* or *since*); *fanboys* also includes *yet* and *so*, which share features of conjunctive adverbs (words like *however*, which you'll see later in this chapter). The *n* of *fanboy* is even further removed from the big three in that it has a built-in negative meaning and is used only with its partner, *neither*, or, sometimes, *not*. (You'll read more about the correlative *neither–nor* later in the chapter.) All of these lesser conjunctions are certainly words you use in writing from time to time, but their in-between status means they do not have the wide range of use that the big three have. And for most of them, their main job is to connect complete clauses rather than structures within the clause.

And *versus* But

There's an important difference between *and* and *but*. While they're both coordinating conjunctions, their meanings are opposite, and their punctuation sometimes reflects that difference:

> I have visited a lot of big cities, *but* never Los Angeles.
>
> I worked most of the night *but* couldn't finish my project.
>
> Melanie's new white rug is beautiful, *but* not very practical.

Notice that two of these sentences include a comma, even where the conjunction joins only predicates, not full sentences.

Although we call *but* a *con*junction, its meaning is related to *dis*junction: It introduces a contrast, and that contrast often calls for a comma. The punctuation rule regarding a two-part compound structure within the sentence, then, is different when the conjunction is *but*. When the compound element is connected with *and*, we use no comma; when it's connected with *but*, however, the comma may be appropriate.

There's also an exception to the comma rule that occurs with *and:* When we want to give special emphasis to the last element in a coordinated pair, we can set it off with a comma:

> I didn't believe him, and said so.
>
> My new white couch is beautiful, and impractical.

The emphasis is even stronger with a dash instead of a comma:

> I didn't believe him—and said so.
>
> My new white couch is beautiful—and impractical.

The dash also sends the message that the punctuation was deliberate—not a comma error, a judgment some readers may make.

Coordination with Correlative Conjunctions

In Chapter 5 you will learn about "power words," words that command special attention; among them are the **correlative conjunctions:**

> *both–and*   *either–or*
>
> *not only–but also*   *neither–nor*

The power of the correlatives lies in their ability to change the rhythm and focus of the sentence in ways that one-word conjunctions cannot do—to set up different expectations in the reader. Read these two sentences aloud and listen to the change in your voice when you add *both:*

> Individuals <u>and</u> nations must learn to think about the environment.
>
> <u>Both</u> individuals <u>and</u> nations must learn to think about the environment.

The change may seem like a small one. But notice what the added *both* does: It shifts the emphasis from the predicate to the subject, which normally gets little, if any. Now the reader expects to read on about the response of nations. Here's another example of the difference that *both–and* can make in contrast to *and* alone. This is a revised version of a sentence you just read:

> The power of the correlatives lies in their ability to change <u>both</u> the rhythm <u>and</u> the focus of the sentence in ways that one-word conjunctions cannot do.

If you listen carefully, you'll notice that the addition of *both* adds stress to *and*.

The same kind of change in emphasis occurs with *not only–but also* (or *not only–but ... as well*):

> As citizens of this global village, we must be concerned <u>not only</u> with our own health and safety <u>but</u> with the needs of others <u>as well</u>.
>
> As citizens of this global village, we must be concerned <u>not only</u> with our own health and safety <u>but also</u> with the needs of others.

In reading these two sentences aloud, you'll notice that in the second there is less emphasis on *others;* main focus falls on *also.*

Probably the least common correlative is *neither–nor;* and it's probably accurate to say that inexperienced writers avoid it. But because it is rare, it sends a strong message, one that says the writer has constructed the sentence carefully:

> <u>Neither</u> individuals <u>nor</u> nations can afford to ignore what is happening to the environment.

The use of *both–and* carries a restriction the other correlatives do not have: It cannot connect full sentences. The other correlatives are more versatile in that they can connect both compound sentences and the slots within the sentence.

> I should *either* spend more time studying *or* get a part-time job.
>
> *Either* I should spend more time studying, *or* I should get a part-time job.

Note that in all of these examples with correlatives, the two parts of the conjunction introduce **parallel** structures: two noun phrases, two verb phrases, two independent clauses. Later in the chapter we look more closely at this concept, an important feature of all coordination.

EXERCISE 7

Revise the following sentences by substituting correlatives *(both–and, not only–but also, either–or, neither–nor)* for the coordinating conjunctions.

1. Japanese blue-collar workers work more hours per day than American workers do and typically do so with more dedication and energy.

2. Workers and schoolchildren in Japan put in more time than their American counterparts.

3. Blue-collar workers and students in the United States do not spend as much time at their respective jobs as their Japanese counterparts.

4. In the game against Arizona last night, our center surpassed his previous single-game highs for rebounds and points scored and broke the school's all-time scoring record.

5. Julie got an A in the final exam and an A in the course.

6. When my parents retire, they plan to sell the house and buy a condo near San Diego or rent the house and buy an RV and travel the back roads.

7. The chairman of the Planning Commission did not allow the citizens' committee to present the petition and would not recognize them when they attempted to speak out at the meeting.

8. Aunt Rosa has promised to fix her famous lasagne for my birthday dinner and bake my favorite lemon cake.

9. My history professor would not let me take a make-up exam when I cut his class and wouldn't accept my paper because it was late.

10. Day care and education are issues that our elected officials will have to address if this country is going to solve its economic and social problems.

Coordination of the Series

In the series, a coordinate structure with three or more components, we use commas to separate the coordinate elements:

> Among the lands on the frozen fringes of the Arctic Ocean are Alaska, Canada, and Greenland.

These commas represent the pauses and slight changes of pitch that occur in the production of the series. You can hear the commas in your voice when you compare the series of three with a two-part compound structure, which of course has no comma:

> Among the lands on the frozen fringes of the Arctic Ocean are Alaska and Canada.

You probably noticed a leveling of your voice in reading the pair, a certain smoothness that the series does not have.

Some writers—and some publications as a matter of policy—leave out the **serial comma,** the one immediately before the conjunction. One such publication is the *New York Times.* Here is the sentence from which the previous example was taken, as published in the *Times:*

> Unlike Antarctica, a continent surrounded by ocean, the Arctic is mostly ocean ringed by land—the frozen, inhospitable fringes of Alaska, Canada, Greenland, Iceland, Scandinavia and Russia.
>
> —Darcy Frey

This open, or light, punctuation style leaves out the comma where a boundary is otherwise marked. Here, of course, the conjunction *and* marks the final boundary of the series.

This punctuation style, however, does have a drawback: It may imply a closer connection than actually exists between the last two elements of the series.

Two other structural principles involved with the series should be emphasized: (1) parallelism; and (2) **climax,** the arrangement of words or phrases or clauses in the order of increasing importance or length. Here's a sentence you will see at the opening of Chapter 10 with a series of verbs:

> You have your own style of writing, just as you have your own style of <u>walking and whistling and wearing your hair.</u>

These verbs are a parallel series of objects in a prepositional phrase—in this case, connected by conjunctions rather than commas. Compare that version with the following:

> You have your own style of writing, just as you have your own style of *walking, whistling, and the way you wear your hair.*

Now the third element is a noun phrase, making the series unparallel.

You can see that "wearing your hair" is placed where it is because of its length. You would hear a kind of offbeat rhythm if the three-word member of the series were first or second:

> … your own style of wearing your hair, walking, and whistling.

Here are some further sentences with coordination in a series, all of which exemplify both principles, parallelism and climax:

> Thus political language has to consist largely of euphemism, question-begging and sheer cloudy vagueness.
> —George Orwell

Note that Orwell omits the serial comma, but his ordering is impeccable: first one, then two, then three words. The following series has the same numerical pattern:

> It [the garden] is subtly divided into distinct sections separated by walls, low hedges, and curving stone paths.
> —Susan Allen Toth

By this time you've probably noticed the prevalence of the three-item series. Clearly, there must be something special about triplets, a natural inclination of some kind that encourages writers to write them and satisfies the readers who read them.

Subject–Verb Agreement

The topic of **subject–verb agreement** is often at issue with sentences that have compound subjects. The concept can perhaps best be illustrated by looking at examples where the subject and verb "disagree." Among the most noticeable kinds of disagreement are speech patterns of certain dialects:

> We was at the movies last night.
>
> He don't work here anymore.

These deviations from what we call standard English—*We was; He don't*—are connected to the *-s* form of the verb, the third-person singular:

	Singular	Plural	Singular	Plural
1st	I was	we were	I do	we do
2nd	you were	you were	you do	you do
3rd	she was	they were	he does	they do

As you know, the verb *be* has two forms in the past tense: *was* and *were*—our only verb that does. In the first example of nonstandard speech, *be* is treated like all other verbs, as if it had only that one past form, *was*. The example with *don't* works the opposite way—that is, omitting the *-s* of *doesn't*—in the negative; this deviation from standard English shows up only in the negative.

In writing, too, the issue of subject–verb agreement is concerned with the *-s* form of the verb and the number (whether singular or plural) of the subject. As you know, in standard English we use the *-s* form only when the subject is singular *and* third person (a subject that can be substituted by *he, she,* or *it*). But when subjects are compound, agreement can get a bit tricky.

When nouns or noun phrases in the subject slot are joined by *and* or by the correlative *both–and*, the subject is plural:

> *My friends and relatives* are coming to the wedding.

However, the coordinating conjunction *or* and the correlatives *either–or* and *neither–nor* do not have the additive meaning of *and*. In compound subjects with these conjunctions, the verb is determined by the closer member of the pair:

Neither the speaker nor <u>the listeners</u> **were** intimidated by the protestors.

Either the class officers or <u>the faculty adviser</u> **makes** the final decision.

Do <u>the class officers</u> or the faculty adviser make the final decision?

Does <u>the faculty adviser</u> or the class officers make the final decision?

If the correct sentence sounds incorrect or awkward because of the verb form, you can simply reverse the compound pair:

Either the faculty adviser or <u>the class officers</u> **make** the final decision.

When both members of the pair are alike, of course, there is no question:

Either <u>the president or the vice president</u> **is** going to introduce the speaker.

Neither <u>the union members not the management representatives</u> **were** willing to compromise.

For most verb forms, you'll recall, there is no decision to be made about subject–verb agreement; the issue arises only when the -*s* form, the present tense, of the verb or auxiliary is involved. In the following sentences with the past tense, there is no choice:

Either the class officers or the faculty adviser <u>made</u> the final decision.

Either the faculty adviser or the class officers <u>made</u> the final decision.

Another situation that sometimes causes confusion about number—that is, whether the subject is singular or plural—occurs with subjects that include a phrase introduced by *as well as* or *in addition to* or *along with:*

*The sidewalk, in addition to the driveway, need to be repaired.

*The piano player, as well as the rest of the group, usually join in the singing.

*Mike, along with his friend Emilio, often help out at the bakery on weekends.

These additions to the subject are parenthetical; they are not treated as part of the subject. In all three sentences, the subjects are singular; the verb should be the *s*-form. To make the subject compound—to include the additions—the writer should use a coordinating conjunction, such as *and:*

The sidewalk <u>and</u> the driveway <u>need</u> to be repaired.

The piano player <u>and</u> the rest of the group usually <u>join</u> in the singing.

Mike <u>and</u> his friend Emilio often <u>help</u> out at the bakery on weekends.

COMPOUND SENTENCES

In the section of Chapter 1 called "Clause and Sentence," you were reminded that the basic sentence patterns you had just studied, when they begin with a capital letter and end with a period or other terminal punctuation, are called **independent clauses.** When we put two or more independent clauses together, we are creating a **compound sentence:**

> Acupuncture has been effective in healing muscular disorders, **and** it has no side effects.

> Acupuncture is cheaper than conventional medicine, **but** most Americans do not understand how it works.

The punctuation convention calls for a comma at the end of the first clause, signaling that another independent clause is on the way. Here, then, is the second punctuation rule in connection with coordination:

> **Use a comma before the coordinating conjunction between the two independent clauses of a compound sentence.**

As you can see, it's important to understand exactly what it is you're compounding: If it's only part of the sentence—that is, a structure within the sentence—then no comma is called for; if it's two independent sentences, then the conjunction needs a comma to send a signal to the reader that another sentence is on the way.

It's not unusual to see in published works compound sentences without the comma, especially when both independent clauses are short. However, most professional writers follow the conventional rule consistently.

Connecting Sentence Patterns

If you've ever encountered a teacher's "CS" or "R-O" notation in the margin of an essay, you're in good company. The **comma splice** and the **run-on sentence** are among the most common—and probably the most perplexing to teachers—of all the punctuation errors that writers make. They are perplexing because they are based on such a straightforward and common situation: a sentence with two independent clauses.

Consider again the sentence patterns you saw in Chapter 1—those simple *subject–verb–complement* sentences. When you write one of those—when you begin it with a capital letter and end it with a period—you've created an independent clause, a sentence that can stand on its own.

It's true, of course, that most of the sentences we write aren't as simple as the bare sentence patterns—and often not as easy to identify. Every subject and every complement can be expanded with all sorts of structures; further, there are all shapes and sizes of adverbials that can fill the optional slots at the beginning and the end of the sentence. So the trick is first to recognize a sentence pattern when you see it—to recognize the boundaries of its various slots—bearing in mind that the slots are themselves sometimes filled by clauses.

In an earlier discussion we saw an example of a nominal clause filling the direct object slot:

Annie Dillard says <u>that a weasel is wild.</u>

This sentence, of course, is more complex than the sample Pattern 5 sentence in Chapter 1—*My roommate borrowed my laptop.* But, in fact, the Annie Dillard sentence has the same three slots:

Someone   says   something.

In the following sentence a *who*-clause is part of the subject slot:

The man <u>who lives upstairs</u> bothers the neighbors.

Again, you can recognize the three slot boundaries when you substitute pronouns for the noun phrases:

He   bothers   them (or us).
(SUBJECT)   (VERB)   (OBJECT)

The pronouns stand in for the entire noun phrases, including all the modifiers. This sentence, by the way, is called a **complex sentence** because it includes a dependent clause.

Now let's add another clause that tells *when*—a subordinate adverbial clause filling an optional slot:

The man who lives upstairs bothers the neighbors <u>when he comes home from work at midnight.</u>

Here the *when*-clause is filling the slot that an adverb like *sometimes* would fill:

The man who lives upstairs bothers the neighbors <u>sometimes.</u>

In terms of punctuation, we treat that clause as we would any other adverbial of time. So there is still no place in this sentence for a comma.

But now we'll add another sentence to make a **compound-complex** sentence out of it:

> The man who lives upstairs bothers the neighbors when he comes home from work at midnight, <u>and</u> I've decided to speak to him about it.

This punctuation follows the highlighted rule you saw in the last section:

Use a comma before the coordinating conjunction between the two independent clauses of a compound sentence.

What would happen if we left out the conjunction?

> *The man who lives upstairs bothers the neighbors when he comes home from work at midnight, I've decided to speak to him about it.

We've produced a *comma splice.* (With neither the comma nor the conjunction, the error would be called a *run-on,* or fused, sentence.) In other words, we've spliced, or joined, two complete sentences together with a comma. But a comma alone is not strong enough: It needs the support of a conjunction. *Remember, we want the reader to know that another complete sentence is coming.*

If you have ever committed a comma splice—left out the *and* (well, maybe *committed* is too loaded a word!)—you may have done so for what you thought was a good reason: to create a tighter connection. The sentence may have sounded or looked better. It's true that sometimes the *and* adds a certain flabbiness; maybe the sentence would be better off without it. There is a solution, and it's often a good one—the semicolon (as in the previous sentence):

> It's true that sometimes the *and* adds a certain flabbiness; maybe the sentence would be better off without it.

And here's the earlier example:

> The man who lives upstairs bothers the neighbors when he comes home from work at midnight; I've decided to speak to him about it.

To make the connection clearer for the reader, you may want to include a conjunction with the semicolon, especially when you use *so* or *yet.* In fact, our sample sentence would probably be more effective with *so* than with *and:*

> The man who lives upstairs bothers the neighbors when he comes home from work at midnight; <u>so</u> I've decided to speak to him about it.

In the version with the semicolon—with or without the conjunction—the reader will give more emphasis to the second clause. We take up semicolons later in the chapter. This use of *so* is also considered a coordinating conjunction, so a comma is also correct for connecting the two clauses (as in this sentence).

How about the conjunction by itself? Is that ever allowed in the compound sentence?

> *The man who lives upstairs bothers the neighbors when he comes home from work at midnight <u>and</u> I've decided to speak to him about it.

Again, the wrong message—another run-on of sorts, although not as serious as the run-on with neither conjunction nor comma. The use of *and* without the comma tells the reader that a coordinate structure *within the sentence* is coming—not that a new independent clause is coming.

It's certainly possible to find examples in both contemporary and older prose of two sentences, usually short ones, put together with the conjunction alone or with the comma alone—deliberate deviations from conventional punctuation practices. And there are writers on punctuation and style who would not have marked that last example sentence an error—as the asterisk indicates it is. However, the standard convention for the compound sentence follows the rule stated earlier: comma-plus-conjunction. That's the rule followed in this book. In most of your writing situations, you are expected to conform to standard conventions. It's important to remember the purpose of punctuation: to give the reader information about the kind of structure that follows.

The importance of accurate punctuation cannot be overemphasized. Not only will readers be guided accurately through your ideas, they will also gain confidence in you as a writer—and as an authority on your topic. It's easy for a reader to conclude—perhaps subconsciously and, yes, perhaps unfairly—that slipshod punctuation equals slipshod thinking. Your image, your credibility as a writer, can only be enhanced when you make accurate, effective, and helpful punctuation choices.

EXERCISE 8

Add punctuation to the following sentences—if they need it.

1. I took piano lessons for several years as a child but I never did like to practice.

2. I surprised both my mother and my former piano teacher by signing up for lessons in the Music Department here at school so now I practice every spare minute I can find.

3. My hands are small but I have exercised my fingers and now have managed to stretch an octave.

4. My fingers are terribly uncoordinated but every week the exercises and scales get easier to play.

5. I was really embarrassed the first few times I practiced on the old upright in our dorm lounge so I usually waited until the room was empty now I don't mind the weird looks I get from people.

6. Some of my friends clap their hands or tap their feet to help me keep time.

7. I have met three residents in the dorm who are really good pianists they've been very helpful to me and very supportive of my beginning efforts.

8. I often play my Glenn Gould records for inspiration and just plain enjoyment.

9. I'm so glad that Bach and Haydn composed music simple enough for beginners and that my teacher assigned it for me to play.

10. I'm looking forward to seeing the look on my mother's face when I go home at the end of the term and play some of my lessons from *The Little Bach Book* she will be amazed.

Conjunctive Adverbs

In the next chapter, on the topic of cohesion, you will read about *metadiscourse*, a term that refers to certain signals that help the reader understand the writer's message. Among the most useful such signals are the **conjunctive adverbs,** also known as *adverbial conjunctions.* As their name suggests, the conjunctive adverbs join sentences to form coordinate structures as other conjunctions do, but they do so with an adverbial emphasis. The following list includes some of the most common simple adverbs and adverbial prepositional phrases that function as sentence connectors:

> *Addition:* moreover, furthermore, likewise, also, in addition
>
> *Time:* meanwhile, in the meantime, afterwards, previously
>
> *Contrast:* however, instead, on the contrary, on the other hand, in contrast, rather
>
> *Result:* therefore, so, conseqeuntly, as a result, of course
>
> *Concession:* nevertheless, yet, still, at any rate, after all, of course
>
> *Apposition:* namely, for example, for instance, that is, in other words
>
> *Summary:* thus, then, in conclusion
>
> *Reinforcement:* further, indeed, in particular, above all, in fact

Conjunctive adverbs differ from other conjunctions in that, like ordinary adverbs, most of them are movable; they need not introduce their clause. It is that movability that makes them such an important tool for writers:

> We worked hard for the Consumer Party candidates; <u>however,</u> we knew they didn't stand a chance.
>
> We worked hard for the Consumer Party candidates; we knew, <u>however,</u> that they didn't stand a chance.
>
> We worked hard for the Consumer Party candidates; we knew they didn't stand a chance, <u>however.</u>
>
> The campaign contributions we had been counting on simply didn't materialize; <u>in fact,</u> the campaign was broke.
>
> The campaign contributions we had been counting on simply didn't materialize; the campaign, <u>in fact,</u> was broke.

Bear in mind, however, that the farther along in the sentence the conjunctive adverb appears, the less value it has as a connector. If the reader needs the signal that the connector carries—such as the message of *however,* indicating that a contrast is coming—you will probably want the reader to get it in timely fashion, not wait until the end, especially when the second clause is fairly long.

A different emphasis occurs when the conjunctive adverb is used with no punctuation. Read these pairs of sentences aloud and note where you put the main stress in the second clause of each:

The contributions we had been counting on simply didn't material-
ize; the campaign was <u>in fact</u> broke.

The contributions we had been counting on simply didn't material-
ize; the campaign, <u>in fact,</u> was broke.

Our main speaker canceled at the last minute; the rally was <u>there-
fore</u> postponed until the following weekend.

Our main speaker canceled at the last minute; the rally, <u>therefore,</u>
was postponed until the following weekend.

In the versions *without* commas, it is the word *following* the conjunctive
adverb that gets main stress; *with* commas, it's the word *preceding.*

This punctuation choice occurs with only a limited number of the conjunctive adverbs; most of them require the commas to send their message.
And it's also important to recognize that without punctuation they lose
some of their connective power, functioning more like adverbials, less like
conjunctions. In our two examples without commas, *in fact* and *therefore*
seem more like modifiers of the words *broke* and *postponed* rather than
comments relating to the clause as a whole.

You'll also want to consider the tone that conjunctive adverbs tend to
convey. Some of them—such as *moreover, nevertheless, therefore,* and even
the fairly common *however*—may strike the reader as formal, perhaps even
stiff. You can often diminish that formality by using coordinating conjunctions: Instead of *however,* use *but;* instead of *moreover,* use *and* (or *also*);
for *nevertheless,* use *yet.*

Compound Sentences with Semicolons

You've seen a great many semicolons used in the discussions throughout
these chapters. And in the previous section you saw them in sentences illustrating the use of the conjunctive adverbs. However, you can't assume from
these examples that you'll find them in great numbers everywhere. Some
people manage to go through life without ever making their acquaintance.
If you belong to that group of non-users, you can be sure of one thing:
Your punctuation is not as effective as it could and should be. But take
heart! The semicolon is easy to use.

In her book *Woe Is I* (Riverhead Books, 1996), Patricia T. O'Conner
calls the semicolon the flashing red of punctuation traffic signals:

> If a comma is a yellow light and a period is a red light, the semi-
> colon is a flashing red—one of those lights you drive through
> after a brief pause. (139)

Think of the semicolon as the equivalent of the comma-plus-conjunction that connects compound sentences. You could even put this relationship into a formula:

$$(, + and) = (;)$$

In the last section you saw semicolons in compound sentences with conjunctive adverbs, but don't get the idea that the conjunctive adverb is required. Semicolons can be used with no conjunction at all:

> There was silence; I stood awkwardly, then moved to the door.
> There was silence; white faces were looking strangely at me.
> —Richard Wright

In compound sentences like these, the semicolon sends a message to the reader: "Notice the connection." To understand the importance of the semicolon, imagine the Richard Wright sentences without the semicolons, with periods instead. The connection of the silence to what follows in each case would be lost.

These two uses of the semicolon to connect clauses—by itself and with a conjunctive adverb—are perhaps the most common; but there are times when you will want to use a coordinating conjunction along with the semicolon, as in this compound sentence you are reading. As you can see, in the second clause the conjunction *but* signals a contrast. In meaning, *but* is very much like *however,* except in its degree of formality; it is less formal.

In Chapter 9 you will read about the one other place we use the semicolon: to separate the parts of a series when the individual parts include punctuation of their own. Here's an example:

> The study of our grammar system includes three main areas: phonology, the study of sounds; morphology, the study of meaningful combinations of sounds; and syntax, the study of sentences.

Because each of the three items in the series includes an explanatory phrase set off by commas, the use of semicolons between them helps keep the reader on track.

Compound Sentences with Colons

Inexperienced writers often avoid using semicolons simply because they don't understand them; even less understood is the colon as a sentence connector. In Chapter 9 you will read about the colon in its more familiar role—as a signal of appositives:

> Three committees were set up to plan the convention: program, finance, and local arrangements.

In this sentence the message of the colon is "Here it comes, the list of committees I promised."

In connecting two complete sentences, the message of the colon is similar. As with the list in the preceding example, the independent sentence following a colon also completes or explains or illustrates the idea in the first clause:

> Rats and rabbits, to those who injected, weighed and dissected them, were little different from cultures in a petri dish: they were just things to manipulate and observe.
> —Steven Zak

> It's not that Japanese consumers are eager to throw their money away: to judge by the way shoppers prowl through the neighborhood supermarket and electronics store, they are extremely cost conscious.
> —James Fallows

> I came to a conclusion that I want to pass on to you, and I hope nobody gets too mad: Medical science does everything it can.
> —Carolyn See

The preceding examples are all taken from essays in popular magazines. The following sentence is from fiction:

> Jem and I found our father satisfactory: he played with us, read to us, and treated us with courteous detachment.
> —Harper Lee *(To Kill a Mockingbird)*

Notice how the first clause sets up an expectation in the reader. The colon says, "Here comes the information you're expecting" or "Here's what I promised." In the second passage, the *not* in the first clause sets the reader up for a contrast in the second. In general, if you can mentally insert *namely* or *that is* or *in fact,* as you can in the preceding examples, you should consider using a colon to connect the sentences.

It's important to recognize that this way of connecting two clauses is quite different from the connection with semicolons. The two clauses connected with the semicolon have parallel ideas. And unless you include a signal to the contrary, your reader will expect the relationship to be an additive one, an *and* connection. If you try to replace the colon with *and,* you'll see that it won't work.

Two other common situations that the colon signals are questions and direct quotations:

> Everyone at the news conference wondered what was coming next: Would the senator actually admit her part in the cover-up?

> A Northwestern University psychiatrist explained the purpose of brain chemicals rather poetically: "A person's mood is like a symphony, and serotonin is like the conductor's baton."
>
> *— Time*

Another situation that calls for the colon as a signal, which you are probably familiar with, is the block quotation—the long indented quotation.

There is one detail of punctuation in these compound sentences that varies. Except in the case of the direct quotation, you have the choice of using either a capital or a lowercase letter following the colon. (The first word of a direct quotation following a colon is generally capitalized, whether or not the quotation is a full sentence.) Some publications capitalize all full sentences following colons (the style of this book); others capitalize only questions; some use lowercase for all sentences except direct quotations. Whichever style of punctuation you choose, be consistent.

THE COMPOUND SENTENCE: PUNCTUATION REVIEW

We have seen five styles of punctuation for joining the clauses in compound sentences. Every writer should understand all five and be able to use them effectively.

1. Comma-plus-conjunction

> My neighbor makes a lot of noise, and I intend to talk to him about it.
> I haven't confronted my neighbor about the noise problem, but I intend to do so very soon.

> Remember that the comma by itself is not strong enough to make that connection; without the conjunction, the result is a comma splice.

2. <u>Semicolon</u>

> My neighbor makes a lot of noise; I intend to talk to him about it.

You can think of this connection as a tighter version of the comma with *and*.

3. <u>Semicolon-plus-conjunction</u>

> I haven't confronted my neighbor about the noise problem; but I intend to do so very soon.

Here the reader stops for the semicolon's flashing red light, a clear stop compared with the brief pause for the comma's yellow light.

4. <u>Semicolon-plus-conjunctive adverb</u>

> I haven't confronted my neighbor about the noise problem; however, I intend to do so very soon.

The meanings of 3 and 4 are essentially the same. The only difference is a matter of formality and emphasis. *However* is more formal; also, it has the advantage of being movable, so you can manipulate the rhythm pattern to focus the emphasis on different words. You can decide how the reader reads the sentence:

> ...; I intend, however, to do so very soon.
> ...; I intend to do so very soon, however.

Strong stress falls on the word preceding the comma.

5. <u>Colon</u>

> The man who lives upstairs has a problem he hasn't heard about yet: He has an unhappy neighbor.

Here the colon is saying, "Here it comes, the problem you're expecting." Note that the full sentence following the colon does not always begin with a capital letter, as it does here. Some publications prefer lowercase in this position.

These, then, are the five methods we use for connecting the two clauses of a compound sentence. Be sure to take time to understand all of them. Using them correctly also means understanding the structure of clauses, their parameters. These two concepts—the structure of clauses and the conventions for connecting them—are basic tools that every writer needs for every writing task.

EXERCISE 9

Add punctuation to the following passages, if necessary. In some cases there may be more than one possibility.

1. Norm doesn't like to dance and he claims that he's not very agile but he wanted to make his girlfriend happy so he signed up for six lessons.

2. The lectures in our astronomy class as well as the assigned reading and the lab work make it clear that I am in the wrong class I have decided to drop the course.

3. Slang is merely a habit and like many other habits it is easily acquired however it is not always easily lost.

4. The defendant stood at the judge's request braced himself against the table and waited for the judge to read the jury's decision.

5. The surface of the lake was neither choppy nor smooth but the wind was right it would be a good day for sailing.

6. There were red and white balloons tied to trees fences and signposts all over the campus not only to celebrate the basketball team's big win but also to signal the beginning of Spring Week.

7. Something always seems to be going wrong with my equipment the fax machine jams the paper the computer sends me error messages I don't understand and the printer refuses to print the bottom line of every page.

8. My equipment is obviously sending me a message I will have to invest in both a new computer and a new printer before the semester ends.

9. The hundreds of separate groups that make up the environmental movement have been speaking out and demonstrating in order to get the support of both their fellow citizens and their legislators they are especially concerned about the quality of life for future generations.

10. Our neighbor is proud of his vegetable garden he built up the soil with compost planted exotic vegetables and erected a fence to keep the rabbits out unfortunately however the deer discovered those tender green shoots and the fence didn't deter them in the least.

PARALLEL STRUCTURE

One of the most important lessons to be learned about coordination is the concept of **parallel structure.** A coordinate structure is parallel only when the two parts are of the same *form*. And the parallel structure is an effective one—and this feature is just as important—only when the *two ideas are equal,* when they belong together. Here, for example, is a compound structure that is unparallel in form:

> *My new exercise program and going on a strict diet will give me a new shape before bikini season.

Here the *and* connects a compound subject:

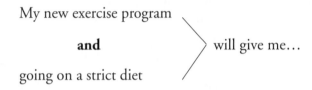

The first one *(My new exercise program)* is a noun phrase in form; the second *(going on a strict diet)* is a verb phrase, a **gerund.** (*Gerund* is the label we give an *-ing* verb when it is used as a noun.) In this case the ideas are equal, so in that sense they belong together. But for the sentence to be grammatical, the two parts of the compound must be the same form:

> My new exercise program **and** a strict diet (NP + NP)
>
> Sticking to my exercise program **and** going on a diet (VP + VP)

In the case of correlative conjunctions, the problem of unparallel structure is usually easy to spot and easy to fix: It's a matter of paying attention to the conjunctions. *Either* signals that *or* is on the way—and your reader knows it! Just be sure that the same form follows both parts of the correlative, because that's what the reader is expecting. The writer of the following sentence suffered a lapse in attention:

> *I will **either** take the train **or** the bus.

Here we have a verb phrase *(take the train)* connected to a noun phrase *(the bus)*. To correct this unparallel structure, simply move *either:*

> I will take **either** the train **or** the bus.

You may be thinking that these incorrect sentences seem perfectly normal—like sentences you say every day. And you're right—they do sound normal. We use sentences like these in our conversation all the time—and no one accuses us of being ungrammatical. But writing is different. We want to be as precise and effective as possible. And as writers, we have a second (and third and fourth!) chance to improve our sentences. We don't have to show that first draft to anyone. Sentences with unparallel features like these can always be improved.

In sentences with compound predicates, unparallel verb forms can sometimes produce a kind of fuzziness. Notice in the following sentence that only one of the two verbs includes an auxiliary:

> Experts in sports medicine <u>emphasize</u> the importance of water intake and <u>are recommending</u> a half-ounce per day for every pound of body weight.

A related source of fuzziness can occur in the compound sentence. The previous example could easily be turned into a compound sentence with the simple addition of a second subject:

> Experts in sports medicine emphasize the importance of water intake
> **, and**
> they are recommending a half-ounce per day for every pound of body weight.

The sentence is now parallel in *form*. But a question remains: Are the two *ideas* parallel? Do they belong together as equal partners? (And remember, that's what the message of *and* is: "These two structures are equal partners.")

If the two ideas were fuzzy partners as predicates—a judgment suggested by the form of the verbs—then they are just as likely to be fuzzy partners as sentences. The problem is not just that one verb has an auxiliary and the other doesn't (*are recommending* and *emphasize*); it's the underlying reason for that difference. We generally use the simple present tense *(emphasize)* to describe an accepted truth or timeless quality; we use the present progressive tense *(are recommending)* for a present action. It's not that the two ideas don't belong together: They do. But not as equal partners. *And* is simply the wrong connection.

Because the sentence is out of context, we don't know which of the two ideas should be emphasized, but a good guess would be the recommendation:

> Experts in sports medicine, who emphasize the importance of water intake, are recommending a half-ounce per day for every pound of body weight.

Here we've used a relative clause for one of the two ideas. Another possibility is the **participial phrase** to open the sentence. (An *-ing* verb used as an adjective is called a **participle** or, as in this case, a participial phrase.)

> Emphasizing the importance of water intake, experts in sports medicine recommend a half-ounce per day for every pound of body weight.

We will look at both of these noun modifiers—the relative clause and the participial phrase—in Chapter 9.

You may find it helpful to think in terms of foregrounding and backgrounding when you have two ideas to combine. Which idea should get the foreground, the prominence of the main clause? Which should be thought of as background? This concept is related to the concept of known and new information, which you will study in the next chapter.

The following sentence illustrates another common coordination problem: a fact and a conclusion based on that fact put together as parallel ideas.

> The African killer bees are less predictable than European bees and tend to attack in vast swarms.

One clue that the two predicates don't belong together is a difference in verb classes: linking and transitive. Again, we need context to know which idea should get the main focus, which idea should be foreground and which should be treated as the background:

> The African killer bees, which are less predictable than European bees, tend to attack in vast swarms.
>
> The African killer bees, which tend to attack in vast swarms, are less predictable than European bees.

A mismatch in verb forms certainly doesn't guarantee a problem, but it's the kind of sentence you'll want to notice when you're revising.

Exercise 10

Revise the following sentences, paying particular attention to the unparallel structures.

1. I can't decide which activity I prefer: to swim at the shore in July, when the sand is warm, or jogging along country roads in October, when the autumn leaves are at their colorful best.

2. The Baltimore Orioles' stadium at Camden Yards has all the virtues of the beloved ballparks of another era and is in the great tradition of classic baseball architecture.

3. I neither enjoy flying across the country nor particularly want to take the train.

4. The movie's starting time and whether we could afford the tickets were both more important to us than were the opinions of the reviewers.

5. Denny lost weight very slowly but said he didn't want to try the new diet drugs.

6. Bowling, like other sports, requires physical exertion and is the number one participation sport in the country.

7. I almost never watch television: There is either nothing on that appeals to me, or the picture disappears at a crucial moment.

8. Blue whales are the largest of all animals and up to 80 percent of them congregate seasonally in Antarctic waters.

KEY TERMS

Backgrounding	Coordinating	Run-on sentence
Climax	conjunction	Semicolon
Colon	Coordination	Serial comma
Comma	Correlative	Series
Comma splice	conjunction	Subject–verb
Compound sentence	Foregrounding	agreement
Conjunction	Independent clause	
Conjunctive adverb	Parallel structure	

RHETORICAL REMINDERS

Parallelism

Do the coordinate structures within the sentence belong together? (Are the ideas equal? Are the forms the same?)

But

Have I reserved *but* for signaling contrasts?

Correlatives

Have I taken advantage of the strong focus that the correlatives provide: *either–or, neither–nor, both–and, not only–but also?*

Conjunctive Adverbs

Have I used the versatile conjunctive adverbs to good advantage?

Have I placed them where I want the reader to focus?

Colons

Have I used the colon to connect those sentences that set up an expectation in the reader?

PUNCTUATION REMINDERS

Have I remembered that in the case of a two-part compound within the sentence no comma is required?

Have I used a comma with the conjunction between the two independent clauses of a compound sentence?

Have I made good use of a semicolon to connect clauses when it would effectively signal a close connection?

Have I used a colon effectively to signal the expected information that follows in a second independent clause?

Have I used a dash (or dashes) to lighten the comma load?

CHAPTER 4

Cohesion

CHAPTER PREVIEW

The topic of **cohesion** is about the connection of sentences to one another, to the flow of a text, to the ways in which a paragraph of separate sentences becomes a unified whole. In our examination of cohesion, we first look at **reader expectation,** which means, simply, imagining yourself—you, as writer—in your reader's shoes. Then we examine four important features of cohesive writing:

- **Repetition:** key words and phrases that keep the reader on course.

- The **known–new contract:** a simple but powerful concept that reflects one aspect of reader expectation—that a sentence will have both known, or old, information as well as new and that the known information will precede the new.

- **Metadiscourse:** signals, or guideposts, that help the reader interpret the writer's message.

- **Parallelism:** the repetition of structures of the same form for purposes of clarity and emphasis.

The final section in this chapter explains a method of paragraph analysis called **levels of generality,** a way of visualizing the connection of sentences that may illuminate places where revision is called for.

With all of these topics, you are essentially learning to put labels on features of the language that often make the difference between merely adequate prose and really effective prose. When you recognize them and learn to manipulate them, they become writing tools at your disposal.

In every aspect of rhetoric—especially in the matter of connections—the writer must keep the reader and the reader's expectations in mind. So before taking up the separate features of cohesion, we will look at this important concept affecting all the connections: reader expectation.

READER EXPECTATION

Have you ever come across a teacher's "awk" noted in the margin of a written assignment, or have you yourself ever judged a piece of writing as awkward? Perhaps in reading a composition of your own or that of your classmate you have felt that something was amiss—but you couldn't quite put your finger on the something. Such problems can sometimes be traced to thwarted expectations. Something may have struck you as awkward simply because you weren't expecting it.

Both in reading and in conversation our language is loaded with expectations; we have a sense of direction about language. Although we may not know exactly what's coming next, when we hear it—or read it—we recognize if it's appropriate. It's when the ideas take an unexpected turn that the "awk" response can set in, when a passage fails to fit that expectation, that sense of appropriateness: "I didn't know exactly what was coming next—but I certainly didn't expect *that!*"

In conversation, we can call a halt to the speaker: "Wait! What was that you just said?" But as readers, of course, we don't have that option. Instead, we find ourselves thinking, "Why am I reading this now?" Even though it's only a fleeting thought, it doesn't take many such interruptions—the pause, the second thought, the backtracking—to obstruct the cohesive flow of a piece of writing.

Where do a reader's expectations come from? Obviously, from what has gone before, from the prior text, or, in the case of an opening paragraph, from the title or, possibly, from the author's reputation. Within a paragraph, reader expectation begins with the opening sentence. The writer, of course, has all manner of possibilities for setting up that expectation. The first sentence of this paragraph, because it is a question, sets up the expectation of an answer—or perhaps a second question.

Following is the opening sentence from a paragraph in an article about the "most glamorous sweepstakes in sports"—the Triple Crown of thoroughbred racing. This paragraph follows the article's opening section discussing the eleven horses that have successfully swept the three races of the Triple Crown since its inception in 1914, the most recent being Affirmed in 1978. The paragraph is preceded by a subheading: "Three races become the ultimate test."

> The sweep is so rare and difficult because each race has unique demands and the series as a whole requires unusual ruggedness.

This opening sentence has no doubt set up an expectation in you about what is coming next, something about the difficulties, demands, and/or ruggedness of the Triple Crown sweep. Now read the complete paragraph:

> The sweep is so rare and difficult because each race has unique demands and the series as a whole requires unusual ruggedness. Racehorses usually do best with about a month between races. In the Triple Crown they must race three times in 36 days, over three different tracks, and at three different distances, all longer than most have ever tried before.
> —Steven Crist *(USAir Magazine)*

That second sentence is surely a letdown: We were expecting something else. The topic has shifted. Not that this new topic is unimportant. But the writer did not prepare us to expect this shift from the ruggedness of the race to the ideal interval between races.

The effective topic sentence nearly always suggests the direction the paragraph will take, calling up a response in the reader: "Prove it" or "Tell me more." The following sentence opens a paragraph in *Time* about the friendship between Abraham Lincoln and Frederick Douglass, the third paragraph in an article by John Stauffer entitled "Across the Great Divide":

> Despite the immense racial gulf separating them, Lincoln and Douglass had a lot in common.

After reading that statement, we expect to read facts that prove the point. The writer meets our expectations, first with what we might call a subtopic sentence and then the supporting details:

> They were the two preeminent self-made men of their era. Lincoln was born dirt poor, had less than a year of formal schooling and became one of the nation's greatest Presidents. Douglass spent the first 20 years of his life as a slave, had no formal schooling—in fact, his masters forbade him to read or write—and became one of the nation's greatest writers and activists.

The paragraph ends with two additional sentences about Douglass as writer and activist. As you can see, the promise of the topic sentence has been kept. It led us to believe we would be given proof of its proposition—and the rest of the paragraph does just that.

While you're in the early drafting stage of your essay, you have lots of details to think about: deciding which ideas to emphasize and how to support your premises, finding just the right words. At this early stage the response of your reader may not even occur to you. But certainly at the various revision stages along the way—and, by the way, revision does go on all the time—you'll want to think about the reader's expectations.

Remember that, as with many other facets of language, a reader's expectations are not necessarily conscious thoughts. A thwarted expectation may constitute only a fleeting break in concentration, a momentary blip in the flow. But remember, too, it's that blip that produces the "awk."

Active readers do more than simply process the words and meanings of a particular sentence as they are reading it. They also fit the ideas of the current sentence into what they already know: knowledge garnered both from previous sentences and from their own experience. At the same time, they are developing further expectations.

To become aware of the reader's expectations means to put yourself in the reader's shoes—or head. It requires the ability to read your own ideas objectively, to see and hear your own words as someone else might read them. All of the sections that follow in this chapter, covering various features of cohesion, emphasize this relationship between writer and reader.

FOR GROUP DISCUSSION

1. Look again at the weasel paragraph at the opening of Chapter 1. Delete the second sentence, the question. Discuss how that deletion alters reader expectation. In what way does the presence of the question change the expectation set up by the opening sentence? Compose an alternative second sentence in the form of a statement, rather than a question. Compare your version to Dillard's in terms of its effect on a reader's expectation.

2. Revise the second sentence of the Triple Crown paragraph to eliminate that blip of awkwardness. In other words, prepare the reader for the information about the time between races; prepare the reader to expect it.

3. Write (or read aloud to your group) a partial paragraph from your current essay assignment. Then ask the other members of the group to predict what's coming next.

REPETITION

Instead of "Repetition," this discussion could be headed "**lexical cohesion,**" a term that refers to the contribution of particular words to the cohesion, or continuity, of text. (*Lexicon,* the noun form of *lexical,* means the words of the language; you can think of your lexicon as the dictionary in your head.) The repetition of words from one sentence to another is an obvious cohesive link, one that logically occurs in a paragraph on a particular topic.

In his book *Constructing Texts,* George Dillon characterizes the conflicting advice about repetition that student writers often encounter as a "no-man's land":

> [A] no-man's-land where they are caught in the crossfire of Never Use the Same Word Twice on a Page and Repeat Key Terms, Use Your Thesaurus to Find Synonyms and Avoid Needless ('Elegant') Variation. (p. 96)

Dillon notes that the journalism class is more often the source of "Never Use the Same Word Twice" and English class the source of "Repeat Key Terms." He points out that sportswriters are especially good at avoiding repetition, at finding synonyms. Here, for example, is a paragraph about a Cubs-Cardinals game from the Associated Press's "National League Roundup" column in the *New York Times* (July 24, 2005):

> [Derrek Lee's] two-run shot off Matt Morris (11-3) with two outs in the fifth sailed over the visitors' bullpen in left before clanging off a guardrail, a drive estimated at 421 feet that put the Cubs ahead, 5-3. Morris gave up all three homers and has allowed 10 this season after surrendering 35 last year.

In the first sentence, the batter's successful hit is referred to as both a *shot* and *a drive;* and the three verbs in the last sentence—*gave up, has allowed, surrendering*—are all synonyms for delivering a home-run pitch. In fact, among the major word classes in the paragraph—nouns, verbs, adjectives, and adverbs—there's not a single repeated word!

It's not only the sports reporters who avoid repetition. News writers in other departments also rely on synonyms. During the 2004 election campaign, for example, we often read news reports that started off with "John Kerry," then changed to "the Democratic candidate," then "the nominee," then "the senator from Massachusetts" in successive sentences or paragraphs. And political writers often use "the White House," "the administration," and "the executive branch" as alternatives to "the president."

On the other hand, you'll find that the paragraphs you've been reading in this textbook reflect the English-class advice that Dillon identifies:

"Repeat Key Terms." For example, the first paragraph in Chapter 1, headed "Chapter Preview," includes the word *sentence* five times in its six sentences and the word *language* three times, with no synonyms for either word—simply because there are no synonyms that would do the job as well. And of course it makes sense to repeat key concepts in a book designed to teach those concepts. But you'll also find from time to time alternative phrasing for the sake of variety or to add a new dimension to the discussion. In the writing you do for your English class, the best advice is probably the middle ground. It would certainly be a mistake to conclude that repetition should be avoided. In fact, the opposite is true: Repetition strengthens cohesion.

But what happens when your teacher writes "rep" in the margin of your essay, a comment usually aimed at unnecessary repetition? How can you tell the difference between the good kind, the repetition that enhances cohesion, and the kind that calls negative attention to itself? Unnecessary repetition goes by the name of **redundancy**. It's possible that the redundant word the teacher noticed is part of a redundant sentence, one that adds nothing new to the discussion. As you'll read in the next section, most sentences contain both known and new information. The lack of new information may be the source of that "rep" comment.

Lexical cohesion also refers to synonyms and other related words, not just actual repetition: *birds/robins, rodents/mice, evening meal/supper, friend/companion, vacation/trip/holiday.* And of course our grammar itself calls for the use of pronouns in lieu of repeating a noun or noun phrase. Such substitutes constitute strong cohesive ties.

THE KNOWN–NEW CONTRACT

Seeing the sentence as a series of slots, as you did in Chapter 1, will help you understand the feature of cohesion called the **known–new contract.** It relates to both what the reader knows and what the reader expects.

The first sentence in a paragraph, like the first paragraph of a chapter or an essay, sets up expectations in the reader about what is coming. Certainly one of those expectations is that the following sentences will stick to the topic. Another is that the sentence will have new information, not just a repeat of what the reader already knows.

The term *known–new* also describes the most common order for that information, with the known, or old or given, information coming first, generally filling the subject slot, and the new information—the reason for the sentence—in the predicate, where the main emphasis of the sentence naturally occurs. This pattern is obvious in the Lincoln/Douglass paragraph, with *Lincoln and Douglass* as the subject of the topic sentence, *they* as the subject of the second, and their separate names as subjects in the sentences that follow. In the Triple Crown paragraph, that blip of awkwardness we encountered occurred in the subject slot of the second sentence. We expected a known subject, old information, such as *each race;* instead we encountered *racehorses.*

The repeated known information is not always repeated in the exact words, as it is in the Lincoln/Douglass example—as the sports reports in the preceding section clearly demonstrate. We saw another example in the paragraph about dams in Chapter 2, where the known information in the second sentence is a paraphrase of the topic in the first:

> Shaping up as an important milestone is <u>the demolition of two large dams</u> in Washington State's Elwha River, which flows from the mountains of Olympic National Park into the Juan de Fuca Strait. <u>Their removal,</u> scheduled to begin in 2008, would occur in stages, and if it goes as planned, the Pacific Northwest will lose only a tiny amount of hydropower and regain a legendary salmon fishery.

In other words, *removal* is another way of saying *demolition.*

The Lincoln/Douglass example illustrates a common pattern wherein the repeated topic, information that the reader knows, remains fairly constant throughout the paragraph, in subject position. In some paragraphs, however, the new information that appears in the predicate of one sentence becomes the known information in the next, filling the subject slot. Here, for example, is a newspaper paragraph written by a meteorologist in response to a reader's question about thunderstorms; it begins with a one-sentence paragraph:

> Thunderstorms can be categorized as single cell or multicell.
> Basically, *a single-cell thunderstorm* is the lone thunderstorm that forms <u>on a hot humid day.</u> The *heat and humidity of the day* is the only trigger for the storm. This type of storm forms in an environment with little difference in the wind speed and direction—or wind shear—between the surface and cloud level.
> —Joe Murgo *(Centre Daily Times)*

Here's a paragraph you read in Chapter 1 in the section headed "Clause and Sentence":

> In summary, then, we can say that all sentences are made up of <u>one or more independent clauses.</u> However, *a clause* need not be an independent, or complete, sentence; it doesn't always have

sentence status. *Understanding the status of clauses*—whether independent or dependent—is basic to understanding punctuation. In fact, it is perhaps the most important concept overall for a writer to have under control.

And here's one you'll read in Chapter 6 in the discussion of contractions:

Contractions affect the rhythm of sentences and, in doing so, affect the reader's perception of the writer's voice. *That voice* will probably strike the reader as more conversational, less formal, when contractions are part of the message. *Contractions* help to close the distance between writer and reader.

The arrows in these examples highlight this pattern: The new information in the predicate of one sentence (underlined) becomes the known information (italicized) in the next one.

In another paragraph pattern, or information pattern, the proposition in the topic sentence is followed by supporting details suggested by the topic and expected by the reader. This pattern of development is fairly standard for writing various kinds of description, where the topic sentence sets up the expectation of the details that will prove its point, specific examples to support the generalization in the topic sentence:

Our trip to Florida for spring break turned out to be a disaster. The hotel room we rented was miserable—shabby and stuffy and downright depressing. The food we could afford made our dining hall remembrances from campus seem positively gourmet. The daily transportation to the beach we had been promised showed up only once and even then was an hour late. . . .

Here the subjects of the supporting sentences are what we can think of as subtopics of the main subject, "our trip to Florida for spring break." Paragraphs like this one generally cry out for more details, and the place to add them is under those subtopic sentences, with specifics of the room and the food and other events that make the trip come alive for the reader—in other words, another layer of detail. If, after finishing the disaster details, you decide to add some happy events of the trip, either in the same paragraph or in the next one (assuming there were indeed some happy events), you'll have to signal that change to your reader with "on the other hand" or "however" or "but" or some other indication that you're shifting gears.

If you are writing a descriptive essay about your apartment, perhaps to let a future roommate know what to expect, chances are you'd use this same pattern. You might begin with an overall assessment of the apartment's adequacy or inadequacy, its efficiency or lack thereof, in your topic sentence. The subjects of the sentences that follow would support that assessment with details about cost, location, furnishings, neighbors, and so on.

It might appear that the sentences of such a paragraph, like those in the description of spring break, contain no known information, when each brings up a new topic, or subtopic. But in both cases the subtopics really are known information; they are all part of the domain, the sphere, of apartment living—or of spring breaks in Florida. We can think of them as essentially given information, information that a reader can be expected to recognize as relevant.

FOR GROUP DISCUSSION

The following paragraphs are from Chapter 15 of *Undaunted Courage*, the story of the Lewis and Clark expedition by Stephen E. Ambrose. The passage here describes an event in October 1804, a year into the trip. As you read the sentences, note the information patterns and cohesive ties that Ambrose has used. You might begin by marking the known information in each sentence and noting its connection to the preceding text:

> Beginning in October, as the expedition made its way through present northern South Dakota, it passed numerous abandoned villages, composed of earth-lodge dwellings and cultivated fields. Some of the fields, although unattended, still had squash and corn growing in them. These had once been home to the mighty Arikara tribe. About thirty thousand persons strong in the year the United States won its independence, the tribe had been reduced by smallpox epidemics in the 1780s to not much more than one-fifth that size. Another epidemic swept through in 1803–4, devastating the tribe. What had been eighteen villages the previous year had been reduced to three by the time Lewis arrived.
>
> On October 8, the keelboat passed a three-mile-long island, near the mouth of the Grand River, home to the three villages of living Arikaras, about two thousand Indians all together. The island was one large garden, growing beans, corn, and squash. Arikaras lined the banks, watching the boat progress to the head of the island and then watching the men make camp on the starboard side. Lewis selected two voyagers who spoke the Arikara language and two soldiers, took a pirogue, and paddled across to meet the Indians on the island. Clark stayed in camp, posting guards on shore and sentinels on the boat and canoes, with "all things arranged both for Peace or War."

EXERCISE 11

Revise the following passages to improve their cohesion. Think especially about reader expectation and the known–new contract.

1. The Gateway Arch at the edge of the Mississippi River in St. Louis is the world's tallest monument. Eero Saarinen designed the stainless steel structure that commemorates the Westward Movement.

2. Psychologists believe that color conveys emotional messages. Advertisers routinely manipulate consumers using color psychology. The pure white backgrounds and bold primary colors of detergent boxes are thought to influence buyers. Cleanliness and strength are associated with those colors.

3. The relentless heat of California's great Central Valley makes the summer almost unbearable at times. Over 110° is not an unusual temperature reading from June through September. Bakersfield often records the hottest temperature in the valley.

4. Getting chilled or getting your feet wet won't cause a cold. Weather is not the culprit that causes the common cold. Viruses are to blame.

5. Pittsburgh's new baseball stadium is the smallest in the major leagues, except for Boston's Fenway Park. Pittsburgh-based PNC Bank Corporation purchased the right to name the new park. PNC Park is the name they chose. They will pay $1.5 million a year for twenty years for the privilege of naming it. April 9, 2001, was the opening date. There are 38,127 seats in the stadium.

6. The federal witness-protection service began in 1968. The U.S. Marshal Service directs the program. Over four thousand people have been relocated under the program. New identities are created for people in the program. The people are in extreme danger because they have testified against criminals.

The Role of Pronouns

Personal Pronouns. Perhaps our most common known element, equally as strong as the repeated noun phrase, is the pronoun. In Chapter 1, you'll recall, we used **personal pronouns**—*he, she, it, they, we*—to identify the boundaries of noun phrase slots. When we use those pronouns in writing (and we often do use a pronoun instead of repeating a noun phrase), we call that noun phrase the pronoun's **antecedent.** You can think of the antecedent as the pronoun's back-up system. And because it has that backup noun phrase, the pronoun is, by definition, known information. But the pronoun will work only when its antecedent is clear to the reader, in the foreground of the reader's consciousness.

Let's look at a portion of the weasel paragraph we saw in Chapter 1:

> (1) A weasel is wild. (2) Who knows what **he** thinks? (3) **He** sleeps in **his** underground den, **his** tail draped over **his** nose. (4) Sometimes **he** lives in **his** den for two days without leaving. (5) Outside, **he** stalks rabbits, mice, muskrats, and birds, killing more bodies than **he** can eat warm, and often dragging the carcasses home.

The pronoun *he* connects the second sentence to the first—only that one word, but clearly a strong grammatical tie. The third sentence repeats *he*. The fourth and fifth sentences both begin with *he*.

Personal pronouns in the **possessive case,** such as *his* in the third and fourth sentences of the weasel passage, function as **determiners,** or noun signalers. A noun phrase can often be identified on the basis of its opening word, its determiner. The most common determiners are the **articles**—*a, an,* and *the;* possessives—both possessive nouns and possessive pronouns—run a close second. In our five sample sentences at the opening of Chapter 1, four of them have determiners, two of which are possessive nouns: *a* weasel, *Jenny's* sister, *Gino's* father, *the* gymnasium.

In the following passage, the possessive pronoun *its* provides strong cohesive ties:

> Portland, sixty miles from the Pacific Ocean, is by no means immune to the suburbanization that has sapped the vitality from many cities. **Its** suburbs now contain about two thirds of the area's 1.4 million residents and about half of the area's jobs. Yet as the suburbs have grown, the downtown has become more attractive and popular than ever.
>
> Downtown Portland has distinct edges. **Its** eastern border is the deep, navigable Willamette River, lined for more than a mile by Tom McCall Waterfront Park, a grassy, mostly level expanse suited to events that draw thousands such as the Rose Festival (Portland calls itself the "City of Roses"), a blues festival, and a summer symphony series. **Its** western border is the steep West Hills, which contain Washington Park, home of the International Rose Test Gardens, where more than 400 varieties of roses are cultivated, and Forest Park, whose 4,800 acres of Douglas fir, alder, and maple constitute one of the largest nature preserves and hiking areas in any American city.
>
> —Philip Langdon *(The Atlantic Monthly)*

In the weasel paragraph, *he* constitutes the entire subject; in the Portland paragraph, in all three cases, *its* stands for the possessive noun *Portland's* and acts as a signal for the headwords: *suburbs, eastern border,* and *western border.* But no matter how it functions—whether it fills the whole slot or acts as a determiner—the pronoun represents known information. It is this known information that helps provide the cohesive tie between sentences. The three *its* sentences here are typical, with the known information in the subject slot, the new information in the predicate.

Demonstrative Pronouns.   Like the personal pronouns, the **demonstrative pronouns**—*this, that, these,* and *those*—take the place of a noun phrase; in doing so, they provide a strong cohesive tie. And, like the possessive pronouns, they also serve as determiners:

> <u>That</u> sounds like a good plan. (noun phrase replacement)
>
> <u>That</u> plan sounds good to me. (determiner for *plan*)

When you read the second sentence aloud, you can hear the special focusing quality that the demonstrative adds to the noun *plan,* a focus that the determiner *the* would not have:

> The plan sounds good to me.

The demonstratives include the feature of proximity, in reference to both space and time, with *this* and *these* indicating closeness, *that* and *those* more distance. You'll find many sentences in these chapters (note the use of *these*) that demonstrate the close proximity indicated by *these* and *this*—in addition to the one you just read—in its role as determiner. Here are examples from Chapter 2:

> In <u>this</u> chapter we focus on the power that short sentences have . . . in <u>these</u> two roles.
>
> Each of <u>these</u> examples is a complete paragraph.

In the following example from Chapter 1, the demonstratives fill the noun phrase slot without a noun headword:

> <u>These</u> seven [sentence patterns] represent the underlying skeletal structure of nearly all our sentences.

When a writer uses a pronoun, the reader has the right to assume that the antecedent is not just known information but that, in fact, the information is located in the foreground of his or her consciousness. The demonstratives, especially *this* and *these,* represent extra emphasis for foregrounding in both capacities: when they serve as determiners and when they fill the noun phrase slot on their own. We saw an example of this emphasis in the Ambrose passage about Lewis and Clark:

> Some of the fields, although unattended, still had squash and corn growing in them. <u>These</u> had once been home to the mighty Arikara tribe.

And in the sentence introducing the quote you just read, there's another example: *this emphasis.*

Writers can easily introduce weak spots when the pronoun filling the noun phrase slot has no clear antecedent. For example, in the following sentence there is no specific noun phrase to back up either *this* or *it:*

> My roommate told me she has decided to drop out of school and look for a job. *This* has taken me completely by surprise, and I know *it* will shock her parents.

The problem here is not one of communication; we can easily figure out what the sentence means. But notice the absence of a specific noun in the first sentence to which the demonstrative *this* refers; rather, the pronoun refers to the idea in the sentence as a whole. This use of the pronoun is called **broad reference.** And while this example may not cause the reader to stumble, sometimes the understood antecedent is a bit tricky to figure out. The point is that we, as readers, shouldn't have to do the figuring: That job belongs to the writer. Often the best way to fix a vague *this* or *that* is to turn the pronoun into a determiner and supply the missing headword:

> *This decision of hers* took me completely by surprise.

By turning *this* into a complete noun phrase, we also provide the vague *it* with a backup antecedent.

When you're revising the first draft of your essay—or perhaps rereading a sentence you just wrote—always pay attention to those sentences with a lone pronoun as subject, especially the demonstratives. Make sure that the antecedent of *this* or *that* or *these* or *those* is clear to the reader. If the noun phrase the pronoun stands for is not obvious, consider turning it into a determiner and adding the headword. Pay special attention to *it* and *they* as well. It's important to recognize that pronouns without clear antecedents are in violation of the known–new contract.

FOR GROUP DISCUSSION

You could make the argument that a bare *this* or *that* or *these* or *those* is perfectly capable of communicating without a noun headword, as the example in the Lewis and Clark passage by Steven Ambrose demonstrates. And the original draft of the sentence that introduces the quotation also had a bare determiner: "We saw an example of *this* in the Lewis and Clark passage."

Do you think the revised version with the word *emphasis* added is an improvement? Would the addition of *fields* improve the Ambrose passage? And how about the roommate example? Did it really need the headword added? Check some of your reading material from this or another class to find out how common it is for demonstratives to fill the noun phrase slots without headwords. Are the missing headwords obvious, easy to retrieve?

EXERCISE 12

Revise the following passages to eliminate the vague pronouns. In some cases the most effective revision will be to turn *this* or *that* into a determiner. Another possibility is to combine the sentences.

1. The contractor for our house is obviously skeptical about solar energy. This doesn't surprise me.

2. The summer heat wave in the Midwest devastated a large portion of the nation's corn crop. That probably means higher meat prices for next year.

3. I know that I should give up junk food to get in shape for summer, but that is never easy to do.

4. We arrived at the airport two hours before our flight. I was glad to do it, realizing the importance of safety procedures.

5. If I would take time to study my computer manual, it would save me a lot of frustration.

6. Jeremy's father died when he was only six years old. That left the burden of raising him and his sister to his mother. Jeremy remembers that it wasn't easy for her.

7. My friend Abe nearly drowned several years ago when his boat capsized in Lake Erie. I assume that is the reason he became a confirmed landlubber and refuses to go fishing with me.

8. Last year my brother Chuck designed and built his own house— a beautiful rustic log cabin. It really amazed me, because when we were kids he did nothing but break things, especially my favorite toys. In fact, he was always in trouble because of that.

The Role of the Passive Voice

It's possible that everything you've heard about the passive voice up to now has been negative; English teachers often declare it out of bounds. Such edicts come about—those "pass" comments appear in the margins—because writers so often use passives when they shouldn't. And it's true that ineffective passives do stand out. But there's a great deal of misunderstanding about the passive. All good prose includes both active and passive voice.

In Chapter 1 you practiced changing active sentences to passive by making the direct object of the active sentence the subject of the passive. That shift of focus is one of the main strengths of the passive voice, one of its purposes: It allows known information to fill the subject slot. Here, for example, is the beginning of a paragraph from a *Time* article by Michael D. Lemonick about the destruction of the Brazilian rain forests. Note how the subject of the passive second sentence provides a cohesive tie:

> If Americans are truly interested in saving the rain forests, they should move beyond rhetoric and suggest *policies* that are practical—and acceptable—to the understandably wary Brazilians. <u>*Such policies* cannot be presented as take-them-or-leave-them propositions.</u> If the U.S. expects better performance from Brazil, Brazil has a right to make demands in return. In fact, the U.S. and Brazil need to engage in face-to-face negotiations as part of a formal dialogue on the environment between the industrial nations and the developing countries. [Italics added.]

In the first sentence, *policies* is new information; in the second it is known. You'll note that the agent is missing from the passive sentence; however, "by the Americans" is clearly understood. Note also how the information patterns work in the two sentences following the passive, with the known information, *U.S.* and *Brazil*—the agents—in subject position and the new information in the predicates.

The following passive sentence, which may look familiar, closes the first paragraph of the section in Chapter 1 called "Sentence Patterns" on page 11; it follows the branching diagram that identifies the subject and the predicate:

> In this pattern the structure following the *be* (in this case *is*) is called a **subject complement** because it says something about the subject....

Here the new information—in this case a term mentioned for the first time—is highlighted by boldface type.

The following example of the passive voice appears in a sentence you read earlier in this chapter in the discussion of the known–new contract. It opens a paragraph:

> In another paragraph pattern, or information pattern, the proposition in the topic sentence <u>is followed</u> by supporting details suggested by the topic and expected by the reader.

Like the previous example, in which the term *subject complement* is introduced, here the term *supporting details* is the new information, so it belongs in the predicate, where it gets the main emphasis. You'll be reading more about this important feature—the connection of information and sentence rhythm—in the next chapter.

Other Sentence Inversions

As you have seen, the *passive transformation*, as the passive voice is called, inverts the active word order, with the original direct object shifted to subject position. Another, much more common, method of rearranging information is to open the sentence with an adverbial modifier, as you saw in Chapter 1 under the heading "The Optional Slot" (page 18). Adverbials are called optional because, with few exceptions, sentences are grammatical without them. However, when we do add them—and adverbials are very common indeed—they are considered modifiers of the verb; that is, they are part of the predicate. But they don't have to stay in the predicate slot. Here are two opening adverbials from the discussion in Chapter 1, the first a prepositional phrase and the second a subordinate clause:

> <u>During the Vietnam War,</u> Gino's dad was a pilot.
>
> <u>Because a weasel is wild,</u> it should be approached with great caution.

In that discussion of adverbials, these examples were presented without context. But let's assume that the second one is the opening of a paragraph following our old standby weasel passage. You probably remember its opening sentence: *A weasel is wild.* Clearly, if our *because*-clause opened a second paragraph on weasels, the clause itself would be adding no new information, so we don't want it at the end of the sentence. We want to save the sentence end for the new idea—in this case, the idea of great caution. The *because*-clause, with its known information, provides the transition from the previous sentence; it is the glue that connects them.

One of the main points of the adverbial discussion in Chapter 1 is the movability—and thus the versatility—of the optional adverbial slot. When you put that feature together with the concept of the known–new contract, you can appreciate how important a tool movable adverbials can be for you as a writer.

Still another inversion of information involves switching the position of the subject and the predicate. Here's the topic sentence of a paragraph you've seen before:

> Shaping up as an important milestone is the demolition of two large dams in Washington State's Elwha River, which flows from the mountains of Olympic National Park into the Juan de Fuca Strait.

Here's the underlying subject-predicate structure:

> The demolition of two large dams . . . is shaping up as an important milestone.

The writer's purpose for making that subject-predicate switch is connected to the previous paragraphs in the article, which relate the history and consequences of dam removal. The word *milestone* refers to that history, so it becomes the transition to the new information about these two particular dams. It's an unusual grammatical situation, for the old information to occur in the verb phrase, the predicate. Using her inversion tool, the writer has set aside the subject-predicate order so that the new information is in line for emphasis. The position at the end of the sentence also makes it easier to add those two long modifiers, a prepositional phrase and a *which*-clause.

We look more closely at word-order variations in Chapter 10.

FOR GROUP DISCUSSION

1. As you know from your reading up to now, grammatical terms are highlighted with boldface type when they are first mentioned, as in the passage from Chapter 1 cited on page 77. Because the terms constitute new information, you probably don't expect to find them as subjects in their sentences. However, in some cases you'll find that they are subjects. The opening of the next section is a case in point. Look through the pages you've already studied to see how the bold terms are placed. Think especially about known and new information. You may want to suggest revisions of those sentences.

2. The following paragraph is the beginning of a short description of Jefferson by Lee A. Jacobus:

> Thomas Jefferson, an exceptionally accomplished and well-educated man, is probably best known for writing the Declaration of Independence, a work composed under the eyes of Benjamin Franklin, John Adams, and the Continental Congress, which spent two and a half days going over every word. The substance of the document was developed in committee, but Jefferson, because of the grace of his style,

was chosen to do the actual writing. The result is one of the most memorable statements in American history.

Explain why the author used the passive voice where he did. Try writing a version of the paragraph using only the active voice. Is it equally effective?

METADISCOURSE

Metadiscourse refers to certain signals that help the reader understand the writer's message. The word *metadiscourse* actually means "discourse about discourse"—in other words, signals that "communicate about communication."[1]

These signals act as guideposts for the reader that clarify the purpose or direction of a particular passage. For example, a word like *thus* tells the reader that what follows is a summary. And when a sentence opens with "for example," as the previous one does, you know the sentence will discuss an example of the concept just mentioned. The phrase may not be necessary—many examples go unmarked—but sometimes that help is very important.

Some of our most common and useful metadiscourse signals are the conjunctive adverbs, or adverbial conjunctions, which you read about in Chapter 3: *however, so, nevertheless,* and prepositional phrases such as *in other words, in addition,* and *in fact* (see the list on page 51). Other text connectors you're familiar with, such as *first, in the first place, second, next, finally,* and *in conclusion,* clearly add to the ease of reading, the flow of the text.[2] Those that signal contrasting pairs of ideas—*on the one hand/on the other hand*—are especially helpful. Signals like these contribute to the sense of cohesion, the flow of the paragraph—and sometimes to its accurate interpretation—by keeping the reader informed of the writer's intentions.

In this book you've seen a number of comments that link the text you are reading to what has gone before, such as the *which*-clause and the parenthetical reference in the previous paragraph, both of which are there to remind you that you've already been introduced to conjunctive adverbs. You saw another such link in the discussion of inversions on page 78, when you were reminded about the section called "The Optional Slot" in Chapter 1. And you've often been informed of discussions you'll encounter

---

[1]The quoted words here are from the article by William Vande Kopple listed under the topic of Metadiscourse in the Bibliography.

[2]It's fairly common, especially in British English, to see an *-ly* added to ordinal numbers when they're used as connectives: *firstly, secondly.* However, your reader will hear a much more natural voice if you use the number without the *-ly.* And the numbers certainly don't need that added ending to make them adverbs, the usual job of *-ly: quick* (adjective); *quickly* (adverb). We use ordinal numbers as adverbs just as they are: *I saw it first; she came in second.*

in future chapters. These links constitute metadiscourse—discourse about the text itself, about the topic under discussion.

And here's one more metadiscourse comment to close this discussion: In Chapter 6 you'll be reading about other metadiscourse signals, those that have a special effect on, that make a difference to, your personal voice.

PARALLELISM

Early in this chapter you read that it's okay to repeat words, that repetition can have a positive effect on the reader. In this section we look at a specific kind of repetition called **parallelism,** the repetition of whole structures, such as phrases and clauses. Parallelism is usually thought of as a device for enhancing a writer's style—and indeed it is that. It can certainly add polish and flavor to prose that otherwise might be the plain vanilla variety. But it can also provide cohesion, especially when the repeated elements extend through a paragraph or from one paragraph to the next.

Parallelism refers to repeated grammatical elements, often combined with repeated words. The quality of being parallel means that the repeated elements have the same structure, such as noun phrases with noun phrases, prepositional phrases with prepositional phrases. One of the most famous sentences in President Kennedy's inaugural address includes parallel verb phrases: "pay any price, bear any burden, meet any hardship, support any friend, oppose any foe." And we're all familiar with Lincoln's "of the people, by the people, and for the people."

Parallelism becomes an especially strong cohesive device when a structure echoes a structure from a previous sentence or paragraph. In the second paragraph of the Portland passage on page 73, the subject "Its eastern border" names one of the "distinct edges" referred to in the opening sentence. The next sentence not only fulfills the reader's expectation with the word *western,* it does so using parallel structure:

Its eastern border is the deep, navigable Willamette River....

Its western border is the steep West Hills....

In the following passage the author's use of repetition adds intensity and drama to his argument:

That knowledge has become the key resource means that there is a world economy, and that the world economy, rather than the national economy, is in control. Every country, every industry, and every business will be in an increasingly competitive environment. Every country, every industry, and every business will, in its decisions, have to consider its competitive standing in the world economy and the competitiveness of its knowledge competencies.

—Peter F. Drucker *(The Atlantic Monthly)*

The repeated series in the two subject slots are the most obvious repetitions, but note also in the first sentence two instances of *world economy* contrasted with *national economy* and a third repetition of *world economy* in the last sentence. And in the second and third sentences we read *competitive standing, competitive environment,* and *competitiveness.*

The repeated series in this paragraph by Stephen Jay Gould from his book *Ever Since Darwin* illustrates another fairly common feature of parallelism, that of **antithesis,** the introduction of contrasting, or dissimilar, ideas:

> Why imagine that specific genes for <u>aggression, dominance, or spite</u> have any importance when we know that the brain's enormous flexibility permits us to be <u>aggressive or peaceful, dominant or submissive, spiteful or generous?</u> <u>Violence, sexism, and general nastiness</u> are biological since they represent one subset of a possible range of behaviors. But <u>peacefulness, equality, and kindness</u> are just as biological—and we may see their influence increase if we can create social structures that permit them to flourish.
>
> —Stephen Jay Gould *(Ever Since Darwin)*

Antithesis also plays a part in the parallelism we see here, in the contrast of *easier* and *harder:*

> The wave of software standardization led by Microsoft products like Windows and Word has made computers simpler to use than they once were. <u>It is easier</u> now than it was a decade ago to sit down at any machine, anywhere, and have an idea of how to make it go. <u>But it is harder</u> for a software developer to introduce a genuinely new approach to word processing, data management, or any other established function. <u>And it is much harder</u> for a company even to keep a program on the market if another product, especially one from Microsoft, seems likely to become the standard in the field.
>
> —James Fallows *(The Atlantic Monthly)*

Note in the following passage how the point of view changes in the middle of the paragraph where the parallel *it*-clauses begin. Each of them introduces a clause in the second person, one with *you* as the subject.

A thin broken strand of islands curves out into the Atlantic Ocean and then back again in a sheltering embrace of North Carolina's mainland coast and its offshore sounds. These are the Outer Banks of North Carolina. For thousands of years these barrier islands have survived the onslaught of wind and sea. Today their long stretches of beach, sand dunes, marshes, and woodlands are set aside as Cape Hatteras National Seashore. <u>It can be a lonely place;</u> you may walk along the beach unseen except by shore birds searching for a meal. <u>It can be a place of discovery;</u> you may visit the 1870 Cape Hatteras Lighthouse, one of many monuments to man's encounter with the sea. <u>It can be a wild place;</u> you may be buffeted by an approaching gale or surprised by the honking of large flocks of migrating geese. <u>And it can be an exciting place,</u> where you may explore many opportunities for recreation: surf fishing, sunbathing, swimming, beach combing, canoeing, sailing, surfing, snorkeling. Part land, part sea, Cape Hatteras offers rewards from each.

—National Park Service Brochure

From all of these examples it should be clear that parallelism is more than mere stylistic décor: The parallel structures are, in fact, among the strongest cohesive ties that the writer has available. They highlight those ideas that should be in the foreground of the reader's consciousness, sending the message that the parallel structures are not only connected but also significant.

Repetition versus Redundancy

Rather than commending these authors for effective parallelism, you may be tempted to accuse them of unnecessary repetition, a problem that goes by the label **redundancy.** How do we distinguish between them? How do we tell the difference between good repetition and bad?

Parallelism of the kind we see here—parallelism as a stylistic device— invariably calls attention to itself. Did these authors intend to do that, to call attention to these structures? Clearly, the answer is "Yes—and for good reason." In all of these passages, the use of repetition has added a dramatic dimension to the prose.

The repetition in these passages might also tempt you to accuse the authors of wordiness; their sentences certainly don't pass the test of brevity or conciseness, features of writing so often touted in composition textbooks. Clarity, of course, is always a goal. And, yes, sometimes clarity calls for brevity, for a lean version of a sentence. But there are many occasions that call for a celebration of words. We certainly don't expect the president to be brief in an inaugural address; neither should we expect a writer to be brief in describing Cape Hatteras or in explaining the concept of a world economy or in arguing for the biological basis of kindness.

In Chapter 8 redundancy is addressed in a section called "The Proliferating Prepositional Phrase." And the use of repetition as a stylistic device is discussed further in Chapter 10, "Choosing Stylistic Variations."

EXERCISE 13

The following question-and-answer is from the beginning of a two-page magazine ad for Microsoft Windows:

> CAN YOU PLUG ALL TYPES OF PEOPLE INTO ONE TYPE COMPUTER?
>
> No.
>
> After all, people are different. Jobs are different. Companies are different. And people need different types of computers to get their jobs done. Some need powerful PC's and workstations. Some need light and powerful laptops. Some need hand-held devices. Some need simple terminals running off a network. And some need a combination of machines.
>
> Computers *must* be different to meet the different demands people have in their jobs.

Following the model of that answer, with its various repetitions, write answers to one or more of the following questions (or others that you or your instructor may come up with):

> Isn't one good restaurant sufficient for everyone on this campus?
>
> Isn't one well-built car good enough for every driver?
>
> Isn't one standard school building design good enough for every neighborhood school in this state?

LEVELS OF GENERALITY

The term *levels of generality* refers to a visual method of paragraph analysis that enables the writer to clarify how each sentence in a paragraph relates to its predecessor. Although introduced for the purpose of developing sentences and paragraphs, the technique also illustrates clearly the cohesive features we examined in this chapter.[3]

To outline the levels of generality, we label the topic sentence—usually, but not always, the first sentence—as Level 1. The level of each succeeding sentence is positioned in relation to its predecessor—as subordinate, coordinate, or superordinate. A more specific second sentence, then, is Level 2. If the third sentence is subordinate to the second, it is Level 3; if coordinate to the second, another Level 2.

Here, for example is the paragraph about Lincoln and Douglass, a portion of which we looked at earlier in connection with Reader Expectation:

Level 1: Despite the immense racial gulf separating them, Lincoln and Douglass had a lot in common.

   Level 2: They were the two preeminent self-made men of their era.

      Level 3: Lincoln was born dirt poor, had less than a year of formal schooling and became one of the nation's greatest Presidents.

      Level 3: Douglass spent the first 20 years of his life as a slave, had no formal schooling—in fact, his masters forbade him to read or write—and became one of the nation's greatest writers and activists.

         Level 4: Though nine years younger, Douglass overshadowed Lincoln as a public figure during the 15 years before the Civil War.

            Level 5: He published two best-selling autobiographies before the age of 40, edited his own newspaper beginning in 1847 and was a brilliant orator—even better than Lincoln—at a time when public speaking was a major source of entertainment and power.

Putting a paragraph into this kind of outline form sometimes shows where revision is needed. Here is a paragraph by Joyce Marcus, published in *Scientific American,* about the Zapotecs of Mexico:

In the 16th century Zapotec society was divided into two classes that did not intermarry. The upper stratum consisted of the

---

[3]The method was introduced by Francis Christensen some forty years ago to describe parts of the sentence; he later applied it to paragraphs. For further information on his work with both sentences and paragraphs, see the Bibliography listing under Levels of Generality.

hereditary rulers *(coqui)* and their families, along with minor nobles *(xoana).* The lower stratum consisted of commoners and slaves. Great emphasis was put on the order of birth of noble children: rulers were frequently recruited from the elder offspring and priests from the younger. Military campaigns were fought by noble officers commanding commoner soldiers. Nobles frequently formed political alliances by marrying into the elite families of other communities; commoners usually married within their village. Royal ancestors were venerated and were thought to have considerable supernatural power over the affairs of their descendants.

Again, the first sentence, Level 1, makes a commitment in its statement about two classes of society:

> **Level 1:** In the 16th century Zapotec society was divided into two classes that did not intermarry.
> **Level 2:** The upper stratum consisted of the hereditary rulers....
> **Level 2:** The lower stratum consisted of commoners and slaves.
> > **Level 3:** Great emphasis was put on the order of birth of noble children....

Sentence 4 has introduced a problem. Although it obviously belongs at Level 3 because it is a specific detail, it is not a detail about sentence three: Rather, it is subordinate to sentence 2, the one about the upper stratum.

There's an easy solution to this problem: The writer can reverse sentences 2 and 3, the two Level-2 sentences, so that the specific details about the upper classes are tied to the Level-2 sentence that begins with "The upper stratum."

In addition to showing where the paragraph might need to be revised, the outline can also suggest where further development is needed. For example, our four-sentence paragraph about spring break would look like this outline, with only two levels:

> 1 Our trip to Florida . . . disaster.
> > 2 The hotel room . . . .
> > 2 The food . . . .
> > 2 The daily transportation . . . .

The place to add details is at levels 3 and 4, more specifics about the ideas in those Level-2 sentences.

The outline can also indicate where a cohesive signal might help the reader. For example, when the paragraph goes from, say, Level 3 or 4 back to 1 or 2, the writer may need to signal the reader:

1

  2

    3

      4

At this point we are probably expecting either another Level-4 sentence or one at Level 5. We will need some help in getting back to Level 2, if that's where the next sentence is taking us—perhaps a metadiscourse signal.

Not every paragraph, of course, conforms to a general-to-specific kind of pattern that can be outlined by levels. However, you will find that thinking about levels of generality in this way—whether or not you actually outline your paragraphs—can be valuable when you're both composing and revising. Considering the relationship of sentences in this way will remind you to consider the needs of your readers.

FOR GROUP DISCUSSION

1. Apply the levels of generality to the following paragraphs:

> The jaguar is the perfect conservation symbol. A mythic animal with great imaginative allure, it has been a major presence in Latin American life. The Aztecs and the Maya revered it. As if to wrap themselves in the jaguar's power and authority, royalty and warriors in these cultures wore jaguar skins and framed their human faces with the intimidating jaws of gaping jaguar mouths. In the temples of Teotihuacan not far from Mexico City, the jaguar has its own palace, with murals portraying the creature in feathered headdress.
>
> —Charles Bergman *(Smithsonian)*

> But if home schooling is flawed, and our public schools are weathered, some believe there's a way to improve both by reinvesting home schoolers in their communities and making public schools more nimble. A few school districts are showing the way. In some states, including California and Texas, school districts now allow home-schooled kids to sign up for such offerings as a physics class or the football team. A growing number of districts are opening resource centers where home schoolers come for class once or twice a week. In Orange County, Calif., two school districts have combined two reform ideas by opening charter schools that offer home-schooling programs.
>
> —John Cloud and Jodie Morse *(Time)*

2. Outline the Cape Hatteras paragraph on pages 82–83 according to its levels of generality. You'll notice that the final sentence summarizes the previous four sentences, so it is at a more general level than those four with specific details.

3. As you read in the footnote at the opening of this section, this method of determining levels of generality was first applied to sentences. Look at the last sentence in the passage about Portland on page 73. Outline it according to levels of generality.

4. Select one or several paragraphs of an essay you are now working on. Outline them according to the levels of generality to identify places where revision or further development may be called for.

KEY TERMS

Antecedent	Determiner	Personal pronouns
Antithesis	Known–new contract	Possessive pronouns
Articles	Levels of generality	Pronouns
Cohesion	Lexical cohesion	Reader expectation
Conjunctive adverb	Metadiscourse	Redundancy
Demonstrative	Parallelism	Repetition
pronoun	Passive voice	Vague pronouns

RHETORICAL REMINDERS

Have I anticipated my reader's expectations?

Do my paragraphs profit from lexical cohesion, the repetition of words?

Is the known information in the beginning of the sentence, where it can provide a cohesive tie to the previous sentence, with the new information in end-focus position?

Have I used metadiscourse effectively to signal the reader where necessary?

Have I taken advantage of parallelism as a cohesive device?

Do my sentences follow logically in terms of their levels of generality? Have I used specific details to support my generalizations?

PUNCTUATION REMINDER

Have I set off conjunctive adverbs and other metadiscourse units with commas where necessary?

Sentence Rhythm

CHAPTER PREVIEW

In this chapter we look at a feature of language you might not have thought about before: its rhythm. Yes, our language has a rhythm, just as music does—a regular beat. When you learn to listen to that beat and think about it when you write, you gain control of an important writing tool.

We begin by examining the valleys and peaks of **intonation** and the connection of those patterns with **end focus,** which is tied up with the known–new contract you learned about in Chapter 4. You will learn how to control sentence rhythm using **cleft sentences,** the *there*-**transformation, power words,** and punctuation.

Even though these terms may be new to your vocabulary, the concepts they name are part of your everyday language, in both speech and writing. This chapter is really about consciousness raising; it's about awareness. That awareness will help you control the message that your reader gets.

INTONATION: THE PEAKS AND VALLEYS

One of the most important aspects of your expertise with sentences is your sense of rhythm. For example, if you read the opening sentence in this paragraph out loud, you'll hear yourself saying "one of the most" in almost a monotone; you probably don't hear a stressed syllable, a beat, until you get to *important:*

one of the most imPORTant

And you probably rush through those first four words so fast that you pronounce "of" without articulating the *f,* making "one of" sound like the first two words in "won a prize."

The rhythm of sentences, what we call the **intonation pattern,** can be described as peaks and valleys, where the loudest syllables, those with stress, are represented by peaks:

Not all the peaks are of the same height—we have different degrees of stress—but they do tend to come at fairly regular intervals. As listeners we pay attention to the peaks; that's where we'll hear the information that the speaker is focusing on. And as speakers we manipulate those peaks and valleys to coincide with our message, reserving the loudest stress, the highest peak, for our main point of focus.

Such sentence manipulation is not something we ordinarily think about, nor is it a skill we were taught; for native speakers it's automatic, part of our native language ability. On the other hand, if you're not a native speaker of English, mastering the rhythm of sentences may be difficult, especially if the sentence rhythm of your native language does not have a regular beat like English. Certainly, a dominant feature of some accents is the absence of that rhythm, with peaks and valleys in unexpected places or missing altogether.

But even for you who are not native speakers, recognizing the relationship between the rhythm of sentences and the message, which we examine in this chapter, will be helpful to you as writers. You will also find it helpful in practicing your own listening skills to focus on sentence rhythm, with its peaks and valleys.

END FOCUS

The rhythm of sentences is closely tied to their two-part structure and to the known–new contract. The sentence subject, when it is known information, is usually a valley or a low peak in the intonation contour; the prominent peak of stress occurs in the predicate, on the new information, generally on the last or next-to-the-last slot in the sentence. Linguists describe this common rhythm pattern as **end focus.**

The contrast between the peaks and valleys of rhythm is easy to demonstrate in short sentences. As you read the following, listen for the syllable that gets main stress:

> The common cold is caused by a virus.
>
> My chemistry book cost almost a hundred dollars.
>
> Barbara wrecked her motorcycle.
>
> Sentence rhythm is characterized by end focus.

We normally don't read sentences in lists, of course; we read them in context. And as readers we count on the context, on the meaning, to guide the reading, to help us put the emphasis where it belongs. Our job as writers, then, is clear: If we want readers to understand our intentions and to focus on the important information, we must help them by taking sentence rhythm into account.

The following passages provide a simple lesson on the way in which end focus and sentence rhythm work together:

> Dennis told me that Barbara had an accident this morning on her
>   way to work. But I think he got his facts wrong. She wrecked her
>   motorcycle yesterday.
>
> Dennis told me that Barbara had an accident this morning on her
>   way to work. But I think he got his facts wrong. Yesterday she
>   wrecked her motorcycle.

As you probably noticed, the one difference in the wording of the two passages is the placement in the last sentence of the adverb *yesterday.* And, when you read the two, that difference probably produced a difference in the rhythm pattern. In both passages the words *but* and *wrong* in the second sentence led you to expect information refuting something in the first sentence: perhaps the fact of the accident itself; if not that, its time or place. And recognizing that *yesterday* fulfilled your expectation, that's the sentence slot that got the main stress. However, by putting *yesterday* in the opening slot, the writer disregarded your expectation as the reader that the new, important information would be in end focus position.

As you have read before in these chapters—in Chapter 1 under the heading "The Optional Slot," in your study of the sentence patterns, and in Chapter 4 in connection with the known–new contract—the movability of adverbials is an extremely important and versatile tool in your writer's toolbox. The term *optional,* of course, refers only to the fact that most sentences do not need adverbials to be grammatical; however, when we do add them, we usually do so for good reason: to add information about time and place and manner and reason and so on. Often that information provides transition from the prior text, so the opening slot is the right place for it. And time adverbials, like *yesterday,* often belong there at the opening. But not always. Not in the sentence we've just looked at, where *yesterday* is the new information.

So in case you're tempted to make that kind of switch—to move an adverbial to the opening slot, perhaps for the sake of variety, to relieve the monotony of starting every sentence with the subject—think again! Remember the principle of end focus. If the adverbial is the new information, save it for the end of the sentence, the point of main stress. Otherwise, when the reader happens to be your composition teacher, you're likely to find "awk" noted in the margin of your essay.

FOR GROUP DISCUSSION

The following paragraph opened a *Sports Illustrated* article called "The Dominance Theory." As you read it, locate the main peaks of stress, keeping in mind both end focus and the known–new contract. Do you have any revision suggestions for the author?

> We watch sports to see great plays and great games, great athletes and, of course, great teams. Dynasties form the foundation upon which sports history is built. The Yankees, the Canadiens, the Celtics, the 49ers: They're the standard against which all other teams are judged.

Notice also the author's use of parallel noun phrases, with the repetition of *great* in the first sentence and the team names in the last. Describe the effect these series have on the stress pattern.

EXERCISE 14

Read the following passages, listening carefully to the intonation contour of each sentence. Indicate the words (or syllables) that get main stress. Compare your reading with that of your classmates.

> 1. Never invest in something you don't understand or in the dream of an artful salesperson. Be a buyer, not a sellee. Figure out what you want (be it life insurance, mutual funds or a vacuum cleaner) and then shop for a good buy. Don't let someone else tell you what you need—at least not if he happens to be selling it.
>
> —Andrew Tobias *(Parade)*

2. Plaque has almost become a household word. It is certainly a household problem. But even though everyone is affected by it, few people really understand the seriousness of plaque or the importance of controlling it. Plaque is an almost invisible sticky film of bacteria that continuously forms on the teeth. Plaque germs are constantly multiplying and building up. Any dentist will tell you that controlling plaque is the single most important step to better oral health.

—advertisement of the American Dental Association

3. Punitive notions of disease have a long history, and such notions are particularly active with cancer. There is the "fight" or "crusade" against cancer; cancer is the "killer" disease; people who have cancer are "cancer victims." Ostensibly the illness is the culprit. But it is also the cancer patient who is made culpable. Widely believed psychological theories of disease assign to the luckless ill the ultimate responsibility both for falling ill and for getting well. And conventions of treating cancer as no mere disease but a demonic enemy make cancer not just a lethal disease but a shameful one.

—Susan Sontag ("Illness as Metaphor")

4. Frank evaluation of its [caffeine's] hazards is not easy. There is a vast literature on the effects of caffeine on the body, and for every study reaching one conclusion, seemingly there is another that contradicts it. Although most major health risks have been ruled out, research continues at a steady clip.

—Corby Kummer *(The Atlantic Monthly)*

CONTROLLING RHYTHM

Because end focus is such a common rhythm pattern, we can think of it as part of the contract between writer and reader. The reader expects the main sentence focus to be in the predicate, unless given a signal to the contrary. But of course not all sentences are alike; not every sentence has end focus. In speech, especially, the focus is often shifted elsewhere. The speaker can easily stress the new information, no matter where in the sentence it appears. Consider, for example, these alternative ways of saying the motorcycle sentence, the variety of messages that are possible for the speaker:

BARBARA wrecked her motorcycle yesterday morning. [Not someone else.]

Barbara wrecked HER motorcycle yesterday morning. [Her own; not someone else's.]

Barbara wrecked her motorcycle yesterday MORNING. [Not in the afternoon.]

And we can add extra stress to *motorcycle:*

Barbara wrecked her MOTORCYCLE yesterday morning. [Not her car.]

Or we can give the whole sentence added emphasis:

Barbara DID wreck her motorcycle yesterday morning. [Believe me, I'm not making this up.]

The speaker is in control of the message that the listener is meant to hear. The spoken language is powerful, much more powerful than writing, far more capable of expressing feelings and nuances of meaning.

The It-*Cleft*

It's true that the speaker has a much easier job than does the writer in getting the message across and preventing misinterpretation. But the writer is certainly not powerless—far from it. As we saw earlier, the careful writer can take control simply by understanding the reader's expectations about the sentence and by making sure that the important information coincides with the prominent stress. You'll recall the first version of the motorcycle passage, where the sensitive reader would almost certainly delay the stress until the word *yesterday.* But in the following revision, the writer has left nothing to chance:

Dennis told me that Barbara had an accident on the way to work this morning. But he apparently got his facts wrong. <u>It was yesterday that she wrecked her motorcycle.</u>

In this version it's impossible for the reader to misinterpret the emphasis on *yesterday* with the *it* construction, known as a **cleft sentence.** This use of *it* is called an **expletive.** (The term *cleft* comes from the verb *cleave,* which means to divide or split.) The *it*-**cleft** enables the writer to shift the emphasis to any slot in the sentence, forcing the reader to focus on the structure following "it was" (or "it is," "it has been," etc.):

It was Barbara who wrecked her motorcycle.

It was her own motorcycle that Barbara wrecked.

Instead of the usual end focus, the reader will recognize that the emphasis belongs on the word or phrase following that opening unstressed valley of "it was" and will automatically make that the highest peak in the intonation contour of the sentence.

The following passages are from a *Time* article on killer microbes by Michael D. Lemonick (the passages are not contiguous):

> It is tempting to think of the tiny pathogens that produce such diseases as malaria, dysentery, TB, cholera, staph and strep as malevolent little beasts, out to destroy higher forms of life. In fact, all they're trying to do is survive and reproduce, just as we are. Human suffering and death are merely unfortunate byproducts.

> It is by killing individual cells in the body's all important immune system that the AIDS virus wreaks its terrible havoc. The virus itself isn't deadly, but it leaves the body defenseless against all sorts of diseases that are.

Susan Sontag used an *it*-cleft in the passage about cancer we saw earlier:

> But it is also the cancer patient who is made culpable.

The *it* construction enables the writer to control the reader's valleys and peaks of stress, to determine precisely what the rhythm of the sentence will be.

The What-*Cleft*

Another kind of cleft sentence uses a *what*-clause in subject position; here a form of *be* separates the original sentence into two parts:

> Barbara wrecked her motorcycle.
> <u>What Barbara wrecked was her motorcycle.</u>

The **what-cleft** can also shift the original verb phrase into subject position; that shift will put the original subject in line for end focus:

> A branch lying across the road caused the accident.
> <u>What caused the accident was a branch lying across the road.</u>

> Thick fog reduced the visibility to zero.
> <u>What reduced the visibility to zero was the thick fog.</u>

Both of these examples could also be revised with the *it*-cleft:

> It was a branch lying across the road that caused the accident.
> It was thick fog that reduced the visibility.

The There- *Transformation*

Another method of changing word order to shift the stress is known as the
***there*-transformation:**

> A stranger is standing on the porch.
> <u>There's a stranger standing on the porch.</u>

> No concert tickets were available this morning.
> <u>There were no concert tickets available this morning.</u>

Again, this reordering puts the main stress on the subject by shifting its
position. Remember that the normal subject position, the opening slot, is
usually an unstressed valley in terms of the intonation pattern. This addition of *there,* like *it* in the *it*-cleft, is also known as an expletive; delays the
subject, thereby putting it in line for stress.

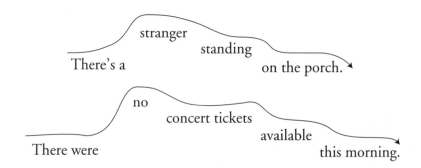

   In addition to their focusing ability, the *there*-transformation and the *it-*
cleft give the writer a way of introducing a new topic, both within the paragraph and at the opening, as the topic sentence. You'll find many such
introductory sentences in this text. In fact, the opening sentence under the
it-cleft heading reads,

> It's true that the speaker has a much easier job than the writer. . . .

And, in the previous chapter, a similar construction opens the discussion
of "The Role of the Passive Voice" on page 77:

> It's possible that everything you've heard about the passive voice up
> to now has been negative.

And at the end of that paragraph, you read,

> But there's a great deal of misunderstanding about the passive.

This use of "there is" is sometimes referred to as "the existential *there*"; in other words, the use of "there is something" affirms that the something is, or exists. For example, in Chapter 1 the section called "The Optional Slot" begins by affirming the existence of a sentence slot in addition to those required in the sentence patterns:

> There's another important slot to add to the discussion, as mentioned in connection with the intransitive pattern: the optional adverbial.

You can hear that same affirmation of existence in the two *there* examples that we looked at in Exercise 14:

> There is a vast literature on the effects of caffeine on the body, and for every study reaching one conclusion, seemingly there is another that contradicts it.
>
> There is a "fight" or "crusade" against cancer.

In all of these *there*-transformations you can hear the main stress focus on the structure following *there is*.

Why, if these are important structures, do handbooks warn writers against starting sentences with the *it* and *there* constructions? You'll find that these warnings generally appear in discussions of wordiness and brevity, with advice about deleting extra words. This is also the reason sometimes given for avoiding the passive voice—another misguided piece of guidance that handbooks invariably expound. And while it's true that "it is" and "there are" do add words, when they are used in the right place and for the right reason, they are not redundant, unnecessary words; they are, in fact, doing an important job.

It's certainly possible to overuse these structures (and the passive voice as well)—and perhaps it's that overuse that teachers and handbooks worry about. So as you reread that first (or second or third) draft, do pay special attention to sentence focus, to the way the reader will read your sentences: Think about end focus, about known and new information, about sentence rhythm. Make sure you have used these focusing tools for the right reason.

EXERCISE 15

Rewrite the following sentences, shifting the focus by using sentence transformations: the *it*-cleft, the *what*-cleft, and *there*. For example, you could use a cleft structure in the first sentence to focus either on Jody or on the flavor; in the second sentence, you could focus on the date or the place or the ship or the iceberg.

1. Jody loves chocolate ice cream.

2. The *Titanic* hit an iceberg and sank in the North Atlantic in 1912.

3. Our defense won the Stanford game in the final three minutes with a crucial interception.

4. Hundreds of angry women were protesting the senator's position on day care at yesterday's political rally in the student union.

5. A month of unseasonably warm weather almost ruined the ski season last winter.

6. Hurricanes of unprecedented force devastated the Gulf Coast in the fall of 2005.

7. Lightning causes many of the forest fires in the Western states.

8. Thousands of guest workers who come to this country from Mexico fill the low-wage jobs that Americans are not willing to do.

FOR CLASS DISCUSSION

The following short essay by Dale Conour accompanies a dramatic two-page photograph in *Sunset* (October 2004) of an enormous black cloud of starlings nearly covering the sky. Notice especially the author's methods of controlling rhythm. Part of that control comes with the use of *it*—seven times, in fact: as an expletive in the *it*-cleft and as the personal pronoun. Can you justify all those *it*s? Consider cohesion as well as the rhythm and focus that they produce. Could the essay get by with fewer *it*s? Is it possible to eliminate all or most of them? Would it be an improvement? Try your hand at revising it.

It's an eerie sight to anyone—a massive swarm of European starlings, some million strong, sweeping over a fallow field off State 46 north of Bakersfield, California. But to birders, it's even more disturbing: They know it's an invasion.

It began in 1890 when New Yorker Eugene Schiffelin made it his quest to introduce to the New World every Old World bird mentioned in Shakespeare's works. Compelled by a single mention of the starling in *Henry IV,* Schiffelin loosed 60 birds in Central Park.

The result today: Millions of starlings—voracious, aggressive, and smart (they're members of the myna family)—have blanketed the U.S., while the number of cavity-nesting songbirds has plummeted.

It may have been *Henry IV* in which the Bard mentions the starling directly, but it's *Henry VI* in which he's prophetic: "Hung be the heavens with black, yield day to night!"

RHYTHM AND THE COMMA

The sentence transformations with *it* and *what* and *there* are not the only ways we have to control the focus and rhythm of sentences. Other ways, in fact, are much more common and, in most cases, more subtle. The phrase *in fact* in the preceding sentence illustrates one such method—a set phrase, an item of metadiscourse that interrupts the rhythm pattern. The inserted phrase not only adds a new intonation contour; it also adds emphasis to the subject. We can illustrate the difference with a picture of the contours:

Other ways are much more common. ⌄

Other ways, in fact, are much more common. ⌄

The visual signal of the comma causes the reader to give added length and stress to the preceding word. And, as the contour lines illustrate, the sentence has gone from having one intonation contour to having three. The main focus is still on the new information at the end, but the sentence rhythm has changed, with part of the reader's attention shifted to the subject. Notice in the second version how much more length and stress you give to the subject headword, *ways,* when it is followed by a comma.

This role for the comma, to shift the peak of stress, is probably one you hadn't thought about before. You've probably considered the comma in the more traditional way, as a signaler of the pause in speech. But, as you learned in Chapter 1 regarding the sentence slots, not every pause translates to a comma in writing. And when we do include a comma, the pause goes beyond simple hesitation. It includes the rising intonation illustrated by the arrows, along with stress and added length given to the preceding word. Even the common *and* gets that extra attention in the second sentence of the previous paragraph. The inserted *as*-clause lengthens the opening *and;* because of the comma, that one word has its own intonation contour:

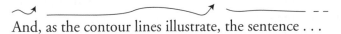

And, as the contour lines illustrate, the sentence . . .

Among the most versatile tools for manipulating sentence rhythm are the metadiscourse signals, such as the conjunctive adverbs, which we saw in Chapter 4. The conjunctive adverbs create cohesion with an adverbial emphasis between sentences, like the phrase *in fact* discussed earlier. Their versatility lies in their movability. That earlier sentence could have been written like this:

Other ways are much more common, in fact.

In this version, the word *common* gets all the attention.

Here are some other examples of sentences with movable phrases—examples from previous passages:

1. One obvious difference, <u>of course,</u> is vocabulary.
2. Consider, <u>for example,</u> these alternative ways of saying the motorcycle sentence....
3. You might choose this order if, <u>for example,</u> you want to put the main emphasis....
4. When you study grammar at school, <u>then,</u> you are studying what you already "know."
5. To be effective, <u>however,</u> writing also requires attention to rhetoric....

Notice especially how many different places in these sentences a conjunctive adverb occurs: in (1) between the subject and the predicate; in (2) between the verb and the direct object; in (3) between a subordinator and the subordinate clause; in (4) and (5) between the introductory adverbial and the main clause.

An important point to understand is that there are other places in all five of these sentences where that word or phrase could have been placed. Writers position these structures to help their readers: How do I want the reader to read this sentence? What is important here for the reader to stress? Will the reader understand how this sentence fits in with what follows?

Other familiar words and phrases in the same category include *in addition, meanwhile, in the meantime, instead, on the other hand, as a result, at any rate,* and *in conclusion.* The conjunctive adverbs are listed on page 51.

FOR GROUP DISCUSSION

1. Several of the sentences in the following passage, from *The Birds* by Roger Tory Peterson, illustrate another method of putting the subject in line for main stress. Read the passage aloud and mark the peaks of stress. Using your understanding of the sentence slots, identify the subject and predicate of each clause. What technique has the author used to control the rhythm? In thinking about the subject-predicate order of the sentence slots, you might want to review the discussion of inversion on page 78. (The sentences are numbered so that the discussion of them will be easier.)

   [1] A bird's feathers have to do many things. [2] Not only must they provide lift surfaces for wings and tail, but they must protect the bird against the weather and insulate

it against loss of heat. [3] Feathers come in almost infinite variety, but they fall into four main categories. [4] Most numerous are the contour feathers which coat the body, giving it a streamlined shape. [5] A house sparrow wears about 3,500 of these in winter, and they are so efficient at sealing in heat that it can maintain a normal temperature of 106.7°F without difficulty in below-freezing cold. [6] Lying beneath them are the soft down feathers, also used for insulation. [7] Scattered among both types are the hairlike filoplumes which sometimes protrude from the coat and may serve as a kind of decoration, or possibly as sensory organs.

2. Read a draft of your own essay (or that of a classmate) with sentence rhythm in mind. (Don't hesitate to read it aloud and listen for your own peaks and valleys.) Think especially about end focus and the difference in rhythm that commas make.

POWER WORDS

We have just seen how conjunctive adverbs set off by commas can override the principle of end focus, the expected rhythm pattern. We've also seen how the use of *it* and *there* can change the emphasis. But some words are powerful enough to interrupt the usual rhythm pattern on their own— even without commas or sentence shifts.

Read the following pairs of sentences aloud and listen for the words that get main stress:

In the first gallery we admired a display of Tiffany glass.

In the first gallery we admired a magnificent display of Tiffany glass.

The senator spoke about the problems of the homeless.

The senator spoke eloquently about the problems of the homeless.

Both its meaning and its length may contribute to a word's inherent attention-getting power, as in the case of the adjective *magnificent* and the adverb *eloquently*. Words that convey strong emotions and words that have a superlative or absolute quality are hard to compete with for attention in most sentences.

Adjectives and adverbs are especially powerful when they are qualified or intensified by another modifier *(absolutely ridiculous, thoroughly disgusting, especially powerful)* and when they are in the superlative degree, ending in *-est* or marked by *most (most aggressively, most incredible)*. Noun phrases too have the power to take control of the sentence, especially when they include one of those powerful modifiers *(complete chaos, dangerous undertaking, overwhelming courage, bewildering array)*.

A word of warning is called for here. To label these words as power words is not necessarily to recommend that you use them. The point to remember is that when you do use them they will command attention. Like movie stars who inevitably create a stir wherever they go, these words change the atmosphere of the sentences they inhabit. Here is what happened to the sentence about the senator's speech:

The senator spoke about the problems of the homeless.

The senator spoke eloquently about the problems of the homeless.

The word *eloquently* shifts the limelight from the topic of the speech to the senator's style of speaking; and, in doing so, it sets up a different expectation in the reader. We would not be surprised if the subject of the next sentence turned out to be *he* or *she* (the senator) rather than *they* (the homeless).

It's important to recognize that in each example the added word—*magnificent, eloquently*—changes a statement of fact into an arguable proposition. The reader has every right to expect supporting evidence for these opinions. What was there about the speech that was eloquent? In what way is the display magnificent? In other words, those power words that change the rhythm also change the reader's expectations.

Correlative Conjunctions

The correlative conjunctions that you read about in Chapter 3—*either–or, neither–nor, both–and, not only–but also*—are among the power words that change the focus and rhythm pattern of the sentence and change the expectation of readers. When you read the following sentence, you probably give the loudest stress to *environment:*

Individuals and nations must learn to think about the environment.

Now add one word. Instead of the simple conjunction *and,* use the correlative *both–and* and listen to your rhythm pattern.

Both individuals *and* nations must learn to think about the environment.

It's important to recognize that these two possibilities—the two different kinds of conjunctions—cannot be used interchangeably. After reading the version with *both–and,* the reader's expectations will be different from those of the version with *and.* The main stress shifted to the subject, especially to *nations,* so the reader is probably expecting to read further about the role of nations. Now try it with *not only–but also* (or ... *as well*):

> *Not only* individuals *but also* nations must learn to think about the environment.
>
> *Not only* individuals *but* nations *as well* must learn to think about the environment.

Now the subject, especially the second half of it, has acquired even more emphasis.

Adverbials of Emphasis

As we saw in the discussion of the optional slot in Chapter 1, the adverbials provide their information of time, place, manner, and the like in a variety of shapes; they also give the writer special flexibility because they are movable. And in the previous section on "Rhythm and the Comma," you saw how the conjunctive adverbs can change the focus by shifting position. But there's another group of adverbials, mainly single-word adverbs, whose purpose is to emphasize a particular structure and thus control the pace and rhythm of the sentence.

Read the following sentences and note where you apply the main stress:

> I could hardly sleep last night.
>
> I slept hardly at all last night.
>
> My roommate also had trouble sleeping.
>
> Some people are always looking for trouble.
>
> Joe tells me that he rarely stays awake past midnight.
>
> The country has never before faced the kind of crisis it faces now with terrorism.

You probably put the emphasis on *hardly, all, also, always, rarely,* and *never before.*

Given these examples, you can think of other words that you use for emphasis: other negatives, such as *seldom, barely, scarcely;* other time and frequency words, such as *afterwards, finally, sometimes;* and others expressing duration, such as *already, no longer, still.*

Negative adverbials produce an even stronger emphasis when they open the sentence, the result of switching the position of the subject and the auxiliary:

> Never before <u>has the country encountered</u> the kind of crisis it now faces with terrorism.

This shift, in fact, requires an auxiliary unless the main verb is a form of *be:*

> I seldom <u>get</u> a good night's sleep on weekends.
>
> Seldom <u>do I get</u> a good night's sleep on weekends.

This is another instance where we call on *do*-support when we need an auxiliary. (This use of *do*-support is discussed briefly on page 10.) And, as you can hear, the auxiliary–subject combination shares the main stress with the adverbial.

It's possible, of course, to write sentences in which these words would not have main stress, where the principle of end focus, for example, would still be in effect. But certainly these are words that you, as a writer, need to recognize; they often wield the power in a sentence, controlling its intonation contour and making a difference in the message.

The Common *Only*.   One of our most versatile—but also most frequently misused—adverbials of emphasis is the common *only*. Like other emphasizers, *only* can change the focus of the sentence by directing the reader's attention to a particular word:

> I'm taking <u>only twelve</u> credits this semester.
>
> The car <u>only looks</u> old; it's really quite new.
>
> Joe isn't <u>only handsome</u>; he's rich too.
>
> Paul cleans house <u>only on Saturdays.</u>

When you read these sentences you'll find yourself putting nearly equal emphasis on both *only* and the word that follows it.

But there's also a common problem with *only:* It's frequently misplaced—and most of the time we don't even notice!

> I'm only taking twelve credits this semester.
>
> Paul only cleans house on Saturdays.
>
> We're only going to be gone for two or three days.
>
> Jane refuses to watch the Super Bowl; she only likes baseball.

Even song writers get it wrong:

> I only have eyes for you.

Perhaps the judgments of "wrong" and "misplaced" are inaccurate—too picky perhaps—when we consider how often this placement of *only* occurs both in speech and in the formal prose of respected writers. Nevertheless, in some cases, the reader will get a clear message when the *only* puts emphasis on a specific detail, to strengthen the sentence focus. That message says, "Pay attention! I've crafted this sentence carefully."

FOR GROUP DISCUSSION

In your peer group, when you are evaluating one another's papers, pay special attention to compound structures where the writer has used *and* and *or*. Consider the possibility of turning the *and* into *both–and* or *not only–but also* and the *or* into *either–or*. Remember however, that the correlative puts extra emphasis on that structure, especially on its second element. You'll want to suggest that change only if you intend for the reader to give it added attention. Pay special attention as well to any adverbials of emphasis, including *only,* and the way in which they affect the pace and rhythm of the sentence.

KEY TERMS

Adverbial of emphasis
Cleft sentence
Conjunctive adverb
Coordinating
   conjunction
Correlative
   conjunction

End focus
Existential *there*
Expletive
Intonation
It-cleft

Power words
Rhythm
Stress
There-transformation
What-cleft

RHETORICAL REMINDERS

Sentence Rhythm

Have I considered my reader's expectations by putting the new information in line for end focus, unless otherwise marked?

Controlling Rhythm

Have I used *there* and cleft sentences effectively—but not too frequently?

Have I placed interrupting words and phrases and clauses where they will be the most effective?

Power Words

Have I considered the impact of power words on the rhythm pattern?

Have I considered the contribution that correlative conjunctions could or do make to the rhythm and the reader's expectations?

Have I placed *only* in its most effective position?

PUNCTUATION REMINDER

In punctuating my sentences, have I taken into consideration that a comma changes the rhythm of the sentence, adding length and stress to the preceding word?

CHAPTER 6

The Writer's Voice

CHAPTER PREVIEW

In the first five chapters we looked at the structure and connection of sentences, including options the writer has for controlling the way the reader reads and interprets them. This chapter continues that discussion, focusing on features of language that affect the writer's voice and, thus, the reader's interpretation: **tone,** the writer's stance, or attitude toward the topic; **diction,** the choice of words; and **point of view,** the perspective from which the writer views the topic. We also continue the discussion of **metadiscourse,** the signals that help communicate the writer's credibility and establish authority.

As you would expect, all of these features depend on the writing situation: the audience, the purpose, and the topic. Your writer's voice in a personal letter, for example, will be quite different from the voice in a letter to a prospective employer. Your voice in a personal essay for your composition class will be different from that of a history research paper. In all of your writing, however, your writer's voice should be your voice, your personal voice.

TONE

In conversation there's nothing very mysterious about tone of voice, about what contributes to meaning:

> "He was his usual cheerful self."
> "She's got attitude."
> "I think he was kidding."

In a face-to-face encounter, of course, it's not only the voice that communicates the tone: There's the red face, the raised eyebrows, the rolling eyes, the smile, the smirk, the pleased expression.

But even on the telephone, without visual cues, we usually have no trouble drawing conclusions about tone. A person's voice may exude confidence or trepidation, hostility or pleasure, anger, bitterness, indifference. "How did she sound?" is a question someone might ask you about a phone conversation—not only, "What did she say?"

But how does your *writer's* voice sound? What determines its tone? Indeed, what does *tone* mean when there is no sound, only words on paper?

To answer these questions, consider what you read in the Introduction about rhetoric—about the choices we make based not only on the topic we're writing about but also on the audience and purpose. In that discussion we compared your writer's voice in a letter to your best friend with one to your great-aunt Millie. Or consider the words you would use in a letter to a prospective employer. You would choose words to convey an earnest and confident and businesslike tone—and of course you'd be careful to dot every *i* and cross every *t*, so to speak.

Clearly, it's the rhetorical situation—the topic, the purpose, and the audience—that determines the tone. For example, newspapers and newsmagazines generally call for a neutral, objective voice. But apparently not always—not in this *Time* article about self-help books:

> In case you haven't noticed, the baby boomers are having families these days. But of course you've noticed. According to the boomer law of cultural tyranny, if the boomers are having families, then we must all turn our attention to the problems of families. Newspapers, magazines, advertising and especially politics are consumed with the subject. Baby boomers have even invented a verb to describe this new craze: "to parent," which suggests the rearing of children is just another one of life's many options—a means of self-fulfillment like mountain biking or enrolling in a clogging class.
>
> With so many affluent, culturally aware parents busy parenting, it's no wonder authors have been busy authoring, cashing in with truckloads of books about you and your child. The trend has even touched the fluffiest genre of nonfiction, the self-help book....
>
> —Andrew Ferguson

The author's tongue-in-cheek tone here is anything but neutral. His use of common phrases—*in case you haven't noticed, we must all turn our attention, it's no wonder*—and his use of the second-person pronoun *you* invite our participation, our agreement; his choice of details—*enrolling in a clog-ging class, parenting, authoring*—keeps us interested.

And in the following short piece, one of several in "Parade's Special Intelligence Report," a regular feature of *Parade* magazine, the use of the word *snafu* in the headline sets the reader up to expect that same kind of flippant tone:

Social Security Snafu

The federal government had to cough up cash last month and mail a "letter of explanation" to 51 million Americans who were short-changed on their Social Security checks. It seems the Bureau of Labor Statistics was supposed to give them 2.5% cost-of-living increases but only added 2.4%, due to faulty math. Recipients won't get rich: It's about $12 to $19 more. (We wonder what it cost to calculate the difference, then print and mail all those letters.) But the blunders didn't stop there: Some folks were sent financial data about their neighbors.

As you can see, the writer fulfills the headline's expectations. It's the choice of words that does it: *cough up, short-changed, faulty math, blunders.* You can be quite sure that a news release on the topic sent by the Bureau of Labor Statistics would have used different words.

In each of these examples, the writer's attitude toward the topic, the writer's take on the topic, clearly sets the tone: tongue-in-cheek, flippant, facetious, derisive. Unlike the "Snafu" article, the following paragraph displays the tone we would expect to find in an article about a serious topic like Social Security. This paragraph, from an article about Robert Ball's involvement with the Social Security program, continues a discussion of where to find the reason for the program's fiscal crisis:

Just where becomes clear when one looks at the reasons why Social Security's long-range projections no longer show the program remaining in balance for 75 years. Some of the slippage has to do with obscure technical matters, such as lowered actuarial expectations about future productivity increases. But the actuaries have also been tracking an economic phenomenon that is entirely external to Social Security but clearly affecting it. That issue is income inequality. It may not be news that the gap between rich and poor in the United States is growing, but the impact of that gap on Social Security's finances has not received much attention. "It should," says Ball.

—Thomas N. Bethel, "Roosevelt Redux"
(The American Scholar)

There's nothing flippant in this passage. We recognize a formal, businesslike tone, one with a ring of authority. In the sections that follow, we consider the aspects of diction, including point of view and the use of contractions, that produce these contrasting voices.

EXERCISE 16

1. Rewrite the "Snafu" paragraph in a neutral tone, as the Bureau of Labor Statistics might have done in a news release. In addition to the informal words mentioned, you'll also want to consider the appropriateness of *It seems* in the second sentence, the reference to getting rich in the third, and the sentence in parentheses.

2. These five short paragraphs open an article by Jeff Gammage entitled "One Significant Swede" about Carl Linnaeus in the "Magazine" section of the *Philadelphia Inquirer* (June 28, 2005):

> At the Swedish museum in South Philadelphia, the staff is getting ready for a gala, year-long celebration of the 300th birthday of Carl Linnaeus.
>
> They face just one pesky problem: Most people don't know who the heck he is.
>
> And that's a shame, sponsors say. Because Linnaeus is not just another guy in a powdered wig.
>
> The Scandinavian scientist came up with a big, world-changing idea, a way to tidy up the clutter of the natural universe: He invented a system to name and categorize everything that lives, has lived or will live. And then he got people to follow his rules.
>
> Remember your high school biology teacher pounding *kingdom-phylum-class* into your head? You can thank—or blame—Carl Linnaeus.

As you can see, the first paragraph covers the standard *who-what-when-where-why* of journalistic reporting in a straightforward way. What has the writer done to change the tone of the last four?

A. Do a revision in which those last four paragraphs conform to the straight reporting of the first one.

B. Do another in which the opening paragraph conforms in tone to the other four.

For the revisions, you might want to combine paragraphs into perhaps just one or two.

....

DICTION

All of the published examples in the preceding section, besides illustrating tone, show clearly the connection between tone and **diction,** the choice of words: They are two sides of the same coin. Both are connected to the writing situation as well as to the essential sense of the words. And it may take only a few words to change the tone from neutral to ironic or bitter or skeptical or enthusiastic—depending, of course, on their meanings.

Where do those meanings come from? While the dictionary can give the core of meaning that a word denotes, its essential sense resides in the language user and in the written or spoken context in which it is used. Communication takes place when that essential sense is shared between speaker and listener, writer and reader.

The words you choose are effective only when they are appropriate in the writing situation, appropriate for the audience and purpose, when they convey your message accurately and comfortably. The idea of comfort may seem out of place in connection with diction, but, in fact, words can sometimes cause the reader to feel uncomfortable. You've probably experienced such feelings yourself as a listener—hearing a speaker whose words for one reason or another strike you as inappropriate and make you feel uncomfortable. Writing can provoke those same feelings in a reader.

As a reader, you will usually spot an inappropriate word simply because it calls attention to itself—negative, uncomfortable attention. And when words are inappropriate, they set up communication barriers. As a writer you must learn to spot your own inappropriate words. Probably the most common such attention-getter is the word that is too formal for the situation. Sometimes, of course, the opposite problem occurs: a word too informal for its purpose. But student writers are more likely to have the mistaken notion that writing calls for a sophisticated vocabulary. And so they look for words that demonstrate that sophistication.

One consequence of that inappropriate word choice is the loss of a personal voice. If what you've written doesn't sound like something you'd actually say, then you should reconsider your choice of words or style of phrasing. This is not to suggest that writing is exactly like speech; it's not, of course. In our everyday conversation with family and friends, we use informal words and phrases that we rarely see in writing, and we commonly use sentence fragments. Further, in writing we use certain modifiers and connectors, such as the *further* at the beginning of this sentence, that we rarely use in speaking. But even when we include such structures, we should be able to recognize our words as our own.

The following passage is the opening of a law school applicant's short essay in response to the question "Why do you want to study law?"

> It has long been a tenet of my value system that as a capable individual I have a social and moral duty to contribute to the improvement of the society in which I live. It seems that the way to make a valuable contribution is by choosing the means that will best allow me to utilize my abilities and facilitate my interests.

In spite of the first person point of view—the use of *I*—there's nothing personal in those lines. Here the author's voice simply doesn't fit the rhetorical situation. If she had been asked in a face-to-face interview why she wanted to go to law school, she certainly would not have begun her answer with "It has long been a tenet of my value system." Never in her life has she begun a sentence that way. Instead, she would have said "I believe" or "I've always thought." But like many inexperienced writers she associated formal writing with lofty phrases and uncommon words.

A personal voice does not, of course, preclude the use of big words or uncommon words. Nor does the expression "big words" refer to the number of syllables. It means pretentious or fancy words, words that call attention to themselves. Pretentious words send the message that the writer is trying too hard. The word *tenet,* as used in the law school statement, is one such pretentious word; it's out of place. Even the Declaration of Independence, with its formal, ceremonial language, uses the simple word *truths:*

> We hold these truths to be self-evident.

Chances are that Thomas Jefferson didn't consider, even in his first draft,

> We hold these tenets of our value system to be self-evident.

There are times, of course, when an uncommon word is called for, a word with the precise meaning you want. All of us have in our passive vocabulary words that we rarely, if ever, use in speaking; and using them when they're called for does not mean giving up our personal voice. The mere fact that a word is infrequent does not make it pretentious. In the opening sentence of the previous paragraph, for example, the verb is *preclude.* It's not a common word, but there's certainly nothing fancy or pretentious about it: It's simply the most precise word for the job.

Another problem with pretentious language is the flabbiness that it produces, such as "utilize my abilities and facilitate my interests." Verbs like *utilize* and *facilitate* may sound impressive, but what do they really mean? *Utilize* simply means *use:* "to use my abilities." And it would probably surprise the law school applicant to learn that *facilitate* does not mean "to carry out," as she apparently assumed; it means "to make easier." So "facilitate my interests" is not only pretentious; it is meaningless.

FOR GROUP DISCUSSION

1. Words are powerful. As a writer you can use to advantage the power that words hold to call up images in the mind of the reader. But to use words effectively, you have to understand as far as possible the meanings, the associations, they are likely to have for the reader. Consider the following sets of related words: What features do the members have in common? What features separate them? In what context would one be more effective than another?

   house/home   slender/skinny/scrawny
   hearth/fireplace   lad/boy/kid
   companion/friend/buddy   slumber/sleep/snooze
   picky/careful/prudent   foolhardy/daring/rash/bold
   cocky/confident   careful/stingy/thrifty/tight

2. Bertrand Russell is credited with the following "conjugation of an irregular verb":

   I am firm. You are obstinate. He is pigheaded.

   Using some of the groups of words in Part 1, and adding to them as necessary, try your own conjugations.

   Example: I am slender; you are skinny; he is scrawny.

3. One characteristic of ineffective diction is the overuse of **clichés,** many of which are **similes,** comparisons that transfer the qualities of one thing (or person or animal) to another. Such comparisons become clichés when the reader knows exactly what's coming—that is, when there is no new information involved. Unlike the message of pretentious words, trying too hard, clichés send the message that the writer isn't trying hard enough. The comparison is much more effective when it evokes a fresh image, when it helps the reader see something or someone in a new way.

Chances are you and most of your classmates can complete the following phrases with identical words:

quiet as a _____	mean as _____
hot as _____	light as _____
cold as _____	pretty as _____
scared as a _____	weak as _____
strong as _____	ugly as _____
fast as _____	tough as _____
avoid like the _____	sell like _____

Now, instead of using the expected word, find one that creates a fresh image. For example, you might say, "Quiet as a sealskin coat."

Note: You'll find it interesting and instructive to compare the answers given by the nonnative speakers of English in the class with those of native speakers.

Contractions

Contractions affect the rhythm of sentences and, in doing so, affect the reader's perception of the writer's voice. That voice will probably strike the reader as more conversational, less formal, when contractions are part of the message. Contractions help to close the distance between writer and reader.

Although contractions are often seen as too conversational, most writers, even in formal contexts, will contract the negative *not* in such words as *don't* and *can't.*

> If you use ready-made phrases, you not only <u>don't</u> have to hunt
> about for words; you also <u>don't</u> have to bother with the rhythms
> of your sentences, since these phrases are generally so arranged
> as to be more or less euphonious.
> —George Orwell ("Politics and the English Language")

Other frequent contractions are those with the auxiliary verbs *have, had, will, would, is, am,* and *are.* Here are some common examples:

Negatives: can't, don't, won't, couldn't, doesn't, isn't

Auxiliaries: I'd, she'll, they're, we've, he's, it's

The contracted forms of *be* can also occur when they function as the main verb:

> <u>You're</u> happy.
> <u>I'm</u> sad.

The contracted *is* is especially common with *it* and *there:*

> <u>It's</u> a nice day today.
> <u>There's</u> a storm due tomorrow.

If you think about—and listen for—sentence rhythm, you'll understand the contribution that contractions make in eliminating or greatly diminishing a syllable. As you read the following passages, consider how different the sentences would be without the contractions they include:

> Cats, I surmise, seem unsocial to us only because we <u>aren't</u> good at recognizing the signals of other species. We interpret cat signals as telling us, for instance, that the cat <u>doesn't</u> care about us and <u>doesn't</u> miss us when <u>we're</u> gone. If people were giving off similar signals, our interpretation would probably be right. But <u>they're</u> not people, and <u>we're</u> wrong.
>
> —Elizabeth Marshall Thomas *(The Atlantic Monthly)*

> All left-handers know that they are different, different in ways that can make everyday life seem like a trip to a foreign country without a phrasebook. Lefties have roughly the first year or two of their lives to prepare for the obstacle course <u>they'll</u> encounter; until <u>they're</u> a couple of years old, infants frequently use both hands interchangeably. <u>It's</u> when children begin to master fine motor skills that a dominant hand emerges.
>
> —Nancy Shute *(Smithsonian)*

You may have noticed that none of the examples, either in the lists or in the quoted passages, involve nouns—only pronouns. Contractions with nouns—"My <u>dog'll</u> eat anything"; "The <u>Senate's</u> accomplished a lot lately"—are fairly common in conversation and in written quotations and dialogue, but they are rare in most writing situations. However, contractions with pronouns are anything but rare.

The advice against using contractions that you may have heard or read simply does not reflect actual usage. Even fairly formal written prose commonly includes the contracted *not,* as the Orwell passage illustrates. And in negative questions, the contracted form is essentially required:

> Hasn't the winter weather been wonderful?
>
> Shouldn't the tax laws be revised?

In the uncontracted form, the *not* predominates, changing the intended emphasis, if not the meaning:

> Has the winter weather not been wonderful?
>
> Should the tax laws not be revised?

An interesting feature in negative statements is that often the writer has more than one contraction to choose from.

> She is not here. ⟶ She's not here *or* She isn't here.

Both contracted forms are less formal than the original, of course, but there's also a difference between the two: In the version with the diminished *not (isn't),* the reader will probably put more emphasis on *here*—and may then expect a different follow-up sentence:

> She isn't here. She's in class.
>
> She's not here. I don't know where she is.

If you want to ensure that the reader puts strong stress on the negative, you can use the uncontracted *not*—with or without the contracted *is.* Another difference between these two contracted versions is the number of syllables. The sentence with *isn't* has four syllables; the one with *not* has only three—a rhythm difference that in a given situation may be important.

In some cases where there's a choice of contractions, you may also notice a difference in formality, with the uncontracted *not* on the more formal side:

> I won't be there. / I'll not be there.
>
> I haven't finished. / I've not finished.
>
> I wouldn't go there if I were you. / I'd not go there if I were you.

Even though the second version in each case includes a contraction, it has a rather formal tone.

It's important to recognize the connection between the level of formality and the use of contractions: In general, the more formal the writing, the fewer contractions you'll find, or want to use, especially contracted auxiliaries. However, in most of the writing you do for school or on the job, the occasional contraction will certainly be appropriate. It's important to recognize the contribution that contractions can make to your personal voice.

FOR GROUP DISCUSSION

Consider the personal voice that you hear in the following advertisements, which appeared during the same week in two different publications. How would you characterize the tone and the diction? In each case the opening paragraph shown is the headline for the ad.

Rewrite each of the ads using the voice and tone of the other one.

1. Looks like this winter will be warmer than the last. Lands' End introduces the newest—and driest—in Polartec outerwear.

   Have you met Polartec yet? If you're into winter sports, betcha you have.

   It's the original man-made fleece. A nubby fabric that weighs nothing—yet keeps you warm when it's umpteen below.

   Well, the folks at Malden Mills who dreamed up Polartec have outdone themselves now.

   They've not only created an even cozier warmer version—they've made it more water repellent, too.

   So much so, that it inspired us at Lands' End to introduce a whole bunch of new Polartec outerwear.
                                                      —*The Atlantic Monthly*

2. A perfect dinner party requires hours of planning and preparation. Having decent appliances doesn't hurt, either.

   Fresh herbs as opposed to dry. Going to the butcher instead of the supermarket. The wedding china, not everyday.

   Her dinner party was that special. Perhaps the brilliant shine of stainless steel inspired her, from a kitchen that was special too. Filled with restaurant-quality appliances—aka the Pro-Style Collection from Jenn-Air.

   From the quintessential cooktop to the matching refrigerator and dishwasher, they're all sleek, gleaming and state-of-the-art. The crème de la crème, as they say.

   True, throwing the perfect dinner party is a major project. But if you've got the perfect kitchen, it's a labor of love.
                                                      —*The New Yorker*

Verbs and Formality

As you might expect, the level of formality in our prose is determined in large part by our choice of verbs—the pivotal slot of the sentence. Among the verbs that send an informal signal to the reader are *phrasal verbs,* a common verb combined with one or more particles, or preposition-like words, to form an **idiom.** The term *idiom* refers to a set phrase whose meaning cannot be predicted from the separate meanings of the words. The meaning of the idiom *give up,* for example, is different from the combined meanings of *give* and *up:* It means "surrender" or "abandon."

Our language is filled with such idioms: *turn down, bring about, bring on, put up with, stand for, think up, take off, take up, look down on, brush aside, get on with, walk out on, come down with, swear off, write off*—the list goes on and on. As you can see, these are common verbs, part of our everyday speech. Like contractions, they lend an air of familiarity, a conversational tone to the writer's voice.

Idioms are certainly appropriate in informal contexts—for example, in a personal essay or narrative, or for a general audience, such as you might address in a letter to the editor of a newspaper. But for research papers or technical reports—and certainly for résumés and letters to prospective employers—a more formal verb may be called for. One way of adding formality, then, is to look carefully at *(scrutinize)* your sentences and do away with *(eliminate)* or at least cut down on *(reduce)* the number of idioms.

EXERCISE 17

A. Substitute a single word for each of the idioms listed in the second paragraph of the preceding discussion. In some cases there will be more than one possibility.

B. The idioms I have used in writing this book certainly influence its level of formality. Here are some of the sentences you have seen so far. Come up with a more formal version of each.

1. Come up with a more formal version of each.

2. The punctuation convention calls for a comma....

3. There are three steps we follow in turning the active voice into passive.

4. All sentences are made up of one or more independent clauses.

5. The first sentence in a paragraph sets up expectations in the reader about what is coming.

6. We can easily figure out what the sentence means.

7. We can <u>think of</u> it as part of the contract between writer and reader.

8. You can be sure that in reading their own prose, whether silently or aloud, they are <u>paying attention to</u> sentence rhythm.

9. The pronoun <u>stands in for</u> the entire noun phrase.

10. We <u>call on</u> *do* when we need an auxiliary....

METAPHOR

As you have seen, the choice of words affects the reader's response to the message and no doubt to the writer as well. The use of contractions tends to close the distance between writer and reader. Another technique for closing that distance is the use of *metaphor,* the application of words from one sphere to another.

You were introduced to the grammar of metaphor in Chapter 1 when you read about the linking-*be* followed by a noun phrase as subject complement. A "something is something" sentence becomes metaphor when that equation is figurative rather than literal—in other words, when the two "somethings" belong to different spheres or domains. Shakespeare's

All the world's a stage

and Charlie Brown's (Charles Schulz's)

Happiness is a warm puppy

illustrate the wide range of possibilities—from the profound to the commonplace.

But *be* sentences, like these examples, are by no means the only form of metaphor, or even the most common. In our everyday language we apply words from one domain to another, creating metaphor with just a simple modifier. Language itself is often described metaphorically: flowery prose, gutter journalism, bathroom words, hard-boiled detective novels. Newsmagazines abound with metaphors, many of them overworked. *Time* reported on "an industrial dinosaur like General Motors" the same week that *Newsweek* described the company as "a sinking ship." In *Time's* story the head of the company "doesn't like sitting in the back seat"; in *Newsweek's* he's helping to steer "a treasure galleon."

Metaphor can often illuminate and lighten a serious or technical discussion. In the following extended metaphor, *New York Times* writers explain the issue of class. This paragraph is from an article by Janny Scott and David Leonhardt called "The Shadowy Lines That Still Divide," the first installment of an eleven-part series called "Class in America":

One way to think of a person's position in society is to imagine a hand of cards. Everyone is dealt four cards, one from each suit: education, income, occupation and wealth, the four commonly used criteria for gauging class. Face cards in a few categories may land a player in the upper middle class. At first, a person's class is his parents' class. Later, he may pick up a new hand of his own; it is likely to resemble that of his parents, but not always.

The following passage opens the third paragraph of a long article by Lauren Resnick and Chris Zurawsky in *American Education,* a publication of the American Federation of Teachers, describing the standards movement in American schools. The two preceding paragraphs introduce the topic in straightforward academic prose.

At about fifteen years of age, the standards movement is in its adolescence, and many are already preparing to kick it out of the house. Before we give up on our unruly teen, however, let's take a clear look at what we have to be proud of, what flaws we need to address, and what might be the benefits of pressing ahead.

After just two sentences of the teenager metaphor, however, the reader is back to serious business, with the questions that the article goes on to address. Undoubtedly, though, in both of these examples, the metaphor has made the reader stop and think about the topic in a new way.

METADISCOURSE

In the discussion of cohesion in Chapter 4, we looked at metadiscourse, or "discourse about discourse": various words and phrases that act as cohesive ties, such as *for example, consequently, thus,* and *in the first place.* We can think of these text connectors as primarily informational, to help the reader understand the message. In this chapter, however, the structures we label as metadiscourse have a different purpose and a different effect: They offer guidance for reading the text, informing the reader of the writer's own attitude about the content of the message.

As you read the following passages, think about the role played by the underlined words. If the sentences look familiar, it's because they have all appeared in earlier sections of this book.

1. Obviously the racehorses are part of the picture—the most important part, of course— ...

2. The point is that we, as readers, shouldn't have to do the figuring.

3. You've <u>probably</u> been told at one time or another to avoid *I* or *you* or the passive voice—and, <u>very possibly,</u> the *it*-cleft as well.

All of these underlined structures qualify as metadiscourse.

Without *obviously* in (1) your reaction to the sentence might have been different: You might have been insulted to think I would assume you have to be told such a self-evident fact; the phrase set off by dashes makes that message even clearer, emphasizing that you didn't really have to be told.

The opening in (2) emphasizes my take on the importance and validity of the proposition.

The use of *probably* and *very possibly* in (3) is called hedging: There's no way I could know for sure that you've been told those things, so I don't want to sound too positive. I don't want you, the reader, to be stopped by a bold statement when it may not be valid in your case. And I certainly don't want you to lose confidence in my authority to write on this topic. Other hedging terms are words like *perhaps,* verbs like *seem* or *indicate* or *suggest* and phrases like *to a certain extent,* as well as the modal auxiliaries *might* and *may* and *could.*

Although you might think that using words like *perhaps* and *probably* would communicate doubt about the author's authority and the reliability of the information, such hedges actually have the opposite effect on the reader. In his book *Constructing Texts,* George Dillon maintains that they "certify the writer as a modest, careful scholar whose tentative conclusions are probably of wider application and greater likelihood than he feels he can claim" (p. 91).[1]

There are many other kinds of metadiscourse markers that affect the writer's personal voice: Some of them comment on the content of the sentence; some of them allow the writer to address the reader directly; some comment on what is coming next—or what the reader has already learned. Here are some further examples, also taken from earlier sections of the book:

> <u>As you probably noticed,</u> the only difference between the two passages is in the rhythm pattern of the last sentence in each.

> The following passive sentence, <u>which may look familiar,</u> closes the first paragraph of the section in Chapter 1 called "Sentence Patterns". . . .

> <u>It is important to recognize</u> that pronouns without antecedents are in violation of the known–new contract.

> <u>And you can be sure</u> that in reading their own prose, whether silently or aloud, they are paying attention to sentence rhythm.

In the following paragraph, from *Saga of Chief Joseph* by Helen Addison Howard, the author translates "Nez Percé" in a parenthetical comment, a

---

[1]Dillon's book is listed in the Bibliography under "Composition Theory."

type of metadiscourse called a *code gloss,* a term applied when the writer clarifies the meaning of a word or phrase. You'll see other obvious metadiscourse signals as well:

> After Lewis and Clark passed through their country (about which more later), French-Canadian trappers came to trade the white man's guns, cloth, metal articles, and trinkets for their pelts of beaver. The French traders, it is claimed, applied the name "Nez Perce" (Pierced Nose) to these Indians because a few members of the tribe used to pierce their noses to insert a shell for ornament. This habit was not a tribal custom, but the name clung to them.

Still another example of metadiscourse appears in the first sentence of the paragraph introducing the previous quotation: The sentence beginning "In the following paragraph" is called an *attributor,* the source of the quoted information. Attributors add authority to the text. In the previous discussion of Dillon's comment about hedges, the attributor phrase begins "In his book"; the opening "According to" is another common lead-in for an attributor.

All of these metadiscourse markers send messages to the reader from and about the writer. They say, in effect, "I'm helping you out here, trying to make your job of reading and understanding easier."

The Overuse of Metadiscourse

It can happen, as you would expect, that inexperienced writers sometimes get carried away with metadiscourse, with those helpful messages, to the detriment of their primary message. The following paragraph is from a paper written by a student participating in a research study on the effectiveness of teaching metadiscourse. The underlined segments were identified as metadiscourse by the researchers:

> In the beginning the television was posed as a real asset for families with children because it would be a big influence in the home. Basically this is what Marie Winn discussed in her article "The Plug-In Drug." As a young adult today I can safely say that the hours one person sits in front of the television has greatly increased from what it was forty years ago. So yes Winn is correct in stating that the television is a major influence on children these days.[2]

Note that the passive verb *was posed* is included as metadiscourse; the researchers call it a "pseudo attributor." Their conclusion about the prolif-

---

[2]Quoted in the article by Cheng and Steffensen listed in the Bibliography under "Metadiscourse."

eration of connectives and markers is that the overuse of metadiscourse resulted in a low level of information in the primary message.

Every writer is sometimes prone to too much of a good thing. That's what revision is all about. This problem of metadiscourse overuse is one you've probably never thought about before, primarily because the whole concept of "discourse about discourse" is new to you. But now that you're aware of its existence, you can see that it's closely connected not only to your writer's voice but also to the principle of the known–new contract and to the awareness of purpose, to the awareness of what each sentence contributes to the whole.

FOR GROUP DISCUSSION

Consider the use of metadiscourse in the following paragraph, the first paragraph in Chapter 9 of Thomas S. Kuhn's *The Structure of Scientific Revolutions*. This chapter is entitled "The Nature and Necessity of Scientific Revolutions."

> These remarks permit us at last to consider the problems that provide this essay with its title. What are scientific revolutions, and what is their function in scientific development? Much of the answer to these questions has been anticipated in earlier sections. In particular, the preceding discussion has indicated that scientific revolutions are here taken to be those non-cumulative developmental episodes in which an older paradigm is replaced in whole or in part by an incompatible new one. There is more to be said, however, and an essential part of it can be introduced by asking one further question. Why should a change of paradigm be called a revolution? In the face of the vast and essential differences between political and scientific development, what parallelism can justify the metaphor that finds revolutions in both?

Identify all the uses of metadiscourse in the paragraph; characterize their purpose and their effect on the reader.

FOR GROUP DISCUSSION

1. Examine the textbooks you use in other classes—for example, history or biology or business—and identify any metadiscourse the authors have included. What kinds of messages does the metadiscourse send?

2. In your peer review group, look for metadiscourse in a classmate's paper. Look for places where adding metadiscourse signals might be helpful for you as a reader.

3. Look again at your own paper with your own writer's voice in mind.

POINT OF VIEW

In discussing **point of view**—the perspective from which the writer views the topic—we again take up the discussion of personal pronouns. In Chapter 1 we saw personal pronouns as stand-ins for noun phrases and used them to determine those phrase boundaries; in Chapter 4 we recognized their role as cohesive devices. Here we look at their relationship to point of view. The writer's decision about point of view is essentially a choice about **person,** a feature of personal pronouns: Shall I write in first person? Second person? A combination? Or shall I stick strictly to third person?

In the following chart, the first forms shown are **subjective case,** the form used when the pronoun functions as the subject or subject complement in its sentence. The forms shown in parentheses are variations of case **(possessive, objective):** The possessive case is used when the pronoun functions as a determiner; the objective case is used in the complement slots (direct object, indirect object, object complement) and as the object of a preposition.

PERSON	NUMBER	
	Singular	Plural
1st	I (my, me)	we (our, us)
2nd	you (your, you)	you (your, you)
3rd	he (his, him)	
	she (her, her)	they (their, them)
	it (its, it)	

(The case of personal pronouns is discussed further on pages 256–260.)

Many kinds of essays are written in first person—more than you might think. Personal narratives, of course, are nearly always first person, but so are many others. In fact, it would probably be accurate to say that most essay writers use first person somewhere in their text—an occasional *we* or *our* or *us.* The exceptions are business and scientific reports and historical essays, which are often strictly third person. Newspapers and newsmagazines also stick to third person when they report the news. But writers of editorials and syndicated columns and feature stories regularly use both first and second person. And in textbooks it's certainly common to see both first and second person. In this one you'll find sentences with *we* or *our* or *you* or *your* on every page.

If it's true that first person is a common point of view, then why do teachers so often rule it unacceptable in the essays they assign? You may have had an English teacher in high school or college who required you to stick to third person. One reason for that proscription against first person is undoubtedly the bad writing that so often results, with *I* turning up as the subject of almost every sentence—as if the writer, the "I," were the topic being discussed.

The most common use of first person in professional writing is the plural—*we* and *us* and *our* rather that *I* and *me* and *my*. The result is a kind of collective first person (sometimes referred to as the "royal *we*" or the "editorial *we*"). You'll find that collective first person in the preamble to the Constitution: "We the people … for ourselves and our posterity…." The *we* in this book is also that collective *we*. And following is another example, a first-person passage from *A Brief History of Time* by Stephen W. Hawking:

> Now at first sight, all this evidence that the universe looks the same whichever direction <u>we</u> look in might seem to suggest there is something special about <u>our</u> place in the universe. In particular, it might seem that if <u>we</u> observe all other galaxies to be moving away from <u>us,</u> then <u>we</u> must be at the center of the universe.

Here the first-person plural is especially effective, where the writer wants the reader to be included in his description of the universe.

Another point of view that teachers sometimes rule out is the second person, the use of *you*. But it too is common for many writing occasions. You'll notice that many of the sentences in the foregoing paragraphs, as well as the sentence you're reading now, include *you* as the subject. This use of *you* not only gets the attention of the reader, it actually involves the reader in the subject matter.

The *Time* article on baby boomers at the opening of this chapter is a good example of this direct appeal, with its informal, personal tone. That informality derives partly from the second person, especially in the opening metadiscourse signal, which establishes a strong bond with the reader. The second sentence, also an example of metadiscourse, continues that connection:

> <u>In case you haven't noticed,</u> the baby boomers are having families these days. <u>But of course you've noticed.</u>

But *you* does not always address the reader; it is often used in a more general sense, with a meaning more like that of the third person. Notice the use of *you* in this passage from *Broca's Brain* by Carl Sagan, describing an excursion into the back rooms of the Museum of Man in Paris:

> Most of the rooms were evidently used for storage of anthro-pological items, collected from decades to more than a century ago. <u>You</u> had the sense of a museum of the second order, in which were stored not so much materials that might be of inter-est as materials that had once been of interest. <u>You</u> could feel the presence of nineteenth-century museum directors engaged, in their frock coats, in goniometrie and craniologie, busily col-lecting and measuring everything, in the pious hope that mere quantification would lead to understanding.

Here *you* takes the place of "one" or "a person"; it is not "you the reader," as we saw in the *Time* article.

Some teachers, however, prefer *one* to this general *you:*

> When <u>one</u> sees the Golden Gate Bridge for the first time, the sight is simply breathtaking.

The use of <u>one</u> adds a formality, a distance that *you* does not have. The sen-tence sounds formal and British, like something Prince Charles would say. In American English, we're more likely to use *you* rather than *one* to convey that third-person indefinite sense:

> When <u>you</u> see the Golden Gate Bridge for the first time, the sight is simply breathtaking.

This use of *you* is technically second person, but the meaning is closer to the indefinite third-person *one*. We saw the use of the formal *one* in the scholarly description of Social Security on page 109.

It is not at all unusual to mix the point of view. A first- or second-per-son passage always includes pronouns in the third person. And many essays that are essentially third person have an occasional *we* or *our* or *you*. There is no rule that says good writing should not have that versatility of view.

EXERCISE 18

The following passage is an adulterated version of the opening of an essay by Annie Dillard, from her Pulitzer Prize–winning narrative *Pilgrim at Tin-*

ker Creek. (Dillard is also the author of the weasel passage in Chapter 1.) You'll notice that these two first-person paragraphs include twelve clauses with *I* as subjects: Four of these *I*'s are *not* in the original. Your job is to put the passage back into its prize-winning form.

> Yesterday, I set out to catch the new season, and instead I found an old snakeskin. I was in the sunny February woods by the quarry; I found the snakeskin lying in a heap of leaves right next to an aquarium someone had thrown away. I don't know why that someone hauled the aquarium deep into the woods to get rid of it; it had only one broken glass side. The snake found it handy, I imagine; snakes like to rub against something rigid to help them out of their skins, and the broken aquarium looked like the nearest likely object. Together the snakeskin and the aquarium made an interesting scene on the forest floor. I thought it looked like an exhibit at a trial—circumstantial evidence—of a wild scene, as though a snake had burst through the broken side of the aquarium, burst through his ugly old skin, and disappeared, perhaps straight up in the air, in a rush of freedom and beauty.
>
> I could see that the snakeskin had unkeeled scales, so I knew it belonged to a nonpoisonous snake. It was roughly five feet long by the yardstick, but I'm not sure because it was very wrinkled and dry, and every time I tried to stretch it flat it broke. I ended up with seven or eight pieces of it all over the kitchen table in a fine film of forest dust.

(You can compare your version with the original in the answers section in the back of the book.)

....

KEY TERMS

Attributor	Metadiscourse	Possessive case
Case	Metaphor	Second person
Cliché	Objective case	Simile
Contraction	Person	Subjective case
Diction	Personal pronoun	Third person
First person	Personal voice	Tone
Hedge	Point of view	Voice

RHETORICAL REMINDERS

What is there in my sentence structure and word choice that has established my tone? Have I avoided words that contradict my tone?

Can I hear my personal voice in the words I've written? Have I avoided unusual words that don't really sound like me—words I probably wouldn't use in speech?

Have I been accurate and complete in attributing the ideas and words of outside sources and in using quotation marks for passages that are not my own?

Are my contractions appropriate, given the level of formality I want to achieve? Are my contractions attached only to pronouns *(she's)* and auxiliaries *(can't)*—not to nouns *(John'll go with us; The teacher's talking)*?

Have I used hedging words appropriately, where I need to hedge? Emphatic words where I want to show emphasis? Have I guided the reader where such guidance would help?

PUNCTUATION REMINDERS

Have I set off metadiscourse markers with commas where an emphasis on the marker would be useful?

Have I included apostrophes in contractions to indicate where a letter (or letters) has been left out?

Have I used quotation marks correctly (e.g., outside the period at the end of a sentence)? (*Note:* See pages 291–292 in the Glossary of Punctuation.)

Choosing Verbs

CHAPTER PREVIEW

You've read about verbs before, of course—in connection with sentence patterns, with cohesion, with parallel structure, with diction, with rhythm. You've no doubt heard the message that verbs are important. In this chapter that message continues. You'll encounter some new terminology in connection with expanded verb forms (but don't worry about memorizing it!); a description of the passive voice, a concept you should feel comfortable with; and discussions on the selection and impact of verbs in your writing.

OUR VERSATILE VERBS

It's probably impossible to count the number of verbs in English. We regularly add new ones when new technology and ideas require them, and we seem to have no qualms about making verbs out of nouns: We *lunch* with our friends; we *Google* to find information; we *e-mail* folks on a regular basis; and, as we saw in Chapter 3, parents engage in *parenting*. We also have a wide array of affixes we can use to change other word classes into verbs: beautify, legalize, darken, activate, encourage, befriend, discourage, derail.

Not only do we have countless verbs, old and new, we have numerous ways of expanding them with auxiliaries for expressing subtle variations in time and duration and completion. In some foreign languages, those variations are accomplished by verb endings; French, for example, has seventy or so different forms for every verb. In English we manage with only five variations (with the exception of *be*). Here are the five, demonstrated by a regular verb (*walk*) and an irregular one (*eat*), along with the eight forms of *be:*

base form (infinitive)	*eat*	*walk*	*be*
present tense	*eats*	*walks*	*am, is, are*
past tense (*–ed*)	*ate*	*walked*	*was, were*
past participle(*–en*)	*eaten*	*walked*	*been*
present participle (*–ing*)	*eating*	*walking*	*being*

The past tense and the past participle are identical in all regular verbs, formed by the addition to the base form of *–ed,* or in a few cases, *–t.* The past participle is often labeled the *–en* form, simply to distinguish it from the past tense: This label is based on the past participle of a number of common irregular verbs: *eaten, beaten, driven, given, spoken, broken,* and the most common of all, *been.*

Verbs are by far the most systematic of our word classes. While we can say that nouns are words that have a plural form, it isn't true of all nouns; for example, most abstract nouns, such as *happiness,* have no plural form, nor do proper nouns. But all verbs, without exception, have these five forms; and whether regular or irregular, all have an *–ing* form and an *–s* form. If you're wondering if a word is a verb, simply ask yourself if it has those two forms. (And while nouns, too, have an *–s* form, they don't have an *–ing.*)

When we combine these forms with the auxiliaries *have* and *be* and the modal auxiliaries (*can, could, would,* etc.), we achieve the variations in meaning that other languages accomplish with suffixes.

Using the Expanded Verbs

The details of these expanded verbs are not listed here for you to memorize—not at all. If you're a native speaker of English, you've been using most of them since before you started kindergarten; they're well established in your internal grammar rules. However, some of them we don't use very often; and in some cases the combinations of auxiliaries we use to express past events have subtle meanings you may not be aware of. So do read through the discussion. It is here to help when you have questions about the accuracy and/or effectiveness of your verbs.

SIMPLE PRESENT: BASE AND -*S* FORM

- *"Habitual"* or *"timeless" present:*
  Kevin <u>has</u> a chemistry exam every Thursday.
  We <u>have</u> earthquakes in California quite often.

- *Present point in time:*

  I <u>understand</u> your position.

PRESENT PROGRESSIVE: -*ING* FORM WITH A FORM OF *BE*

- *Present action of limited duration:*

  Sherry <u>is taking</u> computer science this semester.

  Note: Both this form and the simple present can indicate future time with the addition of an appropriate adverbial:

  The bus <u>leaves</u> at seven.

  We <u>are having</u> pizza tonight.

SIMPLE PAST: -*ED* FORM

- *Specific point in the past:*

  The Assisi earthquake <u>demolished</u> priceless works of art.

- *Span of time in the past:*

  In 1993 we <u>lived</u> in Idaho.

PAST PROGRESSIVE: -*ING* FORM WITH THE PAST OF *BE* (*WAS* OR *WERE*):

- *Past action of limited duration* (often to show one particular action during a larger span of time):

  Larry <u>was sleeping</u> during the history lecture.

  I <u>was trying</u> to study last night during the party, but it was no use.

PRESENT PERFECT: -*EN* FORM (PAST PARTICIPLE) WITH A FORM OF *HAVE:*

- *Completed action extending from a point in the past to either the present or the near present or occurring at an unspecified past time:*

  The leaves <u>have turned</u> yellow already.

  I <u>have eaten</u> dinner already.

  I <u>have memorized</u> several of Frost's poems.

PAST PERFECT: THE PAST PARTICIPLE WITH THE PAST OF *HAVE (HAD):*

- *Past action completed before another action in the past:*

  I <u>had answered</u> only half the questions when the proctor <u>called out</u>, "Time's up."

  By the time the police <u>arrived</u>, the crowd <u>had begun</u> to attack the picket line.

SIMPLE FUTURE: MODAL AUXILIARY *WILL* WITH THE BASE FORM

I <u>will go</u> with you.

Note: Another way of expressing future is with the semi-auxiliary *be going to:*

I'm <u>going to</u> order a salad.

As noted under "present progressive," that form and the simple present are both used to express the future with the addition of an appropriate adverbial:

The bus <u>leaves at seven.</u>

We <u>are having</u> pizza <u>tonight.</u>

FUTURE PERFECT: MODAL AUXILIARY *WILL* ADDED TO THE PRESENT PERFECT.

• *Future action completed before another future action.*

I <u>will have finished</u> dinner by the time you arrive.

The past perfect is one of the tenses most likely to be a problem—most likely to be used ineffectively. In the examples shown at the bottom of page 131, the writer is referring to more than one point or period of time in the past. Actually three different times are included in these sentences, given the writer's point of view in the present:

PAST PERFECT	PAST	PRESENT
prior to "then"	*"then"*	*"now" (at this writing)*
had answered	called out	
had begun	arrived	

Here are some other sentences expressing the past that include more than one clause:

We <u>lived</u> in Colorado when I <u>was</u> a boy.

My family <u>had lived</u> there for six years before we <u>moved</u> to Texas.

Note that in the first sentence the two clauses describe the same period of time; the simple past—*lived* and *was*—is appropriate because the verbs refer to simultaneous happenings. In the second sentence, however, the time expressed by *had lived* precedes the event described in the *before* clause. It's not unusual to see or to hear sentences such as the last one with the simple past in both clauses.

My family <u>lived</u> there for six years before we <u>moved</u> to Texas.

But careful writers would use *had lived* to maintain the time distinction.

Sometimes the meaning is unclear without the time distinction that the past participle contributes:

My dad <u>gave</u> me a motorcycle, which he <u>drove</u> for many years.

In this sentence the time referred to in the second clause could be either prior to *gave* or both prior to and after. It could mean either

which he continued to drive for many years

or

which he had driven for many years.

Another situation that calls for a careful selection of tenses occurs with what is called the "hypothetical past":

If we <u>had invited</u> George, he <u>would have come.</u>

Inexperienced writers sometimes make the mistake of including the modal auxiliary *would* in both clauses:

*If we <u>would have invited</u> George, he <u>would have come.</u>

Here the conditional meaning is expressed by *if,* so *would* is simply redundant.

The *if*-clause can also denote what is called the **subjunctive mood,** to express a condition contrary to fact or contrary to the belief or expectation of the speaker: ˜

If George <u>were</u> here, we would probably be playing charades.

In the subjunctive we avoid the *–s* form of the verb: "If George *were,*" not *was.* We should note, too, that the subjunctive applies in the *if*-clause only when the sentence expresses a wish or a condition contrary to fact or expectation:

If I <u>were</u> rich, I'd be driving a BMW.

If George <u>were</u> here, I just know he'd have us playing charades.

The subjunctive does not apply in *if*-clauses that express contingencies or possibilities:

If the mail *is* late again today, I'm going to complain.

If the store *was* closed, why were you gone so long?

If George *was* here earlier, why didn't he leave a message?

The Modal Auxiliaries

In Chapter 6 in the discussion of metadiscourse we saw the message that modal auxiliaries such as *might* and *may* and *could* send to the reader:

> There's no way I *could* know for sure....
>
> I don't want you, the reader, to be stopped by a bold statement, when it *may* not be valid in your case.

This particular "language about language" is called *hedging*. In traditional grammar, however, the label is **conditional mood.**

A number of the modal auxiliaries, including *could, would, should, may,* and *might* suggest this hedging quality, this conditional implication. The reader assumes from such messages that the writer has certain doubts, doubts that perhaps others may have and should have, thus connecting, as possible fellow doubters, the writer and the reader.

EXERCISE 19

Select a paragraph or page from an essay you have written or one you are currently working on. List the main verbs (with their auxiliaries) in all the clauses.

1. What percentage are a form of *be* or *have?* (Remember that both *have* and *be* can serve as auxiliaries; count them only in their role as main verb.)

2. Consider whether your verbs are as precise as they could be. Use your dictionary or thesaurus to find synonyms that might be more precise.

3. Note the two- or three-word idioms you have used. Try to find single-word substitutes and compare the effect.

4. Note the various forms (tenses) you have used. Do they accurately convey the time relationships?

The Passive Voice

In Chapter 1, where the passive voice was introduced, we used the term *agent* to characterize the subject of the sentence, the performer of the action. This concept might be easier to understand if we use the police department's word *perpetrator* instead of *agent.* The agent in the sentence is the perpetrator— generally human (or animate)—of the action specified by the verb, the responsible party. In the **active voice,** the agent functions as the subject of the sentence, the basic transitive sentence: Agent—Action—Object.

On page 21 in Chapter 1, you saw three steps we follow in turning the active voice into passive: The object becomes the subject and the agent, if it is included, is the object of the preposition *by* (or, in some cases, *for*):

The fans booed the referee. ⟶ The referee was booed by the fans.

My roommate borrowed my laptop. ⟶ My laptop was borrowed by my roommate.

The passive forms are not included in the list of expanded verb forms: Those are all active. The ones with *be* as an auxiliary are labeled *progressive,* and they pattern with the *–ing* form of the verb:

Sherry <u>is taking</u> computer science.

Larry <u>was sleeping</u> during the history test.

The ones with the past participle form are preceded by *have,* not *be:*

I <u>have eaten</u> dinner already.

I <u>had answered</u> only half the questions when the proctor called time.

These are two negative clues, then, that should help you recognize the passive:

1. A form of *be* **without** *–ing* following is passive.
2. A past participle **not** preceded by *have* is passive.

The discussion that follows includes the passive verbs *were laid out, is constructed, can be transmitted, was wounded, was hit.* As you can see, both clues apply.

We can cite good reasons for using the passive voice, as we saw in Chapter 4, where we discussed the role of the passive in cohesion, in enabling the writer to put the known information in the subject slot. The passive voice may also be called for when the agent is unknown or has no bearing on the discussion:

In 1905 the streets of Patterson, California, <u>were laid out</u> in the shape of a wheel.

So far as we know, from Einstein's Special Theory of Relativity, the universe <u>is constructed</u> in such a way (at least around here) that no material object and no information <u>can be transmitted</u> faster than the velocity of light.

—Carl Sagan *(Broca's Brain)*

The Vikings have had a bad press. Their activities <u>are equated</u> with rape and pillage and their reputation for brutality is second only to that of the Huns and the Goths. Curiously, they also <u>have been invested</u> with a strange glamour which contradicts in many ways their fearsome image.

—James Graham-Campbell and Dafydd Kidd *(The Vikings)*

The authors' purpose in the last passage is not to explain who equates the Vikings with rape and pillage or who invests them with glamour. The use of the passive puts these statements in the category of accepted beliefs. In some cases the passive voice is simply more straightforward:

Joe <u>was wounded</u> in Iraq.

And sometimes, in order to add modifiers to the agent, we put it where we can do so more conveniently, at the end of the sentence:

Early this morning my poodle <u>was hit</u> by a delivery truck traveling at high speed through the intersection of James Avenue and Water Street.

Note that if we switched the agent to subject position, the result would be a fairly wide separation of the subject headword and the verb:

Early this morning a delivery <u>truck</u> traveling at high speed through the intersection of James Avenue and Water Street <u>hit</u> my poodle.

The choice, of course, also depends on where the main focus should be.

The passive voice is especially common—and deliberate—in technical and scientific writing, in legal documents, and in lab reports, where the researcher is the agent, but to say so would be inappropriate:

Active:	<u>I increased the heat</u> to 450° and allowed it to remain at that temperature for twenty minutes.
Passive:	<u>The heat was increased</u> to 450° and allowed to remain at that temperature for twenty minutes.

◀ FOR GROUP DISCUSSION

One of the verbs underlined in the passive examples is *have been invested.* It looks as though the past participle, *invested,* is preceded by *have.* How do you explain this passive verb string in light of that rule stated earlier? A past participle *not* preceded by *have* is passive.

EXERCISE 20

It's important to recognize the passive voice when you see it—so that you'll know when you've used it and thus will use it deliberately and effectively. In the first section of this exercise, you'll transform active sentences into the passive voice; in the second part you'll do the opposite—change the passive into the active. And in the third part, the voice of the sentence is not identified: You'll have to figure it out.

A. Transform the following active sentences into the passive voice; remember that the direct object of the active functions as the subject in the passive.

1. My roommate wrote the lead article in today's *Collegian.*
2. Bach composed some of our most intricate fugues.
3. My brother-in-law builds the most expensive houses in town.
4. He built that expensive apartment complex on Water Street.
5. The county commissioners try out a new tax-collection system every four years.
6. Your positive attitude pleases me.
7. Hurricane Katrina devastated the Gulf Coast in 2005.
8. The number of flood victims overwhelmed the available facilities.

B. Transform the following passive sentences into the active voice; remember that the subject of the passive is the direct object in the active. (*Note:* If the agent is missing, you will have to supply one to act as the subject for the active.)

1. The football team was led onto the field by the cheerleading squad.
2. This year's cheerleading squad was chosen by a committee last spring.
3. Bill's apartment was burglarized last weekend.
4. A snowstorm is predicted for this weekend.
5. The election of the student body officers will be held on Tuesday.
6. Your car's oil should be changed on a regular basis.
7. The suspect is being kept in solitary confinement.
8. The kidnap victim has been found unharmed.

C. First decide if the following sentences are active or passive; then transform them.

1. John Kennedy was elected president in 1960.

2. Bill's grandmother nicknamed him Buzz when he was a baby.

3. You should read the next six chapters before Monday.

4. The cities in the Northeast have been affected by migration in recent years.

5. Thousands of manufacturing jobs have been moved to Mexico.

6. After the dot-com bubble burst, many employees of financial institutions were cheated out of their retirement savings.

7. A number of executives from those companies have been sent to prison.

8. The streetlights on campus are finally being repaired.

9. Our company is trying out a new vacation schedule this year.

10. The plant will be closed for two weeks in July.

FOR GROUP DISCUSSION

1. In the following paragraph from Jane Brody's *Good Food Book*, note the underlined passive. The subject (*children's taste for salt*) is the old information in the clause; the *by* phrase—the agent—is new, the point of focus. Identify the other passives.

    Why has Brody used passive instead of active? Would any of them be more effective in the active voice? Why or why not?

    > Human beings are born with the ability to taste salt, but our taste for a high-salt diet is an acquired one. Newborns do not particularly like salty foods. But when given them, after a while they acquire *a taste for salt*, and by early to middle childhood they prefer salted foods to those that are unsalted. A long-term study under the direction of Dr. David L. Yeung, a nutritional scientist at the University of Toronto, showed that <u>children's taste for salt at the age of 4 is determined by how much salt their parents feed them in infancy.</u> A preference for salt does not develop in cultures where salt is not added to foods. In such societies, even the adults do not like salt.

2. Surely the most famous words in our country's history are those written by Thomas Jefferson in the Declaration of Independence. Here is the opening of the Declaration's second paragraph:

    > We hold these truths to be self-evident, that all men are created equal, that they are endowed by their Creator with

certain unalienable Rights, that among these are Life, Liberty and the pursuit of Happiness. That to secure these rights, Governments are instituted among Men, deriving their just powers from the consent of the governed. That whenever any Form of Government becomes destructive of these ends, it is the Right of the People to alter or to abolish it, and to institute a new government, laying its foundation on such principles and organizing its powers in such form, as to them shall seem most likely to effect their Safety and Happiness. Prudence, indeed, will dictate that Governments long established should not be changed for light and transient causes; and accordingly all experience hath shown, that mankind are more disposed to suffer, while evils are sufferable, than to right themselves by abolishing the forms to which they are accustomed.

Underline the passive sentences. Rewrite all or some of them in the active voice and compare the two versions.

The Obscure Agent.   Certainly the passive voice has a place in every kind of writing; it is a legitimate tool—but like any tool it must be right for the job. Too often the purpose of the passive voice is simply to obscure the agent. For example, one of the most common responses that governmental investigative committees hear from individuals accused of mismanagement is

"Yes, Senator, mistakes were made."

And the passive is common in the "official" style used by bureaucrats:

It was reported today that the federal funds to be allocated for the power plant would not be forthcoming as early as had been anticipated. Some contracts on the preliminary work have been canceled and others renegotiated.

Such "officialese" or "bureaucratese" takes on a nonhuman quality because the agent role has completely disappeared from the sentences. In the foregoing example we do not know who is reporting, allocating, anticipating, canceling, or renegotiating.

This kind of agentless passive is especially common in official news conferences, where press secretaries and other government officials explain what is happening without revealing who is responsible for making it happen:

Recommendations <u>are being made</u> to the Mexican government concerning drug enforcement.

A tax hike <u>has been proposed,</u> but several other solutions to the federal deficit <u>are</u> also <u>being considered.</u>

The president <u>has been advised</u> that certain highly placed officials <u>are being investigated.</u>

The faceless passive does an efficient job of obscuring responsibility, but it is neither efficient nor graceful for the writing that most of us do in school and on the job.

Sometimes the inexperienced writer resorts to the passive voice simply to avoid using the first-person point of view. Here is a gardener's active account of spring planting written in the first person *(we):*

In late April, when the ground dried out enough to be worked, we planted the peas and onions and potatoes and prepared the soil for the rest of the vegetables. Then in mid-May we set out the tomato and pepper plants, hoping we had seen the last of frost.

Certainly the first person as used here would seem to be the logical choice for such a passage; nevertheless, some writers take great pains to avoid it—and, unfortunately, some writing texts, for no logical reason, warn against using the first person (see the discussion of point of view on pages 124–127). The result, as applied to the foregoing paragraph, is a gardener's passive account of spring planting—without the gardener:

In late April, when the ground dried out enough to be worked, the peas and onions and potatoes <u>were planted</u> and the soil <u>was prepared</u> for the rest of the vegetables. Then in mid-May the tomato and pepper plants <u>were set out</u> in hopes that the frost was over.

This revision is certainly not as stilted as the earlier examples of agentless prose, but it does lack the live, human quality of the active version.

Here's another example of the passive, typical of the student writer who has managed to avoid using *I,* perhaps because the paper has too many of them already or because the teacher has ruled out the first-person point of view:

The incessant sound of foghorns <u>could be heard</u> along the waterfront.

But remember that English is a versatile language; first person is not the only alternative to the passive. You don't have to write, "I [or we] heard the sound of foghorns…." Here's a version of the sentence using *sound* as the verb:

The foghorns <u>sounded</u> along the waterfront.

And here's one that describes the movement of the sound:

The incessant sound of foghorns <u>floated</u> across the water.

Many times, of course, the writer simply doesn't realize that the passive voice may be the culprit producing the vagueness or wordiness of that first draft. For example, a student writer ended his family Christmas story with an impersonal, inappropriate passive:

That visit from Santa was an occurrence that <u>would never be forgotten by the family.</u>

Clearly, he needed to ask himself, "Who was doing what?"

<u>The family would never forget</u> that visit from Santa.

And if for purposes of transition or rhythm he had wanted to retain *visit* as the subject, he could easily have done so in an active way:

That <u>visit</u> from Santa <u>became</u> part of our family legend.

The student's original sentence ("That visit … was an occurrence") actually has two red flags besides the passive that should have signaled the need for revision: *be* as the main verb and the nominalized *occurrence*—the verb *occur* turned into a noun. All are possible weak spots, the kinds of signals you should be aware of in the revision stage. (*Note:* Nominalized verbs are discussed in the next section.)

EXERCISE 21

1. The writer of the following passage has managed to avoid using the first-person point of view but in doing so has obliterated any resemblance to a personal voice. Revise the passage, avoiding both the passive and the first person. Remember to think about the agent as subject.

> The woods in the morning seemed both peaceful and lively. Birds could be heard in the pines and oaks, staking out their territory. Squirrels could be seen scampering

across the leaves that covered the forest floor, while in the branches above, the new leaves of the birches and maples were outlined by the sun's rays. The leaves, too, could be heard, rustling to the rhythm of the wind.

2. Identify the passive verbs in the following passage from *Stalking the Wild Asparagus* by Euell Gibbons. Why do you think he chose the passive instead of the active voice? Can you improve the passage by revising some or all of the sentences?

> Wild food is used at our house in a unique method of entertaining. Our "wild parties," which are dinners where the chief component of every dish is some foraged food, have achieved a local fame. Many different meals can be prepared almost wholly from wild food without serving anything that will be refused by the most finicky guest. Such dinners are remembered and talked about long after the most delicious of conventional dinners have been forgotten.

THE ABSTRACT SUBJECT

As you learned in the foregoing discussion of the passive voice, the agent—the perpetrator—is not always the subject of the sentence; in some passive sentences it doesn't appear at all. However, the more concrete and active the sentence, the more likely the agent will function as the subject—or at least make an appearance. The more abstract and passive the sentence, the more likely the agent will be missing.

One common cause of abstraction is the sentence with a preponderance of **nominalized verbs**—verbs that have been turned into nouns. The word *occurrence* in the previous discussion is one such example. And in an earlier example of the passive we saw a nominalized verb in subject position:

> Recommendations are being made to the Mexican government concerning drug enforcement.

Our language, of course, is filled with nominalized verbs—most of which are useful, legitimate ways of expressing ideas. In the previous paragraph, for example, you saw *discussion* and *appearance,* both of which began as verbs *(discuss, appear)* and are now ordinary, everyday nouns.

But because nominalized verbs are so common and so easy to produce, they can become a trap for the unwary writer, introducing abstraction where concrete ideas belong. It's during the revision stage of writing that you'll want to be on the lookout. Ask yourself, is the agent there and, if so, is it functioning as the subject? In other words, does the sentence explain *who is doing what?* If the answer is no, your sentence may be a prime candidate for revision.

Another source of abstraction and flabbiness is the sentence with a verb phrase or a clause as subject, rather than the usual noun phrase. When you study these structures in Chapter 9, you'll see that they are grammatical, common substitutes for noun phrases. But because they are abstractions, they too may be pitfalls for the unwary writer. Again, the source of the problem may be that of the missing or misplaced agent:

> The <u>buying</u> of so many American companies and so much real estate by the Japanese is causing concern on Wall Street.
>
> With the opening of the East Bloc nations and China to capitalism, <u>what is happening</u> is that American companies are looking for ways of expanding their markets and their product lines to take advantage of the situation.
>
> <u>Analyzing</u> the situation in China has shown that opportunities for investment are growing.

Although we need context to tell us the best way to revise these sentences, we can see and hear a problem. The sentences seem to be about actions— but they can't show the action in a strong and concrete way because the agents of those actions are not there in subject position. This kind of agentless sentence should send up a red flag—a signal that here's a candidate for revision.

EXERCISE 22

Revise the following passages, paying special attention to ineffective passives, unnecessary nominalizations, and problems of agency. The first three items are the examples from the preceding discussion. Remember to ask yourself, "Who is doing what?"

1. The buying of so many American companies and so much real estate by the Japanese is causing concern on Wall Street.

2. With the opening of the East Bloc nations and China to capitalism, what is happening is that American companies are looking for ways of expanding their markets and their product lines to take advantage of the situation.

3. Analyzing the situation in China has shown that opportunities for investment are growing.

4. In the biography of Lyndon Johnson by Robert Caro, an account of the Senate election of 1948 is described in great detail.

5. When Julie filled out an application for a work-study job, she was surprised to learn that a detailed financial statement would have to be submitted by her parents.

6. Getting his new pizza shop to finally turn a profit has meant a lot of hard work and long hours for Tim.

7. The overuse of salt in the typical American diet has had the result of obscuring the natural taste of many foods. Nutritionists maintain that a reduction in people's dependence on salt would lead to an enhancement of taste and heightened enjoyment of food.

8. The measurement of the Earth's fragile ozone layer was one of the important missions undertaken by the crew of the space shuttle *Atlantis.* The shuttle was launched in October of 1994. The mission lasted ten days. Humans are put at greater risk of skin cancer, cataracts, and other ailments because of overexposure to ultraviolet radiation. Crops can also be spoiled and underwater food sources devastated as a result of too much direct sunlight. A vast ozone "hole" over Antarctica from September to December every year is particularly worrisome to scientists.

SHOWING, NOT TELLING

When writing teachers promote the virtues of "showing" rather than "telling," what do they mean? They mean that you don't have to tell us that the old woman on the park bench looked sad; you can show us:

The old woman on the park bench wept quietly.

You don't even have to tell us that she's old:

Wearing a shawl around her shoulders, the woman on the park bench wept quietly, wisps of gray hair escaping the woolen cap, frail bony fingers clutching her handkerchief.

Annie Dillard doesn't tell us that building a road through the Everglades between Miami and Tampa was an arduous job; she shows us:

To build the road, men stood sunk in muck to their armpits. They fought off cottonmouth moccasins and six-foot alligators. They slept in boats, wet. They blasted muck with dynamite, cut jungle with machetes; they laid logs, dragged drilling machines, hauled dredges, heaped limestone. The road took fourteen years to build up by the shovelful.

—*An American Childhood*

And Barbara Ehrenreich doesn't tell us that she was glad her day of hard work as a housecleaner was over; she shows us:

> I rush home to the Blue Haven [Motel] at the end of the day, pull down the blinds for privacy, strip off my uniform in the kitchen—the bathroom being too small for both a person and her discarded clothes—and stand in the shower for a good ten minutes, thinking all this water is *mine.* I have paid for it. In fact, I have earned it.
>
> *—Nickel and Dimed*

A well-chosen verb not only heightens the drama of a sentence and makes its meaning clear, it also sends a message to the reader that the writer has crafted the sentence carefully, that the idea matters. We certainly get that message from the examples of prose we have just seen.

The potential drama and meaning of your prose are weakened or missing altogether when the verbs don't pull their weight. Sometimes the problem lies in the overuse of *be;* sometimes the culprit is one of our other common, garden-variety verbs, such as *have, make, go, do, say, get, take.* Because these verbs have so many nuances of meaning, you can often find a more precise one. For example, where you have selected the verb *make,* you could probably express yourself more exactly with *constitute, render, produce, form, complete, compel,* or *create,* all of which are indexed under *make* in Roget's *Thesaurus,* along with *make believe, make good* (demonstrate), *make out* (discover, know, interpret), and *make up* (complete).

It's important to note, too, that these alternatives to *make* are not uncommon or esoteric words; they're certainly a part of your active vocabulary. Unfortunately, however, the precise verb doesn't always come to mind when you need it—especially when you're composing the first draft. Rather than stop right there in midsentence or midparagraph to find it, just circle the word you've used—or highlight it with boldface type if you're using a word processor. Then, during the revision stage you can take time to think about it again. At that point, in fact, you may want to consult your dictionary or thesaurus just to remind yourself of some of these more specific verbs.

(*A word of warning:* Every word in the thesaurus is not for you. If it's not your word, if you're not sure of it, if it doesn't sound natural in your voice, then don't use it. Sometimes the dictionary is a better reminder: It usually has each synonym in context, along with the distinctive meanings of each.)

In Chapter 6 we looked at phrasal verbs, idioms that lend informality to the writer's voice: *turn down, bring about, bring on, put up with.* But when a more formal voice is appropriate, you may want to substitute the single-word synonym; it may be more precise—and it's always tighter:

The legislature <u>turned down</u> the governor's compromise
proposal/the legislature *rejected* ...

The lawyers for the defendant <u>turned down</u> the prosecutor's offer
of a plea bargain/the lawyers for the defendant *refused* ...

The police are <u>looking into</u> the rumors about corruption/the police
are *investigating* ...

The police are <u>looking into</u> the evidence/the police are *analyzing* ...

The police are <u>looking carefully</u> at the evidence/the police are
scrutinizing ...

The police are <u>looking below the surface</u>/the police are *probing* ...

Remember that vivid, well-chosen verbs send a clear message to the reader;
the message that the writer has crafted the sentence with care.

EXERCISE 23

Revise the following passages by finding more precise alternatives to the
italicized verbs. In some cases you will have to make changes other than
just the verb substitution.

1. The small band of rebels *fought off* the army patrol for several hours,
   then *gave up* just before dawn. News reports about the event did not
   give any specific details about how many troops were involved.

2. The majority leader *has* a great deal of influence in the White
   House. He can easily *find a way around* the established procedures
   and go directly to the president, no matter what his party affiliation.

3. Several economists are saying that they *look forward to* an upturn
   in the stock market during the second half of the year. Others,
   however, maintain that interest rates must *stop their fluctuating* if
   the bull market is to prevail.

4. The night-shift workers took their complaints to the shop steward
   when the managers tried to *force* them into *giving up* their ten-
   cent wage differential.

5. The chairman of the Senate investigating committee *spoke against*
   the practice of accepting fees for outside speeches. He said that the
   new rules will *put a stop to* all such questionable fund raising. To
   some observers, such practices *are the same thing as* bribery. Several
   senators have promised to *come up with* a new compromise plan.

6. Dorm life changed drastically when colleges *did away with* their
   traditional "in loco parentis" role. In the old days, of course, there

were always students who *paid no attention to* the rules. At some schools, where the administration would not *put up with* violations, students were routinely *kicked out.*

....

THE OVERUSE OF *BE*

Another major culprit contributing to flabbiness is the overuse of the linking-*be* (*am, is, are, was, were, have been, is being, might be,* and so on) as the main verb.[1] You'll recall from Chapter 1 that the *be* patterns commonly serve not only as topic sentences but as supporting sentences throughout the paragraph. You may be surprised, in checking a paragraph or two of your own prose, at how often you've used a form of *be* as the link between the known and the new information. An abundance of such examples—say, more than two or three in a paragraph—constitutes a clear "revise" message.

The following revised examples, sentences from this and earlier chapters, illustrate the substitution of more active, meaningful verbs:

Original: The precise verb <u>isn't</u> always <u>available</u> when you need it.

Revision: The precise verb *doesn't* always *come to mind* when you need it.

Original: As a writer, you must <u>be aware of</u> your own inappropriate words.

Revision: As a writer, you must *learn to spot* your own inappropriate words.

Original: In fact, <u>we are not surprised to see</u> that nonpersonal voice in certain kinds of documents.

Revision: In fact, *we've come to expect* that nonpersonal voice in certain kinds of documents.

Original: Further, in writing <u>there are</u> certain modifiers, such as nonrestrictive clauses and phrases…, that we rarely use in speaking.

Revision: Further, in writing *we use* certain modifiers….

In this last example the culprit is an unnecessary *there are*. In Chapter 5, you'll recall, we looked at this *there*-transformation as well as the cleft transformation *it is,* both of which take *be*—and neither of which should be overused.

---

[1]This overuse of *be* refers only to its role as the main verb. *Be* also has a job to do as an auxiliary in the progressive tenses and in the passive voice, as you saw in previous discussions.

In Chapter 9, in the discussion of appositives, you'll learn about another revision technique for eliminating the linking-*be*. Meanwhile, don't worry if you can't find an alternative. The sentence with a linking-*be* is often the most straightforward, natural structure for making your point (as I concluded in reconsidering this sentence). For further examples of *be* sentences that could be revised, you can turn to almost any paragraph in this book.

KEY TERMS

Abstract subject	Modal auxiliary	Sequence of tenses
Active voice	Nominalized verb	Showing
Agent	Obscure agent	Subjunctive mood
Be	Passive voice	Telling
Conditional mood	Phrasal verb	Tense
Idiom	Point of view	Voice

RHETORICAL REMINDERS

Have I remembered to show, not tell?

Have I kept my use of the linking-*be* to a minimum?

Could I improve the effectiveness of my diction by substituting precise single-word synonyms for my phrasal verbs?

In sentences with more than one clause, do the tenses accurately describe the time relationship?

Have I put the agent in subject position whenever possible?

Have I used the passive voice effectively?

Would any of my nominalized verbs be more effective as verbs rather than nouns?

CHAPTER 8

Choosing Adverbials

CHAPTER PREVIEW

In this chapter you will study in greater detail the "optional slot," which you read about in Chapter 1 when you first met the sentence patterns. The optional **adverbial** slot gives the writer great flexibility in fleshing out the bare bones of the sentence patterns.

Although the term *adverbial* may be unfamiliar, you probably know "adverb" as one of the parts of speech. Among the adverbs are some of our most common words designating time and place: *then, now, here, there, soon, never, always, sometimes, often.* The easiest ones to recognize are those that end in *−ly: slowly, carefully, quickly, peacefully, probably.* We have thousands of such *−ly* adverbs, simply because there are thousands of adjectives like *slow* and *careful* and *quick* and *peaceful* and *probable* that we can convert to *adverbs of manner,* as these adverbs are called, simply by adding *−ly.*

But adverbs are not the only words that add information about time and place and reason and manner to our sentences: Phrases and clauses can also function in an adverblike way. *Adverbial* is the term that names that function. In the following sentences, the adverbial information is provided by prepositional phrases, subordinate clauses, a verb (infinitive) phrase, and a noun phrase, in addition to adverbs:

1. <u>On Tuesday night</u> we ordered pizza <u>because no one wanted to cook.</u>
   (PREP. PHRASE)   (SUB. CLAUSE)

2. The fans cheered <u>wildly</u> <u>when Fernando stepped up to the plate.</u>
   (ADVERB)   (SUB. CLAUSE)

3. <u>Suddenly</u> Paul walked <u>out the door,</u> <u>without a word to anyone.</u>
   (ADVERB)   (PREP. PHRASE)   (PREP. PHRASE)

149

4. There's a film crew shooting a movie <u>near the marina.</u>
   (PREP. PHRASE)

5. I got up <u>early</u> <u>this morning</u> <u>to study for my Spanish test.</u>
   (ADVERB)(NOUN PHRASE)   (INFINITIVE PHRASE)

6. <u>On its last assignment in outer space,</u> *Voyager 2* photographed the
   (PREP. PHRASE)

   rings of Saturn.

We begin by looking at the important opening position that adverbials can occupy. Then we discuss each of the forms—prepositional phrases, clauses, and infinitive phrases.

THE OPENING ADVERBIAL

Adverbials are among the most versatile tools in the writer's toolbox. As the opening list illustrates, they come in a wide array of shapes and sizes—and they are movable. The opening adverbial in a story or essay or paragraph often sets the scene:

> Once upon a time . . .
> When in the course of human events . . .

Many of the Chapter Previews in this book begin with that scene-setting adverbial:

> In this chapter . . .

One important function of the opening adverbial is to provide cohesion, the tie that connects a sentence to what has gone before. In Chapter 4 we saw examples of the cohesion provided by known information, a pronoun or noun phrase that repeats information from the previous sentence. We've also seen the cohesive effects produced by certain stressed words, words that the reader expects because of what has gone before. What opening adverbials do so well is to provide road signs that connect the sentences and orient the reader in time and place. Notice in the following paragraphs from *The Sea Around Us* how Rachel Carson opens her sentences with adverbials. (These are not contiguous paragraphs.)

> <u>In modern times</u> we have never seen the birth of an island as large as Ascension. <u>But now and then</u> there is a report of a small island appearing where none was before. <u>Perhaps a month, a</u>

<u>year, five years later,</u> the island has disappeared into the sea again. These are the little, stillborn islands, doomed to only a brief emergence above the sea.

<u>Sometimes</u> the disintegration takes abrupt and violent form. The greatest explosion of historic time was the literal evisceration of the island of Krakatoa. <u>In 1680</u> there had been a premonitory eruption on this small island in Sunda Strait, between Java and Sumatra in the Netherlands Indies. <u>Two hundred years later</u> there had been a series of earthquakes. <u>In the spring of 1883,</u> smoke and steam began to ascend from fissures in the volcanic cone. The ground became noticeably warm, and warning rumblings and hissings came from the volcano. <u>Then, on 27 August,</u> Krakatoa literally exploded. <u>In an appalling series of eruptions, that lasted two days,</u> the whole northern half of the cone was carried away. The sudden inrush of ocean water added the fury of superheated steam to the cauldron. <u>When the inferno of white-hot lava, molten rock, steam, and smoke had finally subsided,</u> the island that had stood 1,400 feet above the sea had become a cavity a thousand feet below sea level. <u>Only along one edge of the former crater</u> did a remnant of the island remain.

Opening adverbials like these are especially common in narrative writing, the story or explanation of events through time. In fact, you'll notice that most of these adverbial openers—in fact, all but the last one—provide information of time.

THE PREPOSITIONAL PHRASE

No doubt our most common adverbial, other than the adverb itself, is the **prepositional phrase,** a two-part structure consisting of a **preposition** and its **object,** usually a noun phrase. In fact, of the twenty most frequently used words in English, eight are prepositions: *of, to, in, for, with, on, at,* and *by.*[1] Here are examples of adverbial information that prepositional phrases can provide:

Direction:	*toward the pond, beyond the ridge, across the field*
Place:	*near the marina, on the expressway, along the path, behind the dormitory, under the bridge*

---

[1]This frequency count, based on a collection of 1,014,232 words, is published in Henry Kuçera and W. Nelson Francis, *Computational Analysis of Present-Day English* (Providence: Brown University Press, 1967).

Time: *on Tuesday afternoon, at noon, in modern times, in the spring of 1883*

Duration: *until three o'clock, for several days, during spring break, throughout the summer months*

Manner: *in an appalling series of eruptions, without complaint, with dignity, by myself, in a frenzy*

Cause: *because of the storm, for a good reason*

The Proliferating Prepositional Phrase

Our most common prepositions, *of* and *to,* are especially vulnerable to proliferation. Both occur in countless idioms and set phrases. For example, we regularly use *of* phrases with numbers and with such pronouns as *all, each, some,* and *most:*

> one of the guests, all of the people, some of the students, most of the problems, the rest of the time, half of the food, each of the parts

Of is also used to indicate possessive case, as an alternative to *'s:*

> the capacity of the trunk, the base of the lamp, the opening night of the new show, the noise of the crowd

And we use it to show direction and position and time:

> the front of the house, the top of the bookcase, the back of the page, the end of the play

Prepositions also pattern with verbs to form phrasal verbs (we saw these in Chapter 7), many of which are endowed with new, idiomatic meanings:

> look up, bring up, turn on, live down, bring about, bring on, put up with, stand for, hand in, pull through, help out, think up, take off, take up, do away with, get away with, pass out, give up

Because there are so many such situations that call for prepositions, it's not at all unusual to find yourself writing sentences with prepositional phrases strung together in chains. You can undoubtedly find many such sentences in the pages of this book. In fact, the sentence you just read ended with two: "*in* the pages *of* this book." It would be easy to imagine even more: "in the pages of this book about the grammar of English for writers." As you edit what you have written, it's important to tune in to the rhythm of the sentence: A long string of short phrases is a clue that

suggests revision. Ask yourself if those prepositional phrases are proliferating awkwardly.

Awkwardness is not the only problem—nor is it the most serious. The
sentence that ends with a long string of prepositional phrases often loses its
focus. Our usual rhythm pattern, which follows the principle of end focus,
calls for the new information to be the last or next-to-the-last structural unit.
Notice, for example, what happened to that altered sentence in the previous paragraph. Here's the original; read it aloud and listen to the stress:

> You can undoubtedly find many such sentences in the pages of this
> book.

Chances are you put stress on *many* and on *this book*. Now read the altered
version:

> You can undoubtedly find many such sentences in the pages of this
> book about the grammar of English for writers.

Because you expected the sentence to have end focus, you probably found
yourself putting off the main stress until you got to *writers*. But that last
unit (starting with *about*), consisting of three prepositional phrases, is
known information. Not only should it get no stress, it shouldn't be there
at all. That kind of unwanted repetition of known information is what we
call **redundancy.**

Here's another illustration of this common source of redundancy—an
edited version of the opening sentences from the previous paragraph:

> Awkwardness is not the only problem <u>with those extra prepo-
> sitional phrases in our sentences</u>—nor is it the most serious <u>of
> the writer's problems.</u> The sentence that ends with a long string
> of prepositional phrases often loses its focus <u>on the main point</u>
> <u>of the sentence that the writer intended it to have.</u>

Those redundant modifiers add to the total number of words—and that's
about all they add. Clearly, they have added no new information. And they
have obliterated the original focus.

EXERCISE 24

The problem with proliferating prepositional phrases lies not only in their
ungraceful rhythm but also in the resulting lack of focus—a more serious
error. The following are altered versions of paragraphs you read in Chapter
5. Read them aloud, paying particular attention to the intonation, including the points of main stress. Remember that redundant information may

be the culprit that keeps the sentence from having a clear focus. Think about new information as you revise them to give them a clearer focus. (You may compare your edited version with the originals on pages 92–93. They are items 1 and 2 of Exercise 14 and the paragraph following the exercise, headed "Controlling Rhythm.")

1. Never be an investor in something you don't understand or in the dream of an artful salesperson of some product. Be a buyer, not a sellee. Figure out for yourself what you want to buy (be it life insurance, mutual funds or a vacuum cleaner for the home) and then shop for a good buy before making up your mind. Don't let someone else tell you what the necessities for your life are—at least not if he happens to be the salesman who wants to sell it to you.

2. Plaque has almost become a household word in this country. It is certainly a household problem for most people. But even though everyone is affected by it every day few people really understand the seriousness of plaque in their daily lives or the importance of controlling it. Plaque is an almost invisible sticky film of bacteria that in the case of all of us continuously forms throughout the day and night. Plaque germs are constantly multiplying and building up on the teeth. Any dentist will tell you that controlling plaque from forming is the single most important step to better oral health for people everywhere.

3. Because end focus is such a common rhythm pattern in our sentences, we can almost think of it as a contract between writer and reader. The reader has an expectation that the main sentence focus will be in the predicate of the sentence, unless given a signal to the contrary that it has some other focus. But of course all sentences are not alike in every respect; not every sentence has end focus as its rhythm pattern. In speech, especially, the focus is often shifted elsewhere to some other word or phrase. Consider, for example, these alternative ways of speaking the motorcycle sentence in a conversation with someone, the variety of messages that are possible for the speaker to express in saying this sentence.

THE SUBORDINATE CLAUSE

One of the most important adverbial forms is the **subordinate clause.** It's important because, as a subject–predicate structure, it has great information-bearing potential—more potential than other adverbial structures such as the adverb or the prepositional phrase or the verb phrase. In the following sentences you can recognize the subordinate clauses by their opening subordinating conjunctions:

The fans cheered <u>when</u> *Fernando stepped up to the plate.*

We ordered pizza <u>because</u> *no one wanted to cook.*

<u>Although</u> *there was little hope of finding anyone alive,* the fire-fighters continued to search the rubble.

As you can see in these examples, without their opening conjunctions, the subordinate clauses would be complete sentences:

Fernando stepped up to the plate.

No one wanted to cook.

There was little hope of finding anyone alive.

The purpose of the subordinating conjunction is to indicate the relationship of the subordinate clause to the independent sentence, the main clause. The clause introduced by *when* adds time information; *because* adds a reason; *although* adds a concession. We have many such subordinators, words and phrases that connect the clause for a specific purpose:

Time:	*when, whenever, after, as, before, once, since, till, until, now that, while, as long as, as soon as*
Concession:	*though, although, even though, if, while*
Contingency:	*if, once*
Condition:	*if, in case, as long as, unless, provided that*
Reason:	*because, since, as long as*
Result:	*so, so that*
Comparison:	*as, just as, as if*
Contrast:	*while, whereas*

Subordinate clauses are certainly common structures in our language. We use them automatically and often in conversation. But in writing they are not automatic, nor are they always used as effectively as they could be. Two problems that show up fairly often are related to the meaning of the sentence:

1. The wrong idea gets subordinated.
2. The meaning of the subordinator is imprecise.

Here, for example, are two related ideas that a writer might want to combine into a single sentence:

We worked hard for our candidates.
We suspected that our candidates didn't stand a chance.

Here are some possibilities for connecting them:

While we worked hard for our candidates, we suspected they didn't stand a chance.

Although we worked hard for our candidates, we suspected they didn't stand a chance.

We worked hard for the candidates, even though we suspected they didn't stand a chance.

We need context, of course, to know precisely how the relationship between hard work and the chances of winning should be expressed; but given no other information, the last version expresses what would appear to be the logical relationship.

Perhaps an even more common problem than the imprecise subordinator is the compound sentence with no subordination—the sentence with two independent clauses, two equal focuses, that would be more accurate and effective with a single focus. Here, for example, is a passage from an early draft of Chapter 2:

All three sentences look alike, with all three conforming to the "something is something" pattern, but they are actually quite different.

In form this is a compound sentence, two clauses connected by *but,* one of our coordinating conjunctions. But the substance and focus of the two clauses are not equal: The statement in the second clause is clearly the main idea, the new information. The idea in the first clause is information the reader already knows, the known information. It needs to be backgrounded here as a subordinate clause. The short main clause at the end of the sentence will help the reader focus on the new information:

Although all three sentences look alike, with all three conforming to the "something is something" pattern, they are actually quite different.

Although has now subordinated the first clause, signaling the reader that the main idea is coming later. Quite frequently *while*-clauses and *since*-clauses communicate this same kind of message: telling the reader that the information in the subordinate clause is already known, knowledge that the reader and writer share.

EXERCISE 25

Turn the following complete sentences into subordinate clauses by (1) adding a subordinator in the opening position and (2) adding the resulting subordinate clause to another sentence as a modifier, either at the beginning or at the end. You will have to supply the main clause. See page 155 for a list of subordinators; use at least six different ones in your sentences; try for ten.

Example: The party ended at midnight.

We got home earlier than expected because the party ended at midnight.

or

If the party ended at midnight, why did you get home at 3:00 A.M.?

1. The stock market continued to decline during the last quarter.

2. Myra has lost her fortune in the stock market.

3. Cleo couldn't pay her phone bill last month.

4. There is simply no way to avoid the problem.

5. There were several ways we could have solved the computer problem.

6. Ben couldn't decide which SUV to buy.

7. NCAA recruiting violations have been in the news again.

8. The building across the street burned to the ground last weekend.

9. A great many new teachers will be needed when school starts in the fall.

10. The service sector is a large part of the economy.

Punctuation of Subordinate Clauses

There is one standard punctuation rule that applies to the subordinate clause:

> **A subordinate clause that opens the sentence is always set off by a comma.**

This rule applies no matter how short that clause may be:

If you go to the party, I'll go too.

> Even though I'll be bored, I guess I'll go to the party.
>
> When Eric calls, ask him to bring some pizza.

When the subordinate clause closes the sentence, the punctuation will vary, depending on the relationship of the information in the subordinate clause to that of the main clause. As a general rule, when the idea in the main clause is conditional upon or dependent upon the idea in the subordinate clause, there is no comma. For example, the idea of the main clause—the opening clause—in the following sentence will be realized only if the idea in the subordinate clause is carried out; thus, the main clause depends on the *if-* clause:

> Pat will go to Sue's party if you promise to be there.

In other words, Pat may or may not go to the party. But in the next sentence the subordinate clause does not affect Pat's behavior. The comma confirms that lack of effect.

> Pat is going to the party at Sue's on Saturday night, even though she knows she'll be bored.

Here's another pair of sentences that illustrates this distinction:

> I think that Shawn left the office because he felt sick.
>
> I think that Shawn left the office, because I was just there.

Without the comma, the second sentence would have a different meaning.

The use of the comma with a final subordinate clause is probably one of the least standardized of our punctuation rules. It is one situation where you can use your voice to help you decide about the punctuation: If you put extra stress on the last word in the main clause, or if you detect a slight change in the pitch of your voice at the end of the main clause, you probably need a comma.

The Movability of Subordinate Clauses

The movability of subordinate clauses is especially important from a rhetorical point of view. As a sentence opener, the clause often supplies the transition from the previous sentence or paragraph, usually with a cohesive link of known information. The old standard rule of putting subordinate ideas in subordinate clauses and main ideas in main clauses is probably more accurately stated as "known information in the opening clause, new information in the closing clause." And certainly that closing clause could be a subordinate clause, depending on the context. For example, the reason for an action or decision as stated in a *because*-clause could easily be the new information.

Although most subordinate clauses occupy either the opening or closing slots of the sentence, they can also occur in the middle, between the
subject and predicate or between the verb and complement. In this position the clause will be set off by commas, one before and one after:

> I learn later that night, <u>when ties are loosened during a coffee
> break</u>, that I am wrong.
> > —James R. Chiles *(Smithsonian)*

> My brother, <u>when he was only four years old,</u> actually drove the
> family car for about a block.

That interruption in the usual flow of the sentence slows the reader down.
Notice also that it adds stress and length to the word just preceding the
clause, and it changes the rhythm pattern. We saw the same principle at
work in Chapter 5, when we manipulated the intonation contour of the
sentence by shifting word order and changing the punctuation. Ordinarily the subject is in an unstressed valley; it is old information. But a parenthetical comment following it, a word or a phrase or a clause set off by
commas, as in our example, puts the subject in a position of stress; the
reader will give it extra length and emphasis. Compare the stress given to
brother in the previous example with the following revisions, where the subordinate clause either opens or closes the sentence:

> When he was only four years old, my brother actually drove the
> family car for about a block.

> My brother actually drove the family car for about a block when he
> was four years old.

And it's not only a difference in the stress on *brother* that makes the inserted
when-clause noteworthy. That internal positioning of the subordinate
clause is unusual; it sends a message to the reader that says, "Pay attention.
I did this on purpose."

The Because-*Clause Myth*

Because a subordinate clause looks so much like a full sentence (remember,
it consists of a sentence preceded by a subordinator), it is a prime candidate
for fragmenthood—that is, a part of a sentence punctuated as a full sentence.
One of the most common such fragments is, apparently, the *because*-clause:

> Everyone agreed that our midterm was unfair. Because our profes-
> sor included questions about cases we hadn't discussed in class. It
> turns out she hadn't even assigned them.

It appears that some teachers have discovered a sure-fire way to prevent such fragments: Ban *because* as a sentence opener. As a result, many student writers don't understand that *because* can, indeed, open a sentence, just as all the other subordinators can; however, if that *because*-clause is new information, it belongs at the end of the sentence. In the previous example, the *because*-clause should be added to the previous sentence:

> Everyone agreed that our midterm was unfair because our professor included questions we hadn't discussed in class.

It's possible that the *because*-clause is frequently punctuated as a full sentence on the basis of speech. In answer to a spoken question of cause, the natural answer is a subordinate clause:

> Why are you late? *Because I missed the bus.*

In this speech situation, the respondent has simply omitted the known information, the information in the question. The response in the following exchange, which includes the known information, is much less likely to occur:

> Why are you late? *I'm late because I missed the bus.*

EXERCISE 26

Combine each of the following groups of sentences into a single sentence, using coordination and subordination. In some cases you may have to reword the sentence to make it sound natural. You can probably come up with more than one possibility for each.

1. The famous Gateway Arch is in St. Louis.
   Kansas City claims the title "Gateway to the West."

2. Our spring semester doesn't end until the second week of June.
   Many students have a hard time finding summer jobs.

3. Thomas Jefferson acquired the Ozark Mountains for the United States in 1803.
   That was the year of the Louisiana Purchase.
   We bought the Louisiana Territory from Napoleon.

4. Auto companies offered enticing cash rebates to buyers of new cars last January.
   Car sales increased dramatically.

5. The neighbors added a pit bull to their pet population, which now numbers three unfriendly four-legged creatures.
   We have decided to fence in our backyard.

6. The human circulatory system is a marvel of efficiency.
   It is still subject to a wide variety of degenerative diseases.

7. Carbohydrates—starches—are the body's prime source of energy.
   Fad diets that severely restrict the intake of starches are nearly always ineffective.
   Such diets can also be dangerous.

8. By 1890 the buffalo population of the West had been nearly wiped out.
   It now numbers about 60,000.
   About 400 ranchers in Colorado are raising buffalo for meat.

The Elliptical Subordinate Clause

One common variation of the subordinate clause is the **elliptical clause,** one in which something is deleted. Elliptical clauses introduced by the time connectors *while* and *when* are especially common:

> While waiting for the bus, we saw the police arrest a pickpocket at the edge of the crowd.
> When stripped of its trees, the land becomes inhospitable.

Here the deletions of the subject and part of the verb have produced tighter structures, and there is certainly no problem in interpreting the meaning. The understood subject in the elliptical clause is also the subject of the main clause:

> While we were waiting for the bus
> When the land is stripped of its trees

This feature of elliptical clauses—let's call it a rule—is an important one for the writer to recognize:

The subject of the main clause is always the understood subject of the elliptical clause as well.

This rule simply reflects the interpretation that the reader expects. Unfortunately, it is not always followed. Note what has happened in the following sentence:

> *While waiting for the bus, the police arrested a pickpocket at the edge of the crowd.

This sentence reports—no doubt inadvertently—that it is the police who were waiting for the bus. We call that a dangling elliptical clause. The writer should not expect the reader to give the sentence any other interpretation.

The problem of dangling also occurs in adverbial prepositional phrases that have verbs or verb phrases as objects:

> *Since <u>leaving school,</u> good jobs have not been easy to find.
>
> *Before <u>going to class this morning,</u> the bookstore was crowded.

These phrases are almost identical to the elliptical subordinate clauses. The only difference is that they cannot be expanded to full clauses without a change in the form of the verb:

> Since I left school ...
>
> Before I went to class ...

Nevertheless, the underlying clausal meaning is clear, and the same rule applies: The subject of the main clause is also the subject of the verb in the prepositional phrase. Without that subject–verb relationship, the phrase is dangling.

In introductory position the dangling clause or verb phrase is fairly obvious, once you've been made aware of the problem. However, when the dangling phrase or clause closes the sentence, its dangling nature is not as noticeable:

> *Jobs have not been easy to find since leaving school.
>
> *The subway is better than the bus when late for work.

Here the reader gets to the end of the main clause with no unfulfilled expectations and can simply supply a subject for that ending adverbial from the context. Even though the dangling may not be as obvious, the problem of fuzziness remains. Notice that there's no agent—no subject stated—for the verbs *find* and *leaving* in the first sentence; and in the second, who is late? These are the kinds of sentences that can produce a negative response in the reader, a response that undermines the writer's authority.

The Elliptical Clause of Comparison.   The elliptical clause of comparison is different from the other elliptical clauses in that only the elliptical version is grammatical:

> I'm a week older <u>than Terry</u> [is old].
>
> My sister isn't as tall <u>as I</u> [am tall].

or

I'm a week older than Terry is [old].

My sister isn't as tall as I am [tall].

Recognizing such comparisons as clauses will help you understand why it is nonstandard to use *me* in such sentences:

*My sister isn't as tall as me.

*My roommate doesn't work as hard as me.

In standard, formal usage the pronoun is in the subjective case, not the objective, because it is the subject of the underlying elliptical clause:

My roommate doesn't work as hard as I work.

The ellipses in such comparisons can produce ambiguity when the main clause has more than one possible noun phrase for the subordinate clause to be compared with:

Joe likes Tracy better than Pat.

The University of Nevada–Las Vegas beat Fresno State worse than Arizona.

In these sentences we don't know if the comparison is between subjects or objects because we don't know what has been left out. We don't know whether

Joe likes Tracy better than Pat [likes Tracy].

or

Joe likes Tracy better than [Joe likes] Pat.

And we don't know whether

UNLV beat Fresno State worse than [UNLV beat] Arizona.

or

UNLV beat Fresno State worse than Arizona [beat Fresno State].

These elliptical clauses of comparison are especially tricky. Always look them over carefully to make sure you haven't misled your reader.

FOR GROUP DISCUSSION

1. Using your understanding of elliptical clauses, explain how it's possible for both of the following sentences to be grammatical:

My little sister likes our cat better than me.
My little sister likes our cat better than I.

2. The following sentences are both illogical and ungrammatical. Explain the source of the problem.

*The summer temperatures in the Santa Clara Valley are much higher than San Francisco.

*The Pirates' stolen base record is much better than the Twins.

EXERCISE 27

Rewrite the following sentences to eliminate the dangling clauses and phrases. In some cases you may want to complete the clause; in others you may want to include its information in a different form.

1. Before mixing in the dry ingredients, the flour should be sifted.

2. Lightning flashed constantly on the horizon while driving across the desert toward Cheyenne.

3. There was no doubt the suspect was guilty after finding his fingerprints at the scene of the crime.

4. While waiting for the guests to arrive, there were a lot of last-minute details to take care of.

5. If handed in late, your grade on the term project will be lowered 10 percent.

6. After filling the garage with lawn furniture, there was no room left for the car.

7. While collecting money for the hurricane victims, the generosity of strangers simply amazed me.

8. The employees in our company who smoke now have to go outside of the building during their breaks if they want a cigarette, since putting the smoking ban into effect a month ago.

9. When revising and editing your papers, it is important to read the sentences aloud and listen to the stress pattern.

10. Your sentences will be greatly improved by eliminating dangling phrases and clauses.

INFINITIVE (VERB) PHRASES

Another adverbial form in the list of sample sentences at the opening of the chapter—in addition to the adverbs, prepositional phrases, and subordinate clauses—is the **infinitive phrase:**

> I got up early this morning <u>to study for my Spanish test.</u>

The infinitive is usually easy to recognize: the base form, or present tense, of the verb preceded by *to,* sometimes called *the sign of the infinitive.* There's an understood "in order to" meaning underlying most adverbial infinitives:

> I got up early this morning in order to study.

The problem of dangling that comes up with the elliptical subordinate clause also applies to the adverbial infinitive phrase. As with other verbs, the infinitive needs a subject; the reader assumes that its subject will be the subject of the main clause, as it is in the example with *study.*
When the subject of the infinitive is not included, the infinitive dangles:

> *<u>To keep your grades up,</u> a regular study schedule is important.
>
> *For decades the Superstition Mountains in Arizona have been explored in order <u>to find the fabled Lost Dutchman Mine.</u>

Certainly the problem with these sentences is not a problem of communication; the reader is not likely to misinterpret their meaning. But in both cases a kind of fuzziness exists that can be cleared up with the addition of a subject for the infinitive:

> To keep your grades up, <u>you</u> ought to follow a regular study schedule.
>
> For decades <u>people</u> [or <u>adventurers</u> or <u>prospectors</u>] have explored the Superstition Mountains in Arizona to find the fabled Lost Dutchman Mine.

The dangling infinitive, which is fairly obvious at the beginning of the sentence, is not quite so obvious at the end, but the sentence is equally fuzzy:

> *A regular study schedule is important to keep your grades up.

Two rules will help you use infinitives effectively:

The subject of the adverbial infinitive is also the subject of the sentence or clause in which the infinitive appears.

An infinitive phrase that opens the sentence is always set off by a comma.

The punctuation rule does not apply to adverbial infinitives in closing position; in fact, the opposite is generally true: A comma is rarely called for when the infinitive closes the sentence.

And, as with other adverbials, it's possible to insert the adverbial infinitive in an almost parenthetical way, in which case commas—or even dashes—are called for:

> According to nutritionists, dieting, to have lasting effects, should be undertaken as a lifelong program of sensible eating habits.

MOVABILITY AND CLOSURE

The movability of adverbials, which enables us to vary our sentences and to change their emphasis, includes a risk for the unwary writer—the risk of losing the reader. As readers, we expect verbs to follow subjects, complements of various kinds to follow verbs, and adverbial phrases and clauses to open or close the sentence. Deviation from that norm comes as a surprise. As writers, we like to include surprises from time to time, but when we do, we should do so for a reason—and within reason.

In the discussion of movable adverbial clauses, we saw two examples in which the placement of the clause changed the stress pattern of the sentence. Here is one of them:

> My brother, when he was only four years old, actually drove the family car for about a block.

In spite of the interruption of normal word order, the sentence is short and direct enough for the reader to recognize where it is headed and to experience a sense of closure, or completion. The reader experiences a beginning, a middle, and an end. Given a more complex interrupter, however, the reader is likely to be confused:

> My brother, when he was only four years old and so short that all we could see were two small hands holding on to the steering wheel and a tuft of blonde hair, actually drove the family car for about a block.

Here the detour of that interrupting clause takes us too far from the path; we don't have enough information to know where we're headed. And when we do finally get back to our original clause, we've forgotten where we started. We have had to keep too many ideas on hold. Before we can experience a sense of closure, we have to go back to reconsider the opening of the clause. This is the kind of a sentence that produces an "awk" in the margin—when the reader happens to be your English teacher.

EXERCISE 28

(1) Underline all of the adverbial structures in the following sentences. (2) Identify the form of each: adverb, noun (or noun phrase), prepositional phrase, verb phrase, or subordinate clause. (3) Identify the kind of information it provides: time, frequency, duration, place, reason, manner, condition.

1. To save money, I often eat lunch at my desk.

2. After breakfast let's take the bus to the shopping center.

3. After my dad retired from the navy, he started his own business.

4. We furiously cleaned house to get ready for the party.

5. As soon as the guests left, we collapsed in a heap on the couch.

6. The legislature held a special session last week to consider a new tax bill.

7. When October came, the tourists left.

8. Victoria was crowned queen of England when she was only eighteen years old.

9. African killer bees are slowly making their way northward.

10. At last report, they had reached the southern border of Texas.

11. We stayed home last night because of the snowstorm.

12. If there is no further business, the meeting stands adjourned.

For further practice with adverbials, change the form of the adverbial while retaining the information.

◄▬▬▬   **FOR GROUP DISCUSSION**

In his book *Notes Toward a New Rhetoric,* Francis Christensen reports a study undertaken by his students in an English class to discover the kinds of structures other than the subject that professional writers use in the opening sentence slot. They selected works (ten fiction, ten nonfiction) of twenty American authors and counted the first 200 sentences. (They omitted quotations, dialogue, fragments, questions, and sentences with postponed subjects—that is, cleft sentences and *there*-transformations. Here are the findings, based on 4,000 sentences counted:

979 (24.5%) had a sentence opener other than subject;
919—in other words, all but 60—were adverbials, including adverbs, prepositional phrases, clauses, and nouns (adverbial infinitives were counted with the verbal group, listed next);
47 were verbal phrases (including infinitives and *–ing* verbs);
13 were other constructions, including adjective phrases and inverted subjects and predicates.

In addition to the 979 sentence openers, there were 266 sentences (6.65%) that opened with coordinating conjunctions (*and, but, or, nor, so, yet, for*).

Examine the sentence openers in your own writing; then compare your percentages with those of your classmates and with the professionals.

(*Note:* One of the works included in the study was Rachel Carson's *The Sea Around Us,* quoted on pages 150–151. Her numbers were the highest among the twenty writers: 79 nonsubject openers in her 200 sentences, 74 of which were adverbials; and 29 conjunctions as sentence openers.)

THE QUALIFIERS

When you read the description of parts of speech in Chapter 11, you'll discover that we group the words of our language into two general classes: the form classes and the structure classes. **Qualifiers** belong with the structure classes. They qualify or intensify adverbs and adjectives, so their function is actually different from that of the adverbials. We look at them here in connection with choosing adverbials, recognizing that they also pattern with adjectives.

Among the most common words that qualify adjectives and adverbs are *very, quite, rather, too, still, even, much,* and *fairly.* Some adverbs of manner, the *–ly* adverbs, are themselves used as qualifiers with certain adjectives: *dangerously* close, *particularly* harmful, *absolutely* true. In the discussion of "Power Words" in Chapter 5, we saw the effect that qualifiers such as these can have on sentence rhythm.

As a rule, it's a good practice to let a single word do all the work it can. *Rushed* and *dashed* and *bolted* are stronger than *ran very fast;* leaves that *flickered* are more delicate in movement than leaves that *moved slightly.* The experienced writer, instead of describing a person as *really nice* or *very nice* or *very beautiful,* might say instead *cooperative* or *charming* or *stunning.* In most cases the difference is not a matter of knowing "big" words or unusual words. The difference is a matter of precision, of choosing words carefully. Such precision, even in small details, can make a difference in the overall effect on the reader.

One further caveat concerns the use of qualifiers with certain adjectives that have **absolute** meanings. Careful writers try to avoid *very* with *perfect* or *unique* or *round.* Although we might say *absolutely perfect* to emphasize the perfection, to say *very perfect* would probably have a negative effect on the reader. And certainly as careful users of language we should respect the meaning of *unique:* "one of a kind." *Round* and *square* have meanings in our lexicon other than their geometric absolutes, so it is possible for the shape of an object to be "nearly round" or "almost square." But qualifiers such as *very* or *quite* are best reserved for other kinds of qualities.

EXERCISE 29

As you read the following sentences, pay particular attention to the italicized words; replace them with words that are more precise.

1. Ben was so *very careful* about his wardrobe, he had his ties pressed after every wearing.

2. The guest speaker's *really strong* denunciation of our foreign policy seemed *quite out of place* at the awards banquet.

3. The foreman gives his orders in a *very abrupt* manner.

4. To me, the tropical garden is the *most intriguing* display in the conservatory. *Completely covered* with orchids and vines, the towering palm trees and *really unusual* large-leafed plants seem to belong in a fairy tale.

5. It is usually *an absolute waste of time* to argue with radicals of any persuasion; they are unlikely to be influenced by mere reason.

6. Our host's *overly enthusiastic* welcome embarrassed me: First he kissed me on both cheeks; then he bowed and kissed my hand.

7. The basketball players seemed *really tired* as they took the court for the second half.

8. Our history teacher was *extremely upset* when he discovered that almost half the class had cheated on the midterm exam.

9. The choir members were *really excited* about their summer trip to Europe.

10. The members of Congress were *really very surprised* at the extent of voter cynicism toward Washington.

FOR GROUP DISCUSSION

Examine your own essay or, in a peer-review session, that of a classmate for the use of qualifiers with adjectives and adverbs. Be especially alert for *very* and *really*. Consider revising with more precise words that need no qualifiers.

KEY TERMS

Absolute adjective	Elliptical clause	Qualifier
Adverb	Infinitive phrase	Redundancy
Adverbial	Manner adverb	Rhythm
Because-clause	Movability	Subordinate clause
Dangling elliptical clause	Opening slot	Subordinator
Dangling infinitive	Preposition	
	Prepositional phrase	

RHETORICAL REMINDERS

Placement of Adverbials

Have I considered transition and cohesion and the known–new contract in using adverbials?

Do my opening subordinate clauses contain known information?

Proliferating Prepositions

Have I avoided strings of prepositional phrases that obscure the focus of the sentence and add no new information?

Understood Subjects

Is the understood subject in every elliptical clause also the subject of the main clause?

Is the subject of every adverbial infinitive also the subject of the main clause?

Word Choice

Have I selected modifiers with precise meanings so that such qualifiers as *very* and *really* may not be necessary?

PUNCTUATION REMINDERS

Have I used a comma to set off a subordinate clause that opens the sentence?

Have I used a comma to set off an infinitive phrase that opens the sentence?

CHAPTER
9

Choosing Adjectivals

CHAPTER PREVIEW

The word *adjectival,* like the word *adverbial,* refers to a function: **Adjectival** means "modifier of a noun." In other words, an adjectival is any structure that does what an adjective normally does (just as an adverbial is any structure that does what an adverb normally does). And because we have so many places in the sentence for nouns to function—as subjects, direct and indirect objects, subject and object complements, and objects of prepositions—and so many different structures that can modify them, opportunities abound for the writer when choosing adjectivals.

In Chapter 1 we described the sentence as a series of slots; it can be useful to think of the noun phrase in this way too: the headword noun as the central, pivotal slot, with the various structures that function as adjectivals in the slots before and after it:

<u>det</u>   <u>adj</u>   <u>noun</u>   <u>NOUN</u>   <u>prep phrase</u>   <u>participle</u>   <u>clause</u>

The slots before the noun headword are occupied by single words—determiner, adjective, and noun; the slots that follow, in a systematic order, by multiple-word structures—prepositional phrase, participial phrase, and clause. Here are some examples, with the headword noun shown in bold type:

<u>a</u>	<u>strange</u>	**experience**
(DET)	(ADJECTIVE)	
<u>those</u>	<u>city</u>	**slickers**
(DET)	(NOUN)	
<u>my</u>	**cousin**	<u>from Austin</u>
(DET)		(PREPOSITIONAL PHRASE)

<u>an</u>	**aquarium**	<u>filled with exotic fish</u>
(DET)		(PARTICIPIAL PHRASE)
<u>the</u>	**students**	<u>who live across the hall</u>
(DET)		(RELATIVE CLAUSE)

We can even fill all the slots at once:

> an exciting mystery **novel** about international drug dealers written by Lou Hoblitt, which has garnered praise from the reviewers

Another noun modifier we take up in this chapter is the **appositive,** a structure (usually a noun phrase) that renames the headword noun, adding a new detail:

> my cousin from Austin, <u>an associate at Wal-Mart</u>
>
> the students who live across the hall, <u>a group of friends from high school</u>

As you can see, because of their frequency in the sentence and this variety of structures we use to expand them, noun phrases provide a remarkable range of possibilities for putting ideas into words. In this chapter we will take up each of these structures—each of the slots—in turn, beginning with determiners.

DETERMINERS

Most nouns require a **determiner,** the noun signaler that occupies the opening slot in the noun phrase. The determiner class includes articles, possessive nouns, possessive pronouns, demonstrative pronouns, and numbers, as well as a variety of other common words. In both speech and writing you select most determiners automatically. But sometimes in your writing you will want to give that selection deliberate thought.

As the first word in the noun phrase, and thus frequently the first word of the sentence and even of the paragraph, the determiner can provide a bridge between ideas. The selection of that bridge can make subtle but important differences in emphasis, providing transition for the reader— and it can certainly change the rhythm of the sentence:

> <u>The</u> decision that Ben made was the right one.
>
> <u>That</u> decision of Ben's was the right one.
>
> <u>Ben's</u> decision was the right one.
>
> <u>Every such</u> decision Ben made...

<u>His</u> decision…

<u>Such a</u> decision might have been questionable…

<u>A</u> decision like that…

In selecting determiners, then, writers have the opportunity to make subtle distinctions and to help their readers move easily from one idea to the next in a meaningful way.

In Chapter 4 we looked at the special problem of the demonstrative pronouns used as subjects when they would be better used as determiners. As with other pronouns, the four demonstratives—*this, that, these, those*—always refer to known information. Any pronoun can become a problem when it has no clear referent—that is, when the information it represents is not, in fact, known. In the case of demonstratives, the problem can be solved by providing a headword and using the pronoun as a determiner. Here is a sentence from Chapter 4 that illustrates the problem:

My roommate told me she has decided to drop out of school.

This took me completely by surprise.

The problem is easily solved:

This decision took me completely by surprise.

We probably don't give much thought to determiners, either as readers or as writers. But with all the choices available, as writers we certainly should. And sometimes determiners need our special attention.

◀ FOR GROUP DISCUSSION

In Chapter 11 we look briefly at the semantic features of nouns that regulate our selection of determiners. For example, the indefinite article *a* signals only countable nouns, while the definite *the* can signal both countables and noncountables.

All of the determiners are missing from the following passages. Add them to all the nouns that need them. You'll discover, when you compare your versions with those of your classmates, that for some nouns there are choices—not only a choice of determiner but in some cases a choice of whether or not to use a determiner.

A. Dorothy was little girl who lived on farm in Kansas. Tornado struck farm and carried her over rainbow to land of Munchkins. Soon afterwards she met scarecrow who wanted brain, tin man who wanted heart, and lion who wanted courage. On way to Emerald City four friends met wicked witch who cast spell on them in field of flowers. Witch wanted magic shoes that

Dorothy was wearing. When they reached city, as you recall, they met wizard. Story has happy ending.

B. Planet has wrong name. Ancestors named it Earth, after land they found all around them. So far as they thought about planet as whole, they believed for centuries that surface consisted almost entirely of rocks and soil, except for smallish bodies of water like Mediterranean Sea and Black Sea. They knew about Atlantic, of course, but they regarded it as relatively narrow river running around rim of world. If ancients had known what earth was really like they undoubtedly would have named it Ocean after tremendous areas of water that cover 70.8 percent of surface.

—adapted from *The Sea* (Time-Life Books)

There were several nouns in those passages that you left bare, without determiners. Why? How do they differ from the nouns that needed them? In how many cases did you have a choice of adding a determiner or not?

Did you notice a relationship between your use of the articles (*a* vs. *the*) and information—that is, whether known or new information? Which article did you use when a noun was mentioned for the first time? Which for subsequent mentions? What conclusions can you draw about the indefinite *a* and the definite *the?*

ADJECTIVES AND NOUNS

Adjectives and nouns fill the slots between the determiner and the headword. When the noun phrase includes both, they appear in that order:

DETERMINER	ADJECTIVE	NOUN	HEADWORD
a	dismal	weather	forecast
the	new	pizza	shop
your	important	career	decision

The adjective slot frequently includes more than one adjective modifying the headword:

a covert military operation

an unusual financial arrangement

You'll notice that there are no commas in the preceding noun phrases, even though there are several modifiers in a row. But sometimes commas are called for. A good rule of thumb is to use a comma if it's possible to insert *and* between the modifiers. We would not say *a covert and military operation* or *an unusual and financial arrangement.* However, we would say *an exciting and innovative concept*, so in writing that phrase without *and*, we would use a comma: *an exciting, innovative concept.*

In general, our punctuation system calls for a comma between two adjectives when they are of the same class—for instance, when they are both subjective qualities like "festive" and "exciting" and "innovative." However, in the adjective phrases we saw without commas—*covert military operation* and *unusual financial arrangement*—the two adjectives in each pair are different kinds of qualities. The easiest way to decide on punctuation is to remember *and:*

> **Use a comma between prenoun modifiers if it's possible to use *and.***

Sometimes prenoun modifiers are themselves modified or qualified:

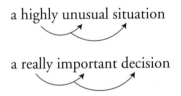

When the first modifier is an *–ly* adverb, as in these two examples, we do not connect it with a hyphen. With other adverbs, however, and with nouns and adjectives as modifiers, we do use a hyphen for these prenoun compound modifiers:

> the English-speaking world
>
> a four-door minivan

Here the hyphen makes clear that *English* modifies *speaking* rather than *world* and that *four* modifies *door*, not *minivan.*

Here are some other examples of hyphens with prenoun modifiers:

a problem-solving approach	a bases-loaded home run
a poor inner-city neighborhood	a small-town high school teacher
a fuel-injected engine	a well-developed paragraph

Another occasion for hyphens in preheadword position occurs when we use a complete phrase in the adjective slot:

an off-the-wall idea   the end-of-the-term party

Modifier Noun Proliferation

There's a pitfall for writers in this system of prenoun modifiers: the temptation to string together too many adjectives or nouns. It's easy to do. For example, the curriculum committee of the faculty is known as the "faculty curriculum committee." And when the committee meets, it has a "faculty curriculum committee meeting." The minutes of that meeting then become the "faculty curriculum committee meeting minutes." And so on. Such strings are not ungrammatical, but they easily become unreadable.

You can make such noun phrases somewhat easier to read by using an *of* phrase in place of the last modifier in the string:

a meeting of the faculty curriculum committee

the minutes of the faculty curriculum committee meeting

EXERCISE 30

Punctuate the following sentences, paying particular attention to commas and hyphens that might be needed in prenoun position. Remember the rule about those commas: If you can add *and*, you probably need a comma. Remember also to apply what you know about punctuating compound sentences and compounds within sentences. You may also have to correct some run-ons.

1. The administration's recent clean air proposals have been criticized as inadequate not only by environmental groups but also by highly placed government officials from several states.

2. A high ranking federal employee testified at a Congressional hearing on Monday.

3. The stock market reached an all time high last week and if inflation can be kept in check will probably keep going up.

4. There was a splendid old table for sale at the auction.

5. A big yellow delivery truck is blocking the driveway and its driver is nowhere to be seen.

6. There was not enough firefighting equipment available this summer for the widespread devastating forest fires in the Northwest.

7. I found an expensive looking copper colored bracelet in the locker room and immediately turned it in to the coach.

8. A commonly held notion among my cynical friends is that big business lobbyists run the country they could be right.

9. I have back to back exams on Wednesday.

10. The highly publicized paper recycling program has finally become a reality on our campus this fall after a year long surprisingly acrimonious discussion.

....

The Movable Adjective Phrase

Before looking at the slots that follow the headword, we should note variations in our use of adjectives when they are modified (with a qualifier like *very* or an intensifying adverb like *highly* or *extremely*) or compounded (with a word like *and*). Such expanded adjectives, or adjective phrases, can be shifted either to the slot following the headword or, if the noun phrase being modified is the subject, to the opening position in the sentence:

Hot and tired, the Boy Scouts trudged the last mile to their campsite.

The Boy Scouts, hot and tired, trudged the last mile to their campsite.

Both of these variations put added emphasis on the subject slot, especially on the modifiers. The subject would not have that emphasis if the adjectives had stayed in their preheadword position:

The hot, tired Boy Scouts trudged the last mile to their campsite.

Here's a sentence with the qualified adjective we saw earlier shifted from its preheadword home-base position. Again, you'll notice how this order changes the rhythm:

Highly unusual, the situation called for extraordinary measures.

The situation, highly unusual, called for extraordinary measures.

And in one of the sentences about weasels in Chapter 1, we saw an opening adjective phrase modifying a personal pronoun:

Obedient to instinct, he bites his prey at the neck....

In this case, the opening slot is the only one that sounds natural; personal pronouns rarely have modifiers in postheadword position.

PREPOSITIONAL PHRASES

The adjectival prepositional phrase, which follows the headword noun, is our most frequently occurring postnoun modifier. It is identical in form to the adverbial prepositional phrase we saw in Chapter 8. In its adjectival role the prepositional phrase identifies the noun headword in relation to time, place, direction, origin, and other such details:

The security guard <u>in our building</u> knows every tenant personally.

We had delicious fish and chips at the new seafood restaurant <u>near the marina.</u>

The meeting <u>during our lunch hour</u> was a waste of time.

Jack is a man <u>of many talents.</u>

Ed finally found an occasion to meet that beautiful girl <u>in our math class</u> <u>with the long red hair.</u>

Because prepositional phrases are so common, both as adverbials and as adjectivals, they can easily get out of hand. In Chapter 8, you may recall, we pointed out the problem of the proliferating prepositional phrase: the tendency for writers to string them together. Such proliferation can easily obscure the sentence focus. One of the examples in that discussion included a string of five prepositional phrases at the end of the sentence, four of which are adjectival:

You can undoubtedly find many such sentences <u>in the pages of this</u> <u>book about the grammar of English for writers.</u>

The last three of those five prepositional phrases are not only unnecessary, they obscure the focus of the sentence, which was intended to be on "this book." Those three superfluous phrases add nothing but words—no new information at all.

In place of certain adjectival prepositional phrases, the writer may have the option of using a prenoun modifier:

an elderly lady with white hair = an elderly white-haired lady

the old gentleman with the beard = the old bearded gentleman

guests for dinner = dinner guests

the soliloquy in the second act = the second-act soliloquy

the problems with the budget = the budget problems

a friend of Amy's = Amy's friend

the final exam in calculus = the calculus final

And sometimes revision may be just a matter of choosing a more precise word:

a bunch of flowers = a bouquet

the main character of the story = the protagonist

birds that fly south in the winter = migratory birds

PARTICIPIAL PHRASES

One of our most versatile adjectivals is the **participial phrase,** a verb phrase headed by the *–ing* or the *–en* form of the verb, known as a **participle.** The noun being modified is the subject of the participle:

The **helicopter** hovering over the roof frightened the dogs.

The **man** sitting by the window is talking to himself.

We were shocked to see all the homeless **people** living on the streets of Los Angeles.

You'll notice that these noun phrases with participial modifiers resemble sentences; the only thing missing is an auxiliary:

the helicopter [is] hovering over the roof

the man [is] sitting by the window

the homeless people [are] living on the streets of Los Angeles

In other words, the noun and the participle that modifies it have a subject–predicate relationship. This is an important feature of participial phrases for you to understand, as you will see later in the discussion of dangling participles.

Why do we use participles? Like adjectives and prepositional phrases, participles add information about the noun headword; and because they are verb phrases in form, they add a whole verbal idea, just as the predicate does. In the first example, the subject, *helicopter,* is the subject of two verb phrases: *hovering over the roof* and *frightened the dogs.* The two verb phrases could have been expressed with a compound predicate:

The helicopter hovered over the roof and frightened the dogs.

or with a main clause and a subordinate clause:

The helicopter frightened the dogs as it hovered over the roof.

The participial phrase, however, allows the writer to include both verbal ideas in a more concise way. Even more important than conciseness is the clear focus of the sentence with a single predicating verb.

The Prenoun Participle

When the participle is a single word—the verb with no complements or modifiers—it usually occupies the adjective slot in preheadword position:

Our <u>snoring</u> visitor kept the household awake.

The <u>barking</u> dog next door drives us crazy.

I should replace that <u>broken</u> hinge.

The old hound growled at every <u>passing</u> stranger.

And, as we saw in the earlier discussion of hyphens, an adverb sometimes modifies the participle:

a <u>fast-moving</u> object

a <u>well-developed</u> paragraph

Remember, too, that if the adverb in that prenoun modifier is an *–ly* adverb, there will be no hyphen:

a carefully conceived plan

The Movable Participle

We can think of the slot following the headword in the noun phrase as the home base of the participial phrase, as it is of the adjectival prepositional phrase. Unlike the prepositional phrase, however, the participial phrase can shift to the beginning of the sentence—*but only if it modifies the subject and if it is set off by commas:*

<u>Looking out the window,</u> my mother waved to me.

<u>Carrying all of their supplies,</u> the Boy Scouts trudged up the mountain in search of a campsite.

<u>Laughing uproariously,</u> the audience stood and applauded.

<u>Shifting his weight from one foot to the other,</u> the man looked impatient as he waited by the fountain.

<u>Pressured by Congress,</u> the president agreed to support an increase in the minimum wage.

Only those participial phrases that are set off by commas can undergo this shift—that is, only those that are nonrestrictive. (Punctuation of phrases and clauses is discussed on pages 187–190.)

While the single-word participle generally fills the preheadword adjective slot, it too can sometimes open the sentence—and with considerable drama:

Exasperated, she made the decision to leave immediately.

Outraged, the entire committee resigned.

You'll note that both of these openers are past participles, rather than the *–ing* present participle form; they are, in fact, the passive voice. The last participial phrase in the first set of examples, *"Pressured by Congress,"* is also passive. There the *by*-phrase offers a clue. (Underlying it is the sentence *"Congress pressured the president."* In the case of the single-word participles here, the *by*-phrase is understood.

That same participial phrase—the nonrestrictive phrase that modifies the subject—can also come at the end of the sentence:

The Boy Scouts trudged up the mountain in search of a campsite, carrying all of their supplies on their backs.

The audience stood and applauded, laughing uproariously.

The man looked impatient as he waited by the fountain, shifting his weight from one foot to the other.

The reason for choosing one position over another has to do with sentence rhythm and focus. At the end of the sentence the participle gets much more attention than it would at the beginning or in the home-base position. At sentence end, participial phrases have great flexibility; there's room to spread out and expand, so it's not unusual to see more than one and to see them with embedded modifiers of their own. In end position they are sometimes called **free modifiers.**

The first two examples are from Jeff Shaara's Civil War story *The Last Full Measure:*

He [Robert E. Lee]'d been awake even before that, staring up at the dark and thinking of Jackson.

He [Grant]'d been up front again this morning, correcting one officer's mistake, adjusting lines of infantry that had dug in too close to the mouths of their own big guns. The men on the front lines had become wary of the rebel sharpshooters, stayed low, flinching from the small bits of lead whistling overhead, sent at them from a hidden enemy very far away.

The following passage is from J. M. Coetzee's *Waiting for the Barbarians:*

They live in settlements of two or three families along the banks of the river, fishing and trapping for most of the year, paddling to the remote southern shores of the lake in the autumn to catch redworms and dry them, building flimsy reed shelters, groaning with cold through the winter, dressing in skins.

And many of the details we learned about weasels in Chapter 1 came by way of participial phrases:

> Outside, he stalks rabbits, mice, muskrats, and birds, killing more bodies than he can eat warm, and often dragging the carcasses home. Obedient to instinct he bites his prey at the neck, either splitting the jugular vein at the throat or crunching the brain at the base of the skull, and he does not let go.

The Dangling Participle

The participial phrase provides a good way to change the focus of the sentence, as we have seen in these variations—but it carries an important restriction:

> **The participle can open or close the sentence *only* if it modifies the subject—that is, when the subject of the participle is also the subject of the sentence and is in regular subject position. Otherwise, the participle will dangle.**

Remember, a participle modifies its own subject. Simply stated, a dangling participle is a verb without a subject:

> *Carrying all of our supplies for miles, the campground was a welcome sight.
>
> *Having swung his five-iron too far to the left, Joe's ball landed precisely in the middle of a sand trap.
>
> * Furiously filling in the bubbles on the answer sheet, the time was up before I could finish the test.

The campground, of course, did not do the carrying, nor did Joe's ball swing the five-iron; and I was the one filling in those bubbles, not "the time." You can fix such sentences (and avoid them in the first place) by making sure that the subject of the sentence is also the subject of the participle:

> Having carried all of our supplies for miles, *we* were exhausted by the time we reached the campground.
>
> Having swung his five-iron too far to the left, *Joe* once again hit the ball into the sand trap.
>
> Furiously filling in the bubbles on the answer sheet, *I* still wasn't able to finish the test before time was up.

Another common source of the dangling participle, and other dangling modifiers as well, is the sentence with a delayed subject—a *there*-transformation, for example, or an *it*-cleft:

> *Having moved all the outdoor furniture into the garage, there was no room left for the car.
>
> *Knowing how much work I had to do, it was good of you to come and help.

In the second sentence, *you* is the subject of the participle, so it's there in the sentence, but it's not in the usual subject position. Sometimes the most efficient way to revise such sentences is to expand the participial phrase into a complete clause. That expansion adds the missing subject:

> <u>After we moved all the outdoor furniture into the garage,</u> there was no room left for the car.
>
> It was good of you to come and help <u>when you learned how much work I had to do.</u>

Even though there is often no problem of communication with dangling and misplaced modifiers—that is, the reader probably knows what you mean—you may in fact be communicating something you hadn't intended: You may be sending a message that says, "Fuzzy thinking."

Our language includes a few participial phrases that we use in sentence-opening position that are not dangling, even though the subject of the sentence is not their subject. They function as sentence modifiers rather than as noun modifiers. The most common are the "speaking of" phrases:

> <u>Speaking of</u> old movies, have you seen *Gaslight?*
>
> <u>Speaking of</u> the weather, we should probably cancel the picnic.

There are other *–ing* words that have the status of prepositions. They often open a sentence in order to set up the topic:

> <u>Regarding</u> your job interview, the supervisor called to change the time.
>
> <u>Concerning</u> the recent book about the Kennedys, several reviewers have doubted its credibility.

Because of their common use, such expressions have achieved the status of set phrases. Nevertheless, they may be regarded by some readers as too casual or informal for certain writing situations.

EXERCISE 31

Rewrite the following sentences to eliminate the dangling participles. In some cases you may want to expand the participles into full clauses.

1. Having endured rain all week, the miserable weather on Saturday didn't surprise us.

2. Hoping for the sixth win in a row, there was great excitement in the stands when the band finally played "The Star Spangled Banner."

3. Known for her conservative views on taxes and the role of government, we were not at all surprised when the Republican county commissioner announced her candidacy for the General Assembly.

4. Exhausted by the heat and humidity, it was wonderful to do nothing but lie in the shade and drink iced tea.

5. Having spent nearly all day in the kitchen, everyone agreed that my superb gourmet meal was worth the effort.

6. Feeling pressure from the environmentalists, the Clean Air Act was immediately put on the committee's agenda.

7. Obviously intimidated by a long history of defeats in Morgantown, there seems to be no way that our basketball team can beat the West Virginia Mountaineers on their home court.

8. Arriving unexpectedly on a weekend when I had two papers to finish and a big exam coming up, I didn't feel exactly overjoyed at seeing my parents.

RELATIVE CLAUSES

Another slot in the noun phrase following the noun is filled by the **relative clause,** sometimes called the *adjective clause.* Because it is a clause—that is, a structure with a subject and a predicate—this adjectival modifier is a powerful tool; it enables the writer to embed a complete subject–predicate idea into a noun phrase.

In many respects, the relative clause and the participial phrase are alike. The participial phrase, in fact, is actually a shortened version of the relative clause. All of the examples we saw earlier could easily be expanded into clauses with no change in their meaning:

The helicopter that is hovering over the roof frightened the dogs.

The man who is sitting by the window is talking to himself.

We were shocked to see all the homeless people <u>who are living on the streets of Los Angeles.</u>

One feature the participle has that the clause does not is its movability: The clause rarely moves out of the noun phrase; it almost always follows the noun it modifies.

The Relatives

The relative clause is introduced by either a **relative pronoun** (*that, who,* or *which*) or a **relative adverb** (*where, when,* or *why*); the relative plays a part in the clause it introduces. In the case of the relative pronoun (the most common introducer), the part will be that of a noun: a subject, direct object, indirect object, subject complement, object of the preposition, or, as possessive nouns generally function, a determiner.

The relative pronoun *who* has different forms depending on its **case,** its role in the clause—*who* (**subjective**), *whose* (**possessive**), and *whom* (**objective**):

The man <u>who called last night</u> wouldn't leave his name.

Here *who* is the subject in its clause.

The student <u>whose notes I borrowed</u> was absent today.

Here the possessive relative, *whose,* is the determiner for *notes.* (You'll recall that "determiner" is the role played by all possessive pronouns.) The clause, in normal left-to-right fashion, is "I borrowed whose notes."

Our dog, Rusty, <u>whom we all dearly loved,</u> was recently killed on the highway.

Here the objective relative, *whom,* is the direct object in its clause: "We all dearly loved whom."

When the relative pronoun is an object in its clause, it can be deleted if the clause is restrictive—that is, if the clause is not set off by commas. In the previous example, the clause is *non*restrictive, so the relative *whom* cannot be deleted. And you'll notice also that *whom* makes the sentence sound formal, not like something you would say. But in the following example, the *whom* can be omitted, and in speech it certainly would be. Most writers would probably omit it too.

King Edward VIII gave up the throne of England for the woman <u>(whom)</u> <u>he loved.</u>

The relative pronoun *that* always introduces restrictive clauses; in other words, *that*-clauses are never set off by commas:

You choose a color that you like.

A boy that I knew in junior high called me last week.

A truck that was going too fast for road conditions hit our dog.

In the first two preceding sentences, *that* can be omitted. Some writers, in fact, would insist on leaving it out in the second one because it refers to a person; some writers insist on *who* and *whom* in reference to people—not *that*. The easiest and smoothest solution is simply to omit the relative:

A boy I knew in junior high called me last week.

However, the relative *cannot* be omitted when it functions as the subject in its clause, as in the sentence about the truck. Nor can it be omitted if the clause is nonrestrictive—no matter what role the pronoun fills:

Rob Miller, whom I knew in junior high, called me last week.

We should note, too, that in speaking this sentence we are more likely to say *who*, even though the objective case of the pronoun is called for; most listeners wouldn't notice the difference. (*Who* actually sounds correct because it's at the beginning of the clause, where the subjective case is found.)

The relative pronoun *which* is generally reserved for nonrestrictive clauses—those set off by commas:

My roommate's financial problems, which he finally told me about, have caused him a lot of stress this semester.

The relative adverbs *where, when,* and *why* also introduce adjectival clauses, modifiers of nouns denoting place (*where* clauses), time (*when* clauses), and of the noun *reason* (*why* clauses):

Newsworthy events rarely happen in the small *town* where I lived as a child.

We will all feel nervous until next *Tuesday,* when results of the auditions will be posted.

I understand the *reason* why Margo got the lead.

PUNCTUATION OF PHRASES AND CLAUSES

Does this modifier need to be set off by commas? That's the question to be answered about the punctuation of participial phrases and relative clauses in the noun phrase. The question also comes up in the case of certain appositives, which we discuss in a later section of this chapter.

The answer to the question has to do with the purpose of the modifier: Is it there to identify the referent of the noun being modified—that is, to restrict its meaning—or simply to comment on it. (The traditional terms for the difference are *restrictive* and *nonrestrictive.*)

You may recall back in Chapter 1 you saw the word *referent* in the discussion of sentence patterns: When the subject complement in the *be*-pattern or the linking-verb pattern is a noun or noun phrase, it has the same referent as the subject (*Mary* is *my sister*). *Referent* means the thing (or person, event, concept, and so on) that the noun or noun phrase stands for: *Mary* and *my sister* refer to the same person. The term *referent* is useful here, too, in thinking about the purpose of the modifier as well as the knowledge of the reader: Is the referent of the noun clear to the reader without the modifier?

In the following sentence, with no other context, the relative clause is needed to identify the referent of the noun phrase *the president:*

> The president <u>who was elected in 1932</u> faced problems that would have overwhelmed the average person.

Ordinarily we would say that the noun phrase *the president* has many possible referents; the *who*-clause is needed to make the referent clear; it defines and restricts *the president* to a particular man, the one elected in 1932. But what if the reader already knows the referent from previous context?

> Franklin Delano Roosevelt took office at a time when the outlook for the nation was bleak indeed. The president, <u>who was elected in 1932,</u> faced decisions that would have overwhelmed the average person.

In this context the referent of *the president* is already defined by the time the reader gets to it: The clause is simply commenting, so it needs to be set off by commas. In other words, the commas are sending the message that the *who*-clause is extra information, just a comment. You don't need this information to know who is being discussed here. In contrast, the lack of commas in the earlier sentence without context sends the message that the *who*-clause is needed to identify the referent of *president.* In other words,

Restrictive (no commas) = identifying

Nonrestrictive (commas) = commenting[1]

---

[1] *Comment* and *identify* are terms that Francis Christensen introduced in his book *Notes Toward a New Rhetoric.* It is listed under "Levels of Generality" in the Bibliography.

Punctuation of participial phrases works the same way. When the participial phrase provides information for identifying the referent, there are no commas:

The merchants <u>holding the sidewalk sales</u> are hoping for good weather.

This lack of commas, then, implies that not all merchants are concerned about the weather—only those who are holding the sidewalk sales. The *holding* phrase is there to tell which merchants are hoping for good weather. In other words, there's another group of merchants who may or may not be concerned about the weather. The lack of commas identifies a particular subgroup of concerned merchants.

Use commas around a nonrestrictive modifier when the modifier is only commenting on the noun rather than defining it—when the reader already knows the referent or if there is only one possible referent.

In the punctuation of relative clauses, the relative pronoun provides clues:

1. The *that* clause is always restrictive; it is never set off by commas.
2. The *which* clause is generally nonrestrictive; it is set off by commas. If you want to figure out if your *which* clause needs commas, try substituting *that*. If you can do so without changing the meaning, then the commas can, and perhaps should, be omitted.
3. If the relative pronoun can be deleted, the clause is restrictive:
   The bus (that) I ride to work is always late.
   The woman (whom) I work with is always early.

The next two rules of thumb apply to both clauses and phrases:

4. After any proper noun, the modifier is nonrestrictive:
   Willamette University, which was established seven years before the Gold Rush of 1849, is within walking distance of Oregon's capitol.
   In Alaska, where the distance between some cities is vast, many businesses and individuals own private planes.

5. After any common noun that has only one possible referent, the modifier will be nonrestrictive:

The highest mountain in the world, which resisted the efforts of climbers until 1953, looks truly forbidding from the air.

Mike's twin brother, who lives in Austin, has a personality just like Mike's.

My mother, who is sitting by the window, is talking to herself.

EXERCISE 32

Decide whether the participial phrases in the following sentences are restrictive (defining) or nonrestrictive (commenting) and punctuate them accordingly.

1. Many coal miners in West Virginia refused to approve two sections of the contract offered by management last week. They maintain that the two sections covering wages and safety represent no improvement over their present contract expiring on Friday at midnight.

2. A group of students held a protest rally in front of the administration building yesterday. The students hoping for a meeting with the provost were demonstrating against the tuition hike recently approved by the trustees. The increase expected to take effect in September will raise tuition almost 15 percent.

3. The senator and her husband sitting next to her on the speaker's platform both looked calm as they waited for the mayor to finish the introduction. Then the mayor turning to look directly at the senator shocked both the audience and the listeners on the platform.

EXERCISE 33

Combine the following groups of sentences into single sentences by embedding some of the ideas as modifiers. You will probably want to use adverbial modifiers as well as adjectivals—participial phrases and relative clauses you have just been studying in this chapter. In some cases you may have to make other changes in the wording as well.

1. In many parts of the country, citizens are mobilizing against crime and drugs.
   They are driving drug dealers out of their neighborhoods.

2. More and more public officials are supporting the legalization of certain drugs.
   They argue that there is no other way to win the drug war.

3. Fingerprints have been used for criminal identification since 1891.
   A police officer in Argentina introduced the method.
   The computer has revolutionized the storage and retrieval of
   fingerprints.

4. The leaning tower of Pisa is 179 feet high.
   It is over 800 years old.
   It leans 17 feet off the perpendicular.
   The distance is gradually increasing.

5. In 1997 an earthquake struck the Assisi region of Italy.
   Many priceless mosaics from the 14th century were destroyed.
   The mosaics decorated the walls and ceiling of the Basilica of
   St. Francis.

6. The highest incidence of colon cancer in the United States occurs
   in the Northeast.
   The Northeast also has the highest levels of acid rain.
   Cancer researchers suspect that there is a causal link between
   the two.

7. The rate of colon cancer is related to the amount of carbon diox-
   ide in the air.
   Carbon dioxide absorbs ultraviolet light.
   Ultraviolet light fuels the body's production of vitamin D.

8. Influenza, or flu, is a viral infection.
   It begins as an upper respiratory infection and then spreads to
   other parts of the body.
   Flu causes aches and pains in the joints.

9. Flu viruses mutate constantly.
   We cannot build up our immunity.
   New varieties spread from person to person and from place
   to place.

10. The sodium intake of the average American is far higher than
    necessary.
    The recommended level is 400 to 3,300 mg per day.
    The average American consumes over 4,000 mg per day.

THE BROAD-REFERENCE CLAUSE

As we have seen, the relative clause is part of a noun phrase—and the
antecedent of the relative pronoun that introduces it is the headword of
that noun phrase:

The **students** who live across the hall are quiet today.

I came to see the **dress** that you bought for the prom.

Joe's **car,** which he bought last week, looks like a gas guzzler to me.

However, the relative clause introduced by *which,* instead of referring to a particular noun, sometimes has what is called **broad reference:**

> Joe bought a gas guzzler, which surprised me.
> Tom cleaned up the garage without being asked, which made me suspect that he wanted to borrow the car.

Here the antecedent of *which* in both cases is the idea of the entire main clause, not a specific noun.

One way to revise this vague broad-reference clause is to furnish a noun that sums up the idea of the main clause, so that the clause will have specific, rather than broad, reference. Note in the revisions that the relative *that* has replaced *which,* and the clauses now have nouns to modify:

> Joe bought a gas guzzler, a decision that surprised me.
> Tom cleaned up the garage without being asked, a rare event that made me suspect he wanted to borrow the car.

This solution to the vague antecedent is sometimes called a **summative modifier.**

There are other solutions to the broad-reference *which*-clause besides the summative modifier. For example, we could revise the following sentence,

> I broke out in a rash, which really bothered me,

in at least three ways. The first is the summative modifier:

> I broke out in a rash, a problem that really bothered me.
> Breaking out in a rash really bothered me.
> The rash I got last week really bothered me.

The earlier example about the clean garage also has other possibilities:

> When Tom cleaned up the garage without being asked, I suspected that he wanted to borrow the car.

Tom's cleaning of the garage without being asked made me suspect that he wanted to borrow the car.

While it's true that broad-reference clauses often have a vague quality, sending a message of carelessness, there are times when a *which* in reference to the whole clause makes the point clearly—and, in fact, may be preferred:

The men my two sisters married are brothers, which makes their children double cousins.

EXERCISE 34

Revise the following sentences to eliminate any instances of the broad-reference *which*.

1. My roommate told me she was planning to withdraw from school, which came as a complete surprise.

2. The first snowstorm of the season in Denver was both early and severe, which was not what the weather service had predicted.

3. The college library has finally converted the central card catalog to a computer system, which took over four years to complete.

4. The president had some harsh words for Congress in his recent press conference, which some observers considered quite inappropriate.

5. Wendell didn't want to stay for the second half of the game, which made Harriet rather unhappy.

6. We're having company for dinner three times this week, which probably means hot dogs for the rest of the month.

7. In his State of the Union message, the president characterized the last two years as a period of "unprecedented prosperity," which one economist immediately labeled "sheer hype and hyperbole."

8. The Brazilian government has grudgingly agreed to consider new policies regarding the rain forests, which should come as good news to everyone concerned about the environment.

FOR GROUP DISCUSSION

The following paragraph, the first one in "Revival Road," a short story by Louise Erdrich, contains nine sentences, with a total of sixteen clauses, seven of which are either adjectival or adverbial. You'll notice, however, that there are many more than sixteen verbs in the sentence. List all of the verbs that you find; name their function. Then consider their effect on the over-all description.

> From the air, our road must look like a length of rope flung down haphazardly, a thing of inscrutable loops and half-finished question marks. But there is a design to Revival Road. The beginning of the road is paved, though with a material inferior to that of the main highway, which snakes south from our college town into the villages and factory cities of New Hampshire. When the town has the money, the road is also coated with light gravel. Over the course of a summer, those bits of stone are pressed into the softened tar, making a smooth surface on which the cars pick up speed. By midwinter, though, the frost has crept beneath the road and flexed, creating heaves that force the cars to slow again. I'm glad when that happens, for children walk down this road to the bus stop below. They walk past our house with their dogs, wearing puffy jackets of saturated brilliance—hot pink, hot yellow, hot blue. They change shape and grow before my eyes, becoming the young drivers of fast cars that barely miss the smaller children, who, in their turn, grow up and drive away from here.

OTHER NOMINALS

The term **nominal** refers to the functions of the noun phrases we've been looking at here, to all of the slots in the sentence patterns that noun phrases fill: subject, direct object, indirect object, object complement, subject complement, and object of the preposition. The heading "Other Nominals" refers to structures other than noun phrases that fill those nominal slots. Just as we use verb phrases and clauses as adverbials and adjectivals—that is, to modify verbs and nouns—we use them as nominals too. In this section, then, we look briefly at verb phrases and clauses in their nominal function.

Verb Phrases

In form, the verb phrases that fill the nominal functions look exactly like those that function as adjectivals and adverbials: They are infinitives (the base form with *to*) as well as *-ing* verbs, known as **gerunds** when they function as nominals.

> That young man jogging along the highway looks exhausted.
> *(participial phrase, as adjectival)*

<u>Jogging along the highway</u> can be dangerous. *(gerund, as subject)*

<u>To lose weight before summer,</u> I am going to take up aerobics. *(infinitive, as adverbial)*

I plan <u>to lose weight before summer.</u> *(infinitive, as direct object)*

Obviously these are not unusual sentences, nor are they the kinds of structures that we ordinarily make mistakes with, even in writing. There are, however, two aspects of verb phrases in nominal roles that deserve special mention, both having to do with gerunds.

The Dangling Gerund.   You may recall from the discussions of infinitives and participles that when a verb phrase opens the sentence, the subject of the main clause in the sentence is also the subject of the verb in that opening phrase:

> <u>To do well in school,</u> **a student** should set aside study time on a regular basis.
>
> <u>Having finished the decorations,</u> **the homecoming committee** celebrated with a keg of root beer.

Remember that an opening verb phrase sets up an expectation in the reader that the subject of that verb will follow. When something else follows, the opening verb phrase dangles:

> *<u>Having finished the decorations,</u> the ballroom looked beautiful.

The problem of this dangling participle is obvious: It seems to be saying that the ballroom did the decorating. Remember that a participle modifies its own subject. In this sentence the participle has no subject.

This same kind of dangler, this thwarted expectation, can occur when the sentence opens with a prepositional phrase in which the object of the preposition is a gerund:

> *<u>After finishing the decorations,</u> the ballroom looked beautiful.
>
> *<u>Since cutting down on fats,</u> my cholesterol level has dropped.

The rule about opening verb phrases is straightforward:

> **When a verb phrase opens the sentence (whether an infinitive, a participle, or a gerund in a prepositional phrase), the subject of that verb will be the subject of the sentence.**

Shifting the prepositional phrase to the end of the sentence does not solve the problem. The error may not seem quite as obvious, but the dangling nature of the phrase is still there:

> The ballroom looked beautiful <u>after finishing the decorations.</u>
>
> My cholesterol level has dropped <u>since cutting down on fats.</u>

So whether that verb phrase opens the sentence or simply *could* open the sentence, the subject–verb relationship must be there. A good way to fix these dangling gerunds is to expand the prepositional phrase into an adverbial clause:

> The ballroom looked beautiful after we finished the decorations.
>
> My cholesterol level has dropped since I cut down on fats.

The Subject of the Gerund.   Another feature of gerunds that you'll want to be aware of is the form that their subjects sometimes take. In many cases the subject of the gerund does not appear in the sentence, especially when the gerund names a general activity:

> <u>Jogging</u> is good exercise.
>
> <u>Raising orchids</u> requires patience.

However, when the subject of the gerund appears in the gerund phrase itself, it is usually in the possessive case, especially when the subject is a pronoun:

> I objected to **their** <u>arriving in the middle of the meeting.</u>
>
> **My** <u>objecting</u> didn't make any difference.
>
> There is no point in **your** <u>coming</u> if you're going to be so late.

When the subject is a simple noun, such as a person's name, it too is possessive:

> I was surprised at **Terry's** <u>refusing the job offer.</u>

The possessive noun or pronoun fills the role of determiner. However, when the noun has modifiers, or when it is compound, then the possessive is generally not used:

> I was surprised at **Bill and Terry** <u>turning down that beautiful apartment.</u>

An alternative structure, which may sound more natural, is the use of a clause instead of the gerund:

I was surprised <u>when Bill and Terry turned down that beautiful apartment.</u>

We look briefly at nominal clauses in the following section.

Nominal Clauses

One of the most common nominal clauses is the one introduced by the expletive *that,* as in the following examples. A clause can fill most of the nominal slots in the sentence, but its most common function is as direct object:

> I suspect <u>that our history exam will be hard.</u>
>
> The president recently announced <u>that he will ask Congress for more aid to Afghanistan.</u>

You'll see that in these examples we have taken a complete sentence and turned it into a part of another sentence:

> Our history exam will be hard.
>
> He will ask Congress for more aid to Afghanistan.

Any declarative sentence can be turned into a nominal clause simply by adding the expletive *that*—and you'll discover that sometimes we don't even need *that:*

> I suspect [＿＿] our history exam will be hard.
>
> He said [＿＿] he would be late.

In many cases, however, the *that* is necessary as a signal to the reader that a clause is coming; its omission may cause the reader momentary confusion:

> Last week I suspected my friend Tom, who never goes to class, was getting himself into academic trouble.
>
> My uncle knows the stockbroker handling his retirement funds never takes unnecessary risks with his clients' money.

Here the expletive *that* would be helpful to signal the reader that *my friend* and *the stockbroker* are subjects, not objects.

The expletive *that* also allows us to turn a direct quotation into indirect discourse:

> *Direct:* He said, "For the past two years the economy has experienced impressive growth."
>
> *Indirect:* He said that for the past two years the economy had experienced impressive growth.

The writer can use indirect discourse to summarize or paraphrase:

The president reported that the economy had been growing during the past two years.

Not all nominal clauses are introduced by the expletive *that*. Many are introduced by interrogative, or question, words:

I wonder **what** <u>our history exam will cover.</u>

Congress is now considering **how much** <u>foreign aid it should appropriate for Afghanistan.</u>

Unlike the expletive, the interrogatives cannot be left out; they provide— or at least ask for—information that is part of the nominal clause.

APPOSITIVES

Appositives will turn out to be very familiar, once you begin to recognize them. You'll probably find them on every page in this book. In the opening section of this chapter, "Determiners," there's one in the first sentence:

Most nouns require a determiner, <u>the noun signaler that occupies the opening slot in the noun phrase.</u>

You can sense that appositives are like nominals in both form and function. They are usually noun phrases in form. And while they don't fill the noun phrase slot, they could. Yet they're also like adjectives, in that they add information to the noun phrase, as other modifiers do. Here are other examples:

Do you know Tim, <u>the deli manager at Giant Foods?</u>

The security guard in our building, <u>an ex-Marine who once played professional football,</u> makes us feel very secure indeed.

And here's one you read in Chapter 6:

I don't want you, <u>the reader,</u> to be stopped by a bold statement, when it may not be valid in your case.

In each of the following examples, also from previous chapters, the appositive is there to remind you, the reader, of a term's definition:

Another point of view that teachers sometimes rule out is the second person, <u>the use of *you*.</u>

Save the important information for the end of the sentence, <u>the point of main stress.</u>

Another function of that opening adverbial is to provide cohesion, the tie that connects a sentence to what has gone before.

We'll also continue the discussion of metadiscourse, the signals that help communicate the writer's credibility and establish authority.

In the next two examples, again from previous chapters, the appositives are verb phrases in form. Any structure that can fill a noun phrase slot, including infinitives and *–ing* (gerund) phrases, can also serve as an appositive:

This role for the comma, to shift the peak of stress, is probably one you hadn't thought about before.

By not putting expected information in the subject slot, not leading off with *they* or *races,* he has violated the known–new contract.

In that last example, the appositive is a gerund phrase renaming the first gerund phrase, the object of the preposition *by.*

The relationship of the appositive to the structure it renames is like that of the subject complement to the subject, which you learned about in Chapter 1 when you studied the linking verbs. In fact, we could easily turn these appositives into subject complements by using the linking-*be:*

Tim *is* the deli manager at Giant Foods.

The security guard in our building *is* an ex-Marine who once played professional football.

The end of the sentence *is* the point of main stress.

You probably won't have occasion to do that: Most writers don't need help in constructing *be* sentences. But you might want to perform the opposite function: turning the subject complement in a linking-*be* sentence into an appositive:

"The Lost Colony" is an outdoor symphonic drama that tells the story of the British settlement on Roanoke Island. It has been performed in Manteo, North Carolina, every summer since 1937.

Rewrite:

"The Lost Colony," an outdoor symphonic drama that tells the story of the British settlement on Roanoke Island, has been performed in Manteo, North Carolina, every summer since 1937.

It's quite common, as in this example, to use two sentences to identify a topic, with *be* as the main verb in one of them. Here's another example:

Alan B. Shepard was the first American to fly in space. He was launched on a 302-mile suborbital shot over the Atlantic in 1961.

Rewrite:

Alan B. Shepard, the first American to fly in space, was launched on a 302-mile suborbital shot over the Atlantic in 1961.

As you can see, this kind of sentence-combining helps solve the problem of choppy sentences, as well as the overuse of *be.* Both are problems that readers often notice and tend to associate with inexperience. The appositive sends the opposite message, the message that this writer has sentence structure under control.

It's possible that the context might call for a different combination of the ideas in the last example, a different focus:

Alan B. Shepard, launched on a 302-mile suborbital shot over the Atlantic in 1961, was the first American to fly in space.

Here, instead of getting rid of the linking-*be,* we have turned one of the sentences into a participial phrase.

Often the appositive is simply a name:

Jack's friend Blane does a great job of cutting his hair.

Sometimes that name needs commas:

The senator's husband, Morrie, stays home with the kids.

Because the senator has only one husband (she wouldn't have been elected otherwise!), the purpose of the appositive is different from the first one: It's only a comment. We know who stays home with the kids, even if we don't have the husband's name. But in the first example, if the sentence read simply,

Jack's friend does a great job of cutting his hair.

the reader would have a question: Who is it? Which friend? Here we don't know who does that great hair-cutting job because Jack has more than one friend. <u>Blane</u> defines <u>friend.</u>

The Introductory Appositive

The appositive that renames the subject is often movable; you may want to shift it to the opening slot in the sentence:

The first American to fly in space, Alan B. Shepard was launched on a 302-mile suborbital shot over the Atlantic in 1961.

In opening position, it tends to put more stress on the subject, which then is no longer an opening valley in the intonation contour. The opening appositive also sends a message to the reader that the sentence has been constructed with special care; it's not your everyday appositive.

The opening appositive is even more dramatic when it consists of a series of appositives, not just a single one. The following passage is part of a description of Queen Victoria written by Winston Churchill:

> <u>High devotion to her royal task,</u> <u>domestic virtues,</u> <u>evident sincerity of nature,</u> <u>a piercing and sometimes disconcerting truthfulness</u>—all these qualities of the Queen's had long impressed themselves upon the mind of her subjects.

The subject of the sentence is *all these qualities;* the list of appositives names the qualities.

In the following passage, the series of noun phrases that opens the second sentence describes the array mentioned in the first one and functions as an appositive to *mixture:*

> The Buffalo Bill Museum is a wonderful array of textures, colors, shapes, sizes, forms. <u>The fuzzy brown bulk of a buffalo's hump,</u> <u>the sparkling diamonds in a stickpin,</u> <u>the brilliant colors of the posters</u>—the mixture makes you want to walk in and be surrounded by it, as if you were going into a child's adventure story. For a moment you can pretend you're a cowboy too; it's a museum where fantasy can take over. For a while.
>
> —Jane Tompkins

Often the opening noun phrase series is in apposition to a pronoun as subject, in this case *they:*

> <u>Political and religious systems,</u> <u>social customs,</u> <u>loyalties and traditions,</u> they all came tumbling down like so many rotten apples off a tree.
>
> —William Golding

This stylistic device, the opening appositive series, may seem a bit dramatic for your purposes. You might think it would call too much attention to itself if you're writing an essay on politics or economics or history or literature. But it needn't be quite as dramatic as those examples. It can simply be a tight, authoritative way of presenting facts:

> <u>Poland, Hungary, Czechoslovakia, Romania</u>—they all caught the democratic fever that was sweeping across Eastern Europe.

The Colon with Appositives

In Chapter 3 we saw the colon in its role as a connector of clauses in compound sentences. Here we see it in its more common role, as a signal for an appositive:

> I'll never forget the birthday present my dad bought me when I was ten: a new three-speed bike.

This sentence can also be written with a comma or a dash instead of a colon:

> I'll never forget the birthday present my dad bought me when I was ten—a new three-speed bike.

Like the dash, the colon is a strong signal, putting emphasis on the appositive; you can think of the dash as an informal colon.

One of the most common uses of the colon is to signal a list:

> Three committees were set up to plan the convention: program, finance, and local arrangements.

Here the list is actually a list of appositives renaming the noun *committees.* The colon is a way of saying, "Here it comes, the list I promised." Sometimes the separate structures in the list have internal punctuation of their own, in which case you will want to separate them with semicolons:

> The study of our grammar system includes three areas: phonology, the study of sounds; morphology, the study of meaningful combinations of sounds; and syntax, the study of sentence structure.

Here each of the three noun phrases in the list has a modifier of its own, set off by a comma; the semicolons signal the reader that the series has three items, not six. This is one of the two occasions in our writing system that call for the semicolon. (The other, you will recall, is the semicolon that joins the clauses in a compound sentence.)

When an appositive series is in the middle of the sentence, we use a pair of dashes to set it off:

> Three committees—program, finance, and local arrangements—were set up to plan the convention.

> All three areas of our grammar system—phonology, morphology, and syntax—will be covered in the grammar course.

If we had used commas instead of dashes, the reader might have been confused:

> *All three areas of our grammar system, phonology, morphology, and syntax, will be covered in the grammar course.

We need the two different marks of punctuation—the dashes as well as the commas—to differentiate the two levels of boundaries we are marking. You'll read more about this issue, the hierarchies of punctuation, in Chapter 13.

Avoiding Punctuation Errors

The use of the colon with appositives is the source of a common punctuation error, but one simple rule can resolve it:

> **A complete sentence precedes the colon.**

Notice in the earlier examples that the structure preceding the colon is a complete sentence pattern, with every slot filled:

Three committees	were set up	to plan the convention.
SUBJECT	VERB	ADVERBIAL

The study of our grammar system	includes	three areas.
SUBJECT	VERB	DIRECT OBJECT

Because the colon so often precedes a list, the writer may assume that all lists require colons, but that's not the case. In the following sentences, the colons are misused:

> *The committees that were set up to plan the convention are: program, finance, and local arrangements.
>
> *The three areas of the grammar system are: phonology, morphology, and syntax.

Your understanding of the sentence patterns will tell you that a subject complement is needed to complete a sentence that has a form of *be* (here it's *are*) as the main verb. (You can review the patterns in Chapter 1.)

One common variation for the sentence with a list includes the noun phrase *the following:*

> The committees that were set up to plan the convention are the following: program, finance, and local arrangements.

That noun phrase *the following* fills the subject complement slot, so the sentence is indeed grammatical. But it's not necessarily the most effective version of the sentence. When you read the sentence aloud, you'll hear yourself putting main stress on the word *following*—a word with no information. If you want to use a colon in such a sentence for purposes of emphasis, the earlier version is smoother and more efficient:

> Three committees were set up to plan the convention: program, finance, and local arrangements.

It certainly makes more sense for the word *convention* to be emphasized rather than *following*.

The Sentence Appositive

Another effective—and dramatic—stylistic device is the sentence appositive, a noun phrase that renames or, more accurately, encapsulates the idea in the sentence as a whole. It is usually punctuated with the dash:

> The musical opened to rave reviews and standing-room-only crowds—<u>a smashing success.</u>

Compare that tight sentence with a compound sentence that has the same information:

> The musical opened to rave reviews and standing-room-only crowds; it was a smashing success.

Here are two other examples, in which the reader's attention will be focused on the final sentence appositive:

> A pair of cardinals has set up housekeeping in our pine tree—<u>an unexpected but welcome event.</u>
>
> In August of 2005 Hurricane Katrina hit the Gulf Coast with winds that clocked 150 mph—<u>the worst natural disaster in the nation's history in over 100 years.</u>

The sentence appositive is similar to the appositives we saw earlier, except that instead of simply renaming a noun, the sentence appositive offers a conclusion about the sentence as a whole in the form of a noun phrase.

The sentence appositive also resembles the summative modifier, which you saw in Chapter 8. You may recall that the summative modifier serves as an alternative to the broad-reference *which*-clause:

Joe bought a gas guzzler, <u>a decision that surprised me.</u>

Tom cleaned up the garage without being asked, <u>a rare event that made me suspect he wanted to borrow the car.</u>

In the next section you'll read about the resumptive modifier, another appositive-like structure at the end of the sentence.

The Resumptive Modifier

Unlike the summative modifier, which modifies, or summarizes, the main clause (see "The Broad Reference Clause" on pages 191–193), the **resumptive modifier** picks up on a particular word in the main clause, adding information or descriptive details connected to that word. The resumptive modifier often includes a *that*-clause, as these examples from previous chapters illustrate:

> Remember that well-chosen verbs send a message to the reader, <u>the message that the writer has crafted the sentence with care.</u>
>
> That kind of agentless prose should send up a red flag, <u>a signal that here's a candidate for revision.</u>
>
> The reader assumes from such messages that the writer has certain doubts, <u>doubts that perhaps others may have, thus connecting, as possible fellow doubters, the writer and the reader.</u>

In the following sentence from a book review about the work of Edith Wharton, the reviewer uses a dash instead of a comma to set off a resumptive modifier:

> Wharton depicted women caught between constraint and the possibilities of a new sexual freedom—<u>a freedom that she herself enjoyed, though at a high cost.</u>
>
> —Margaret Drabble

And in the following example, the word repeated in the modifier has been converted from a verb to a noun:

> The prosecutor obviously believed in the defendant's guilt, <u>a belief obviously not shared by the jury that acquitted him.</u>

Coming at the end of the sentence, in the position of end focus, these modifiers are going to command the reader's attention. And, clearly, they offer the writer a way of adding information, information that might otherwise require a sentence of its own.

EXERCISE 35

A. Add resumptive modifiers to the following sentences:

1. In 1912, the Japanese government gave 3,020 cherry trees to the United States, a gift that _____.

2. The novels of Charles Dickens serve as a window to nineteenth-century England, a time when _____ a place where _____.

3. The Jewish holiday of Rosh Hashana occurs in September, a celebration that _____.

4. Mean solar time is determined by the meridian that runs through Greenwich, England, a line that _____.

5. Acronyms are pronounceable combinations of the initial letters or syllables of a string of words, combinations that _____ _____.

6. The least frequently used member of our alphabet, as you might imagine, is *Q,* a letter that _____.

7. Every state government, along with many county and municipal governments as well, have offices concerned with consumer protection, agencies that _____.

8. Video games were invented in 1972 by Noland Bushnell, an invention that _____.

B. Check your own or a classmate's paper for places where resumptive modifiers could add information or where combining two sentences could make use of this construction.

EXERCISE 36

Revise the following passages, turning some of the sentences into modifiers. Experiment with commas, colons, and dashes.

1. The cost of repairs to the nation's public transportation facilities is an expenditure that cannot be delayed much longer if the system is to survive. Roads, bridges, and railroads are all in need of repair.

2. To many people, the mushroom is a lowly fungus. It has little food value. To other people, it is a gourmet's delight.

3. Since the early 1980s the Chinese have banned the import of certain American goods, such as cotton, synthetic fibers, and soybeans. The restriction has had an adverse effect on the U.S. economy. It has especially affected the farmers.

4. The paper nautilus octopus is a rare marine animal. It normally lives in the coastal waters of Japan. It was found recently in the squid nets off Santa Catalina in California.

5. The ivory-billed woodpecker is one of North America's rarest birds. It is North America's largest woodpecker. There have been documented sightings of this woodpecker in recent years.

6. Potatoes have the reputation of being fattening. A medium potato has only 100 calories. It's the butter and gravy that make the potato fattening. Potatoes are highly nutritious. They contain vitamin C and a number of trace minerals. They are low in sodium, high in potassium, and thus the ideal food for preventing high blood pressure. The potato is even high in vegetable protein. All in all, the lowly potato is a nutrient bargain. (Information adapted from Jane Brody's *Good Food Book*)

PUNCTUATION REVISITED

The very first punctuation lesson you learned in this book, back in Chapter 1, concerned the slot boundaries:

Do not use a single comma to separate the slots in the basic sentence.

The punctuation lessons in this chapter perhaps explain why the word *single* was included in that rule. In this chapter you have seen many sentences in which a modifier that falls between two slots is set off with two commas:

My mother, sitting by the window, is talking to herself.

You may be tempted to think that here the subject and predicate are separated by a single comma, the comma after *window.* But they are not. It's important to recognize that the second comma has a partner and that the purpose of these commas is to allow the participial phrase into the noun phrase as a modifier. *That particular participle wouldn't be allowed without its two commas.* In other words, that comma is not *between* slots: It is part of the subject slot.

You have learned a great many punctuation rules so far in this book—and there are more to come in the next chapter! Learning those rules in connection with the expansion of sentences, as you are doing, should help you recognize their purposes and use them well. And you can be sure that using punctuation well—using it to help the reader and doing so according to the standard conventions—will go a long way in establishing your authority.

EXERCISE 37

Do a style inventory similar to the one described on page 35. This time count the kinds of sentences you have used in your essay, whether simple, compound, complex, or **compound-complex.** (The latter refers to a compound sentence that includes a dependent clause—that is, a clause that functions as an adjectival or adverbial or one that fills a nominal slot.) Compare your essay with one written by a professional—perhaps an essay that you've read in your English class or one that your instructor suggests.

	Your Essay	Professional
1. Number of sentences per paragraph	_____	_____
2. Total number of compound sentences	_____	_____
a. number connected with *and*	_____	_____
b. number connected with *but*	_____	_____
c. number with other conjunctions	_____	_____
3. Percentage of compound sentences	_____	_____
4. Number of complex sentences	_____	_____
5. Percentage of complex sentences	_____	_____
6. Number with correlative conjunctions		
a. within the sentence	_____	_____
b. between clauses	_____	_____
7. Number of semicolons used	_____	_____
8. Number of dashes used	_____	_____

KEY TERMS

Adjectival
Adjective
Adjective phrase
Appositive
Broad-reference clause
Commenting
  modifier
Dangling gerund
Dangling participle

Defining modifier
Determiner
Free modifier
Gerund
Headword
Nominal clause
Nonrestrictive
  modifier
Noun

Noun phrase
Participial phrase
Participle
Prepositional phrase
Relative adverb
Relative clause
Relative pronoun
Restrictive modifier
Summative modifier

RHETORICAL REMINDERS

Prenoun Modifiers

Have I paid attention to commas and hyphens in the noun phrase?

Have I avoided strings of nouns as modifiers?

Postnoun Modifiers

Do opening and closing participles modify the subject of the sentence?

Have I thought about sentence focus in placing the participles?

Does the punctuation distinguish between restrictive (defining) and nonrestrictive (commenting) phrases and clauses?

Have I made a conscious choice in my use of participles and clauses, and appositives?

Have I avoided fuzzy broad-reference *which*-clauses?

PUNCTUATION REMINDERS

Have I used a comma between prenoun modifers where it's possible to use *and?*

Have I used commas around a nonrestrictive modifier when the modifier is only commenting on the noun rather than defining it—when the reader already knows its referent or if it has only one possible referent?

Have I used a comma to set off a verb phrase that opens the sentence (whether an infinitive, a participle, or a gerund in a prepositional phrase)? And have I made sure that the subject of the sentence is also the subject of the verb in that verb phrase?

Have I remembered that a complete sentence precedes a colon?

Choosing Stylistic Variations

CHAPTER PREVIEW

Everything we say, we say "with **style**," in one sense of the word—when the word refers simply to an individual's way of writing. You have your own style of writing, just as you have your own style of walking and whistling and wearing your hair. We also use the word *style* to characterize the overall impression of a piece of writing, such as the plain style, the pompous style, the grand style, the official style. When you follow advice about being brief and using simple words, the outcome will be a plain style; words that are too fancy will probably result in a pompous style.

The word *style* is also used in connection with variations in sentence structure, with the structural and punctuation choices that you as a writer can use to advantage. For example, in the second sentence of the previous paragraph, three verb phrases in a series are connected with two *and*s and no commas:

walking and whistling and wearing your hair

It could have been written with two commas and only one *and:*

walking, whistling, and wearing your hair

Or only commas:

walking, whistling, wearing your hair

Such stylistic variations have traditionally occupied an important place in the study of rhetoric. In fact, the Greeks had names for every deviation from ordinary word order or usage, and Greek orators practiced using them. Some of the more common ones, you're familiar with, such figures of speech as simile, metaphor, and personification. But many of them, you probably don't even notice—such as the shift, in both this sentence and the previous one, of the direct object to opening position. The Greeks called this inversion of usual word order **anastrophe** (pronounced a-NAS-tro-fee).

In studying this chapter you will use your understanding of grammar as you study stylistic choices. You'll look more closely at variations in the series, along with repetition, ellipsis, antithesis, and sentence fragments.

For some of these variations you'll learn the term the Greeks used. But is that important—to learn their labels? Yes and no. Yes, it's important to know they have labels. It's important to know that stylistic choices like these are used deliberately by good speakers and writers. But no, it's not really important that you remember their names. It's enough that you make their acquaintance, that you recognize them when you see them again.

We begin this chapter with a description of a structure you saw way back on the first page of Chapter 1, but one you haven't seen often since then in these pages: the **absolute phrase.** Rather than an adverbial or adjectival, the absolute is considered a sentence modifier because it functions as a kind of loner, standing beyond the sentence. It has a familiar form—that of noun phrase—but it fills none of the noun phrase slots. We include it here in the discussion of stylistic variations not only because it lends a special flair to a descriptive or narrative passage but also because the well-chosen absolute phrase sends the reader a message, a message about the writer's craftsmanship and ability and style.

The purpose of this chapter, then, is to raise your consciousness about style, to encourage you to make the kinds of stylistic choices that send a message to your reader: "Pay attention! Read this carefully. It's important."

ABSOLUTE PHRASES

You saw two absolute phrases on the first page of Chapter 1 in our old familiar weasel paragraph:

A weasel is wild. Who knows what he thinks? He sleeps in his underground den, <u>his tail draped over his nose. . . .</u> One naturalist refused to kill a weasel who was socketed into his hand deeply as a rattlesnake. The man could in no way pry the tiny weasel off, and he had to walk half a mile to water, <u>the weasel dangling from his palm,</u> and soak him off like a stubborn label.

If you recall the formula for the noun phrase that opened the last chapter, you'll recognize that both of these examples follow the pattern:

determiner + noun headword + participial phrase

Absolute phrases are, indeed, noun phrases. This pattern, with a participial phrase as the postheadword modifier, is our most common form of the absolute, although sometimes that modifier is a noun phrase, sometimes a prepositional phrase.

Our two weasel examples illustrate one of the two styles of absolutes, the phrase that adds a detail or point of focus to the idea stated in the main clause. Notice in the third sentence how the main clause describes the overall scene, the weasel asleep in his underground den; the absolute phrase moves the reader in for a close-up view, focusing on a detail, just as a filmmaker uses the camera. The example in the last sentence works the same way: The main clause gives us the long shot of the man walking; the absolute focuses on the weasel dangling from his palm.

With only one small addition to these absolutes, the relationship of the noun headword and its modifier becomes clear:

His tail (is) draped over his nose.

The weasel (is) dangling from his palm.

In other words, the absolute actually adds a subject–predicate relationship to its sentence, but does so without actually adding another clause. That third sentence,

The weasel sleeps in his underground den, his tail draped over
    his nose,

is neither "compound" nor "complex"; in fact, it would be classified as "simple" in traditional grammar, since it has only one clause. However, you can see that it has the impact of a complex sentence, given that it includes what is essentially a subordinate subject–predicate construction.

As you read the sentences containing these two examples, you can probably hear your voice giving emphasis to the noun headword of the absolute phrase. The absolute invariably calls attention to itself, sending a "Pay attention!" message to the reader. For that reason, writers often reserve the absolute for important details. It also sends a more subtle message: "I have crafted this sentence carefully; I know what I'm doing." Even though a reader may not be able to name, perhaps not even to consciously recognize, the absolute phrase, that reader will certainly recognize a writer in control. The well-chosen absolute can add to the writer's authority.

The absolute phrase that adds a focusing detail is especially common in fiction writing, much more common than in expository writing—such as the prose in this textbook and probably your texts for other classes. In the following passages, all from works of fiction, some have a participle as the post-noun modifier, just as Annie Dillard has in her weasel description; however, you'll also see some with noun phrases, others with prepositional phrases.

> There was no bus in sight and Julian, <u>his hands still jammed in his pockets and his head thrust forward,</u> scowled down the empty street.
> —Flannery O'Connor
> ("Everything That Rises Must Converge")

> He smiled a little to himself as he ran, holding the ball lightly in front of him with his two hands, <u>his knees pumping high, his hips twisting in the almost girlish run of a back in a broken field.</u>
> —Irwin Shaw ("The Eighty-Yard Run")

> He saw the city spread below like a glittering golden ocean, <u>the streets tiny ribbons of light, the planet curving away at the edges, the sky a purple hollow extending to infinity.</u>
> —Anne Tyler *(The Accidental Tourist)*

> Silently they ambled down Tenth Street until they reached a stone bench that jutted from the sidewalk near the curb. They stopped there and sat down, <u>their backs to the eyes of the two men in white smocks who were watching them.</u>
> —Toni Morrison *(Song of Solomon)*

> The man stood laughing, <u>his weapons at his hips.</u>
> —Stephen Crane ("The Bride Comes to Yellow Sky")

> To his right the valley continued in its sleepy beauty, mute and understated, <u>its wildest autumn colors blunted by the distance,</u> placid as a water color by an artist who mixed all his colors with brown.
> —Joyce Carol Oates ("The Secret Marriage")

A second style of absolute phrase, rather than focusing on a detail, explains a cause or condition:

> <u>Our car having developed engine trouble,</u> we stopped for the night at a roadside rest area.

We decided to have our picnic, <u>the weather being warm and clear.</u>

<u>Victory assured,</u> the fans stood and cheered during the last five minutes of the game.

The first example could be rewritten as a *because-* or *when-* clause:

<u>When our car developed engine trouble,</u> we stopped....

or

<u>Because our car developed engine trouble,</u> we stopped....

The absolute allows the writer to include the information without the explicitness of the complete clause; the absolute, then, can be thought of as containing both meanings, both *when* and *because.* The absolute about the weather in the second example suggests an attendant condition rather than a cause.

Here's a familiar (and hotly debated) absolute of this style:

A well-regulated militia being necessary to the security of a free state, the right of the people to keep and bear arms shall not be infringed.

This rendering of the Second Amendment does not include two commas that appear in the original: one following *militia* and one following *arms.* Punctuation conventions have changed in the past two centuries.

As you can probably hear, this second style of absolute adds a formal tone to the sentence, formal almost to the point of stiffness. It's certainly not a structure that's used in speech. In fact, neither of these two styles of absolute phrases is used in speech—in speeches, perhaps, but certainly not in everyday speech.

◀ **FOR GROUP DISCUSSION**

We could add *with* to most, if not all, of the examples, thus turning the absolute phrases into prepositional phrases:

The man stood laughing, <u>with his weapons at his hips.</u>

There was no bus in sight and Julian, <u>with his hands still jammed in his pockets and his head thrust forward,</u> scowled down the empty street.

Try the other examples as well, with the added *with.*

How would you characterize the difference in the two styles? Has the meaning changed at all?

EXERCISE 38

Expand the following sentences by adding the modifiers called for. (You might want to review participial phrases and relative clauses in Chapter 9.)

1. Add a *who*-clause that tells what one of your relatives is usually like: My cousin (aunt, uncle, sister, etc.), who _____

   _____,

   surprised everyone at the family reunion.

Now add a subordinate clause that explains what your relative did that was so surprising. Now add an absolute phrase at the end of the sentence—a close-up detail.

2. Add a series of participial phrases that tell what the cyclists were doing: From the window we watched the cyclists _____

   _____.

Now add an appositive at the end of the sentence as a comment on the whole scene.

3. Use an appositive to describe the trucker: At the far end of the counter sat a trucker, _____

   _____.

Now add two prenoun modifiers to explain what sort of counter it is so that the reader will be better able to picture the scene—and an absolute at the end that provides a close-up detail.

4. Start this sentence with an adverbial clause or phrase that tells when: _____

   _____,

   endless cars jammed the freeway.

Now add a series of absolute phrases that describe the cars.

5. Write a sentence or paragraph describing your classroom or campus. Use the modifiers you have been practicing with.

THE COORDINATE SERIES

Many of the variations that writers use for special effects occur in connection with coordinate structures—pairs and series of sentences and their parts. One of those changes is a deviation in the use of conjunctions. Let's go back to the variations possible for the second sentence in the Chapter Preview:

> You have your own style of writing, just as you have your own style of walking and whistling and wearing your hair.

This style, with that extra *and,* was labeled **polysyndeton** by the Greek rhetoricians. You'll recall from the discussion of the serial comma in Chapter 3 that the usual punctuation for the series includes commas until the final *and:*

> walking, whistling, and wearing your hair

Opposite of the extra *and* is the series with no conjunction at all, just commas, a style called **asyndeton:**

> walking, whistling, wearing your hair

The differences are subtle but meaningful. Polysyndeton puts emphasis on each element of the series with a fairly equal beat: _____ and _____ and _____. As Arthur Quinn notes in his book *Figures of Speech* (see the Bibliography), polysyndeton slows us down, perhaps adds a sense of formality, while asyndeton speeds us up. And asyndeton, the variation with no *and*s, also suggests that the list is open-ended. It seems to suggest, "I could go on and on; I could tell you much more."

In the following passage, Winston Churchill describes Stonewall Jackson using asyndeton in both series; he has embedded one such series within another:

> His character was stern, his manner reserved and unusually forbidding, his temper Calvinistic, his mode of life strict, frugal, austere.

The omission of the conjunctions contributes to the strictness and frugality of style that echo the words themselves. With conjunctions, the sentence would lose that echo:

> His mode of life was strict and frugal and austere.

In Chapter 2 we saw an example of asyndeton in Margaret Atwood's description of a woman's feelings, which evokes that same kind of austerity—in this case, the feeling of being caged in an ever-shrinking space:

> She feels caged, in this country, in this city, in this room.

To add the *and* would be to add space.

In the following sentence from her book *A Not Entirely Benign Procedure: Four Years as a Medical Student,* Perri Klass uses asyndeton to help convey the pressure of medical school:

> The general pressure in medical school is to push yourself ahead into professionalism, to start feeling at home in the hospital, in the operating room, to make medical jargon your native tongue—it's all part of becoming efficient, knowledgeable, competent.

And in the following sentence by Annie Dillard, this one from her memoir, *An American Childhood,* she uses both stylistic variations: asyndeton in the opening and the final series; polysyndeton in the series with *or:*

> As for loss, as for parting, as for bidding farewell, so long, thanks, to love or a land or a time—what did I know of parting, of grieving, mourning, loss?

Perhaps the series is not a feature of language that you've thought much about in your writing. But as these examples illustrate, a well-constructed series can add a great deal of stylistic flair. And while it's not important that you remember their labels, now that you know about polysyndeton and asyndeton, you can add these devices to your collection of writers' tools with the assurance that using them will make the reader pay attention and, what's even more important, recognize your competence and authority as a writer.

REPETITION

Repetition has come up before in these pages—in both a positive and a negative sense. On the positive side, repetition gives our sentences cohesion: The known–new contract calls for the repetition, if not of words, then of ideas. It is part of the glue that holds paragraphs together. But we also have a negative label for repetition when it has no purpose, when it gets in the reader's way: Then we call it *redundancy.* You may recall the discussion of redundancy in connection with flabby prepositional phrases that added nothing but words to the sentence and kept the reader from focusing on the new information.

If you've heard warnings about redundancy, if you've seen "red" in the margins of your essays, you might hesitate to use repetition deliberately. But don't hesitate. It's easy to distinguish redundancy from good repetition, from repetition as a stylistic tool. You saw examples of good repetition in the discussion of parallelism as a cohesive device in Chapter 4.

In an essay on redundancy and ellipsis as writing strategies, listed in the Bibliography, Keith Grant-Davie reports that redundancy "is widely seen as a kind of linguistic cholesterol, clogging the arteries of our prose and impeding the efficient circulation of knowledge" (455). On the other hand, effective redundancy contributes "good cholesterol," especially in the field of technical writing.

While "good cholesterol" was not a term they used, the Greek rhetoricians had a label for every conceivable kind of good repetition—from the repetition of sounds and syllables to that of words and phrases in various locations in the sentence. We confine our discussion to repetition in coordinate structures that make the reader sit up and take notice. Again, to emphasize their importance as tools, we use their ancient labels.

Consider the Gettysburg Address. Which of Lincoln's words, other than "Fourscore and seven years ago," do you remember? Probably "government of the people, by the people, and for the people." It's hard to imagine those words without the repetition: "Of, by, and for the people" just wouldn't have the same effect. Lincoln's repetition of the same grammatical form is called **isocolon.** And think about President Kennedy's stirring words, with his repetition of *any* to signal five noun phrases:

> [We] shall pay any price, bear any burden, meet any hardship, support any friend, oppose any foe to assure the survival and the success of liberty.

Notice, too, Kennedy's use of asyndeton. He seems to be saying, "I could go on and on with my list."

You don't have to be a president to use that kind of repetition, nor do you have to reserve it for formal occasions. Whenever you use a coordinate structure, there's an opportunity for you to add to its impact with repetition, simply by including words that wouldn't have to be included. The following sentence, from an essay in *Time* by Charles Krauthammer, could have been more concise, but it would have lost its drama:

> There is not a single Western standard, there are two: what we demand of Western countries at peace and what we demand of Western countries at war.

The following example of isocolon, the repetitions in the *of*-phrases, is part of a paragraph from Virginia Woolf's essay "How Should One Read a Book?" Notice also the asyndeton in the paragraph's opening sentence:

> It is simple enough to say that since books have classes—fiction, biography, poetry—we should separate them and take from each what it is right that each should give us. Yet few people ask from books what books can give us. Most commonly we come to books with blurred and divided minds, asking of fiction that it shall be true, of poetry that it shall be false, of biography that it shall

be flattering, of history that it shall enforce our own prejudices. If we could banish all such preconceptions when we read, that would be an admirable beginning.

A series of clauses too can be dramatized by repetition. The following sentence by Terrence Rafferty is from a review of the movie *Mountains of the Moon,* which appeared in the *New Yorker.* Here too the repetition helps to persuade the reader of the accuracy of the description "an intellectual adventurer":

> He [Sir Richard Burton] <u>had travelled</u> widely, in Europe, Asia, and Africa; <u>he had mastered</u> a couple of dozen languages; <u>he had written</u> seven books; and <u>he had made</u> a reputation as an intellectual adventurer, a man whose joy was to immerse himself in other cultures, to experience everything—even (or perhaps especially) things that his countrymen loathed and feared.

The Greeks called this repetition of clause openings **anaphora.**

The repetitions we have seen so far are contained within sentences, in compound structures—verb phrases in Kennedy's speech, clauses in the Krauthammer and Rafferty sentences, prepositional phrases in the Woolf passage. But whole sentences with obvious repeated elements not only add a stylistic flair beyond the sentence level, they contribute a great deal to the cohesion of a paragraph and beyond. We saw a number of examples in Chapter 4. You may recall the paragraph about Portland (page 73) where one sentence begins with *Its eastern border is* and the following one with *Its western border is.* In a paragraph illustrating parallelism (page 82), three successive sentences begin with repetition: *It is easier, But it is harder, And it is much harder.* These are both examples of anaphora, the repetition of clause openings.

These kinds of repetition are obviously not the artery-clogging kind of redundancy. Rather than hindering the flow of the sentence or paragraph, they enhance it. And they certainly send a message to the reader that the writer has crafted the work with care.

◀ ## FOR GROUP DISCUSSION

Shakespeare, of course, was a master of all kinds of stylistic variations. If you've read *The Merchant of Venice,* you may remember these well-known words, spoken by Shylock in Act III, Scene I:

> He hath disgrac'd me, and hind'red me half a million, laugh'd at my losses, mock'd at my gains, scorn'd my nation, thwarted my bargains, cool'd my friends, heated mine enemies; and what's his reason? I am a Jew. Hath not a Jew eyes? Hath

not a Jew hands, organs, dimensions, senses, affections, passions? Fed with the same food, hurt with the same weapons, subject to the same diseases, heal'd by the same means, warm'd and cool'd by the same winter and summer, as a Christian is? If you prick us, do we not bleed? If you tickle us, do we not laugh? If you poison us, do we not die? And if you wrong us, shall we not revenge?

A. Identify the various rhetorical figures that Shakespeare has used here. In what ways does the sentence style enhance the meaning of Shylock's words?

B. Examine your own use of compound structures or those of a classmate in a peer review session. Look for places where one or more of the stylistic variations you have read about here—polysyndeton, asyndeton, isocolon, and anaphora—would enhance the effectiveness of the writing. For example, you might add details by turning a compound structure into a series. You'll want to bear in mind that these variations can affect the focus and rhythm.

WORD-ORDER VARIATION

A number of the classical rhetorical schemes have to do with variation in normal subject-verb-complement word order, as we saw in the examples of *anastrophe* in the Chapter Preview. Such deviations are especially common in poetry. In reading poetry, we're always on the lookout for subjects and predicates in unexpected places. Here, for example, is the opening of Robert Frost's famous poem "Stopping by Woods on a Snowy Evening":

Whose woods these are, I think I know.

In this line the opening clause is the direct object of *know:*

I think I know *something.*

This inversion of word order can also be effective in prose, mainly because we're not looking for it. It can put stress on the verb, just as it did in Frost's line. In one of the earlier examples cited from this chapter,

But many of them, you probably don't even notice,

the verb is in line for end focus. And in the following sentence, Charles Dickens made sure that the reader would hear the contrast between *has* and *has not:*

Talent, Mr. Micawber has; money, Mr. Micawber has not.

Another variation in word order occurs with certain adverbs in opening position, when a shift of subject and auxiliary is required:

Never before <u>had I seen</u> such an eerie glow in the night sky.

Rarely <u>do I hear</u> such words of praise.

You'll notice that the opening adverbial is a peak of stress. The reader will focus on that opening negative—and will pay attention.

The following sentence, written by Winston Churchill, illustrates yet another kind of shift in word order. Here the very last noun phrase in the sentence is the grammatical subject:

> Against Lee and his great Lieutenant [Stonewall Jackson], united for a year of intense action in a comradeship which recalls that of Marlborough and Eugene, were now to be marshalled the overwhelming forces of the Union.

When you read this sentence aloud, you can hear your voice building to a crescendo on *overwhelming forces,* just as Churchill planned. In fact, it's hard to read the sentence without sounding Churchillian. The sentence leaves the reader in suspense until the end.

The inversion in this passage, from *The Templars* by Piers Paul Read, produces something of that same Churchillian effect:

> The conversion of Constantine was of momentous consequence for Christianity. Equally significant for the future of the Empire was his decision to move its capital from Rome to Byzantium on the Bosphorus.

In Chapter 9 we saw another variation in the expected word order when we shifted adjective phrases from their usual preheadword position:

<u>Hot and tired,</u> the Boy Scouts trudged the last mile to their campsite.

The Boy Scouts, <u>hot and tired,</u> trudged the last mile to their campsite.

<u>Highly unusual,</u> the situation called for extraordinary measures.

The situation, <u>highly unusual,</u> called for extraordinary measures.

These shifts are less dramatic than Churchill's, but they do change the emphasis and call attention to themselves. In both versions, they put the strong stress on the subject, rather than on the predicate, its usual place. The reader of the Boy Scout sentence will not be surprised to read on about the physical condition of the boys. If the writer had not called attention to the adjectives, the reader might have expected to read about the campsite in the next sentence. Likewise, in the other example, both versions put strong stress on the subject. Read them aloud, then compare your reading with this version:

The highly unusual situation called for extraordinary measures.

You probably heard the highest peak of stress on the word *extraordinary* rather than on the subject. The reader of this version will expect to learn more about those measures; in the other two versions the reader probably expects to read more about the situation and what makes it unusual.

All of these word order variations change the rhythm patterns and thus the messages that the reader will get. As a writer, you will want to construct your sentences with the reader and the reader's expectations in mind.

FOR GROUP DISCUSSION

In the following paragraph, the opening paragraph of Chapter 5 in Daniel J. Boorstin's *The Discoverers,* you'll find two sentences that illustrate anastrophe:

> While man allowed his time to be parsed by the changing cycles of daylight, he remained a slave to the sun. To become the master of his time, to assimilate night into the day, to slice his life into neat, usable portions, he had to find a way to mark off precise small portions—not only equal hours, but even minutes and seconds and parts of seconds. He would have to make a machine. It is surprising that machines to measure time were so long in coming. Not until the fourteenth century did Europeans devise mechanical timepieces. Until then, as we have seen, the measuring of time was left to the shadow clock, the water clock, the sandglass, and the miscellaneous candle clocks and scent clocks. While there was remarkable progress five thousand years ago in measuring the year, and useful week clusters of days were long in use, the subdivided day was another matter. Only in modern times did we begin to live by the hour, much less by the minute.

   A. You'll notice that the two sentences illustrating anastrophe also include the shift of the subject and the auxiliary verb. What do they have in common with those examples with *never before* and *rarely* in the discussion? Note as well other figures of speech that Boorstin uses here.

B. Note the variation in sentence length. Where do you find the topic sentence in this paragraph?

C. In Chapters 4 and 6 you read about metadiscourse; you'll find two examples in this paragraph. What effect do they have on you as a reader?

ELLIPSIS

Another fairly common stylistic variation—another that the Greeks used in their oratory—is **ellipsis,** which refers to a sentence in which a part is simply left out, or understood. As you might expect, they had many names for this variation, depending on the kind of structure deleted. We use the umbrella term *ellipsis* for all of them.

One example we've already seen is Churchill's description of Stonewall Jackson:

> His character was stern, his manner reserved and unusually forbidding, his temper Calvinistic, his mode of life strict, frugal, and austere.

And you saw this sentence as an illustration of the series without conjunctions, asyndeton; however, it's also a good example of ellipsis, where all the clauses except the first are missing the verb: "his manner [was] reserved... his temper [was] Calvinistic," and so on. Here are some other, similar, examples, where part of the second clause or phrase is left out to avoid repetition:

> The first day of our vacation was wonderful; the second, miserable.
>
> For breakfast we had eggs; for lunch, eggs; and for dinner, eggs again.
>
> Some of our games this season were awesome; others awful.
>
> Percy always orders the extra-large latte for himself; for me, the medium. He gets his with sugar; I get mine without.

Note that within the sentence a comma sometimes signals the omission, depending on the rhythm, where the pause produced by the comma may be needed to help the reader. As you can hear when you read these sentences, this use of ellipsis gives them a tight, controlled quality that would be missing if the clauses were complete.

In Chapter 7, in the discussion of elliptical adverbial clauses, we saw some in which the ellipsis was required by our grammar:

I'm a week older than Terry [is old].
My sister isn't as tall as I [am tall].

or

I'm a week older than Terry is [old].
My sister isn't as tall as I am [tall].

These structures are not a problem for native speakers; we use them automatically. But some elliptical subordinate clauses are not quite as obvious; they can be left dangling, as we saw in the discussion on pages 161–163.

*While waiting for the bus, the police arrested a pickpocket at the edge of the crowd.

As you may recall from Chapter 8, the subject of that *while*-clause must be the same as the subject of the main clause:

While [we were] waiting for the bus, we saw the police arrest a pickpocket at the edge of the crowd.

In this case, if you prefer to stay with *the police* as the subject of the main clause, there's an easy solution: Simply get rid of the ellipsis; write out the clause in full:

While we were waiting for the bus, the police arrested …

When well used, ellipsis can create a bond of sorts between the writer and the reader. The writer is saying, in effect, I needn't spell everything out for you; I know you'll understand.

You may be thinking at this point that if you actually used such sentences in your essays your teacher would mark them as sentence fragments and ask you to correct them. But that's not likely. Clearly, these elliptical sentences are not accidental; in fact, the opposite message will get through to the reader: "Pay attention. I crafted this sentence carefully."

We should note that *ellipsis* is also the term we use to refer to the string of periods, or *ellipsis points,* that indicate to the reader that we have left something out of quoted material. You can read more about this punctuation convention on pages 288–289 in the Glossary of Punctuation.

ANTITHESIS

In his book on classical rhetoric, referred to in an earlier chapter (also listed in the Bibliography), Edward P. J. Corbett defines **antithesis** as "the juxtaposition of contrasting ideas, often in parallel" (464); among his examples illustrating this figure of speech are the words of Neil Armstrong as he stepped on the moon in 1969:

That's one small step for a man, one giant leap for mankind.

This example is from George W. Bush's second inaugural address:

Across the generations we have proclaimed the imperative of self-government because no one is fit to be a master and no one deserves to be a slave.

Benjamin Franklin included this example of antithesis in a letter he wrote in 1783:

There never was a good war, or a bad peace.

Don't get the idea that world-changing events and presidential speeches are the only occasions for antithesis. Advertisers often use the same kind of juxtaposition of contrasting ideas. Here are some headlines from magazine ads published in *Atlantic* and *Harper's:*

Before our engineers design our cars, our racing programs design our engineers.

Felt but not seen. Because our miracle is on the inside...[mattress ad]

We only live once. But we sit many, many times. [chair ad]

You can't see the innovative technology. But you can certainly hear it. [sound system]

The first one is a clever play on words; in the last three, the negative comment is there to contrast with, and thus enhance, the positive quality being promoted. Earlier we saw an example of antithesis in a quotation from Dickens used to illustrate word order variation:

Talent, Mr. Micawber has; money, Mr. Micawber has not.

The following example is a portion of the paragraph that follows the Boorstin paragraph about clocks quoted in the Group Discussion activity on page 222. It includes the kind of antithesis that you are likely to see in works you are reading—and also to use—where contrasts are included to emphasize the point:

The first steps toward the mechanical measurement of time, the beginnings of the modern clock in Europe, came not from farmers or shepherds, nor from merchants or craftsmen, but from religious persons anxious to perform promptly and regularly their duties to God. Monks needed to know the times for their appointed prayers. In Europe the first mechanical clocks were designed <u>not to *show*</u> the time <u>but to *sound*</u> it.... [author's emphasis]

In his autobiography, *Long Walk to Freedom,* Nelson Mandela uses antithesis to explain the importance of education:

Education is the great engine of personal development. It is through education that <u>the daughter of a peasant can become a doctor,</u> that <u>the son of a mineworker can become the head of the mine,</u> that <u>a child of farmworkers can become the president of a great nation.</u> It is what we make out of <u>what we have,</u> <u>not what we are given,</u> that separates one person from another.

In the discussion of cohesion in Chapter 4 we also saw antithesis, where Stephen Jay Gould contrasts "violence, sexism, and general nastiness" with "peacefulness, equality, and kindness." And one of the examples of anaphora we saw earlier, the repetition of sentence openers, also illustrates antithesis: "It is easier...It is harder...It is much harder...."

THE DELIBERATE FRAGMENT

The sentence fragments used for their stylistic effect are not the kind that teachers mark with a marginal "frag"; those are usually the result of punctuation errors, often a subordinate clause punctuated as a full sentence. But experienced writers know how to use fragments deliberately and effectively—noun phrases or verb phrases that add a detail without a full sentence and invariably call attention to themselves. Here are two examples from the novels of John le Carré:

Our Candidate begins speaking. <u>A deliberate, unimpressive opening.</u>

—*A Perfect Spy*

He began packing up his desk. <u>Precisely.</u> <u>Packing to leave.</u> <u>Opening and shutting drawers.</u> <u>Putting his file trays into his steel cupboard and locking it.</u> <u>Absently smoothing back his hair between moves, a tic that Woodrow had always found particularly irritating in him.</u>

—*The Constant Gardener*

In the following paragraph from *Love Medicine* by Louise Erdrich, we are hearing fragmented thoughts—ideal candidates for sentence fragments. You'll notice that some are simple noun phrases, some are absolutes—a noun with a modifier following—and some are subordinate clauses. But, obviously, all are deliberate:

Northern lights. Something in the cold, wet atmosphere brought them out. I grabbed Lipsha's arm. We floated into the field and sank down, crushing green wheat. We chewed the sweet kernels and stared up and were lost. Everything seemed to be one piece. The air, our faces, all cool, moist, and dark, and the ghostly sky. Pale green licks of light pulsed and faded across it. Living lights. Their fires lobbed over, higher, higher, then died out in blackness. At times the whole sky was ringed in shooting points and puckers of light gathering and falling, pulsing, fading, rhythmical as breathing. All of a piece. As if the sky were a pattern of nerves and our thought and memories traveled across it. As if the sky were one gigantic memory for us all. Or a dance hall. And all the world's wandering souls were dancing there. I thought of June. She would be dancing if there was a dance hall in space. She would be dancing a two-step for wandering souls. Her long legs lifting and falling. Her laugh an ace. Her sweet perfume the way all grown-up women were supposed to smell. Her amusement at both the bad and the good. Her defeat. Her reckless victory. Her sons.

And in the following passage from *The Shipping News,* E. Annie Proulx conveys a tentative quality of the characters' feelings:

Wavey came down the steps pulling at the sleeves of her homemade coat, the color of slushy snow. She got in, glanced at him. A slight smile. Looked away.
    Their silence comfortable. Something unfolding. But what? Not love, which wrenched and wounded. Not love, which came only once.

Both ellipsis and sentence fragments contribute to that tentativeness.

EXERCISE 39

Examine the style of one of your essays or, if working in groups, an essay written by a classmate.

1. Calculate the average length of the sentences. Then count the number that surpass the average length by at least ten words and the number at least five words below the average.

2. Note any series of three or more structures. Do they follow the order of climax, with the longest and/or most important member last in the string? Do any have variations in their punctuation, either asyndeton or polysyndeton?

3. Are there any places where a compound structure could be expanded into a series to add stylistic interest or further information?

4. Is there any clause-level punctuation other than commas and periods—semicolons, colons, dashes? Are there places where alternative punctuation might enhance the effectiveness?

5. How many sentences begin with opening phrases or clauses that precede the subject slot? Check for other word-order variation, such as subject–verb shifts.

6. Count the instances of any repetition, ellipsis, and antithesis.

7. Count the number of appositive and absolute phrases.

Write an evaluation of the essay based on these findings.

FOR GROUP DISCUSSION

The writers of the following passages have used a great many stylistic tools to good advantage. Identify the places where they have sent that special message to the reader: "Pay attention! I've crafted this sentence carefully."

[George Caleb] Bingham's greatest paintings depend upon an open rhetoric, an uncannily frank relation to their audience. We view his subjects from a perspective that includes us within the painting, and the direct looks we meet there usually recall the openness of Bingham's own disposition, itself characteristically American. Looking at *Fur Traders Descending the Missouri* as if from a canoe or from the Missouri's bank, we are obliged to remember that rivers have mouths and sources. *Fur Traders* can certainly be read as a painting in which the wilderness is brought into the frame of civilization, tending ever downriver. But it is more ambiguous than that, and ambiguity is an important source of its effect. Backlit by the diffuse light of the rising sun, offset by an island still in shadow, barely accented by a line of ducks wheeling over the far shore, these exotic figures are just as redolent of where they have been as of where they are going. And as time moves the viewer farther and farther downstream from the wilderness, it seems more and more as if this painting leads us upstream in imagination to the wilder country from which this man and boy have just descended.

—Verlyn Klinkenborg *(Smithsonian)*

Now I know that China is still ruled by her three great symbols: the Yellow River, the Great Wall, and the Dragon. The Yellow River is believed to have given birth to Chinese civilization thousands of years ago in its rich alluvial soil and to have established China as a river country, not an ocean country. She still lives by the yellow river waters, not the blue of ocean seas, turning inward instead of outward, as did the men of the Renaissance and the privateers of Queen Elizabeth. Not yet have the people and their rulers begun to see that the Great Wall keeps the people in, as well as the invaders out; that the walls and courtyards in which they contain themselves, the great magenta walls that surround the Forbidden City and Zhongnanhai, confine minds as well as bodies. And the Dragon is still supreme, China's benevolent dragon that protects the nation, protects the throne, protects the dynasties, protects the people—so long as they do not threaten its order.

—Harrison E. Salisbury *(Tiananmen Diary)*

The general pressure in medical school is to push yourself ahead into professionalism, to start feeling at home in the hospital, in the operating room, to make medical jargon your native tongue—it's all part of becoming efficient, knowledgeable, competent. You want to leave behind that green, terrified medical student who stood awkwardly on the edge of the action, terrified of revealing limitless ignorance, terrified of killing a patient. You want to identify with the people ahead of you, the ones who know what they're doing. And instead, I have found it necessary to retain some of the greenness, so I could explain the hospital to people for whom it was not familiar turf.

—Perri Klass *(A Not Entirely Benign Procedure)*

(*Note:* You saw the opening sentence of this paragraph in the discussion of anaphora.)

It is so known through the length and breadth of its watershed.
The Bay. There is no possible confusion with any other body
of water, no need for more precise description. It is, after all,
the continent's largest estuary. Its waters are rich, the main supply of oysters, crabs, clams and other seafoods for much of the
Atlantic seaboard. Its shorelines cradled our first settlements. It
is the Chesapeake.

                    —William W. Warner *(Beautiful Swimmers)*

(*Note:* This paragraph opens the book's first chapter, "The Bay.")

On two occasions, the contractor hired a group of Mexican
aliens. They were employed to cut down some trees and haul
off debris. In all, there were six men of varying age. The
youngest in his late twenties; the oldest (his father?) perhaps
sixty years old. They came and they left in a single old truck.
Anonymous men. They were never introduced to the other
men at the site. Immediately upon their arrival they would follow the contractor's directions, starting working—rarely resting—seemingly driven by a fatalistic sense that work which had
to be done was best done as quickly as possible.

    I watched them sometimes. Perhaps they watched me. The
only time I saw them pay me much notice was one day at
lunchtime when I was laughing with the other men. The Mex-
icans sat apart when they ate, just as they worked by themselves.
Quiet. I rarely heard them say much to each other. All I could
hear were their voices calling out sharply to one another, giving directions. Otherwise, when they stood briefly resting, they
talked among themselves in voices too hard to overhear.

                    —Richard Rodriguez *(Hunger of Memory)*

Yet above all else the spectator of sport desires the poetic
moment: The shortstop diving long to his left, stopping a
ground ball the eye can't follow, then rising to throw in an
impossible gyration and beating the runner by a millisecond
(and afterward, adjusting his cap, nonchalant and inscrutable).
Or the elegant point guard slashing in from the left who leaves
the ball behind his head for the teammate trailing after him, a
silky forward who must leap and double-pump his graceful
legs, then wait while his off-balance defender descends just half
a beat ahead of him, and at the last moment move the ball
from right to left to lay it softly off the glass at a high angle—

all as if this were an ordinary act he can perform without particular duress. Or the wide receiver going long and longer still, the football apparently just slightly overthrown, and even while we judge from our limited perspective whether the quarterback hasn't given it too much arm, already here is this improbably swift receiver, not only leaping but flinging himself, as if flying from the edge of a precipice, the ball now poised on the tips of three fingers, the opposing team's cornerback arriving at exactly this moment to hurl himself at the receiver's head, and all the while the gravityless receiver just catches the ball, balancing it on his fingertips, then drawing it into his outstretched palm, then clutching it against his side, against his ribs, while the defender pummels him out of bounds, seeking to thrash free the ball from his grip, and still he has the graceful presence to nestle both feet against the neatly drawn sideline before he is slammed full-tilt toward the turf, where rather than curling in contorted pain he performs an amazing, one-handed cartwheel, easily rights himself, slows to a trot, releases the ball from the grip of his right hand, and turns once again in the direction of his teammates with his shirt still neatly tucked inside his pants.

—David Guterson *(Harper's Magazine)*

KEY TERMS

Absolute phrase	Figures of speech	Redundancy
Anaphora	Fragment	Repetition
Anastrophe	Isocolon	Style
Antithesis	Polysyndeton	Word order variation
Ellipsis		

RHETORICAL REMINDERS

Have I taken advantage of the stylistic possibilities of absolute phrases and of various kinds of repetition, word-order variation, antithesis, and ellipsis to heighten the drama and/or call attention to particular passages?

In my series of three or more structures, have I considered order of importance and/or length?

PUNCTUATION REMINDERS

Have I used any punctuation variations for any series, such as asyndeton or polysyndeton?

Do my punctuation choices help the reader, especially in long sentences with internal punctuation?

Have I used colons, semicolons, and dashes accurately and effectively?

CHAPTER
11

Word Classes

Your intuitive understanding of sentences in your native language is more than matched by your remarkable way with words. The sentences that you automatically generate whenever the need arises are, of course, strings of individual words, which you select from an inventory, or **lexicon,** of many thousands of entries—an internal dictionary of sorts. The extent of your lexicon is impossible to measure with any accuracy, but chances are if you have grown up with English you understand well over half of the 150,000 words in a standard desk dictionary. How many of them are part of your active vocabulary is another matter; it's possible you use only 5,000 to 10,000 for most of the speaking and writing you do. No matter what the extent of your active vocabulary, like all literate people, you recognize and understand many more words than you actually use, words that constitute your passive vocabulary.

Although it's useful to compare our internal lexicon to the dictionary, the analogy is not a very accurate one. Individual entries in our lexicon and their definitions are quite different from those in a standard dictionary. Our definitions are bound up with experience and memory, so they include all of the associations that the word holds for us, negative and positive. For example, think about your own personal definition of *mother* and *kindergarten* and *picnic* and *train* and *football;* it's obvious that no dictionary can describe the pictures that those words conjure up for you.

Although the size of an individual lexicon varies from one person to another and from one language to another, this remarkable way with words is universal: It holds true for native speakers of every language. If English is not your first language, your experience will determine the number of words in your vocabulary and the definitions you have for them. And in the discussion that follows, you will probably recognize, from your study of English, some of the restrictions on the ways in which words are arranged—restrictive rules that your classmates who are native speakers have never thought about before.

LEXICAL RULES

Even more impressive than the number of words and their associations in our memory are the grammatical rules and restrictions that determine how we put our words together into sentences. The following pairs of sentences illustrate how those rules and restrictions work—or fail to work:

Kevin had some trouble last night with his homework.
Paul had a trouble last night with his homeworks.

Dr. Carroll owns a BMW.
His wife is owning a pickup.

Sue is being funny.
Rob is being tall.

Pam walked to school.
Kate walked to home.

Jim walked to town.
Joe walked to city.

You probably recognized that in each case the second sentence is ungrammatical—that is, it is not a sentence that a native speaker would say. A comparison of the two sentences in each pair should illuminate the kinds of lexical rules that operate in English.

The first pair illustrates the restriction that prevents us from saying "homeworks," a distinction we make between the **countable** and **noncountable** nouns in our lexicon: *Homework* is noncountable; it's a kind of **mass noun;** others in the class are *sugar* and *water* and *oil* and *cotton.* Another noncountable class is that of **abstract nouns,** such as *happiness* and *peace.* The first pair of sentences also demonstrates the restriction built

into the **indefinite article,** *a* (or *an*), one of our **determiners,** or noun signalers. Noncountable nouns, such as *homework* and *happiness,* cannot be
signaled by *a,* nor do they have a plural form: Native speakers simply do
not say "homeworks" or "a happiness."

The verb *own,* as illustrated in the second pair of sentences, is called a
stative verb; it describes an unchanging condition, or state. Because no
change—no progress—is implied, the progressive form of the verb (the
–ing form preceded by a form of *be* as an auxiliary) is simply not used.

The next pair illustrates the semantic qualities of adjectives: *Tall* is stative,
so it cannot be used with the progressive "is being," which suggests a
dynamic, or changeable, quality. The adjective *funny* includes both possible
meanings: "Sue is funny" suggests a permanent characteristic of Sue's personality; "Sue is being funny" suggests a condition of the present moment.

FOR GROUP DISCUSSION

If you were to hear someone say the following sentences, you could be quite
sure you were hearing a nonnative speaker:

*We're going shopping for a new furniture.

*Our furnitures are getting shabby.

*My family's healths are important to me.

*Kaleena is seeming sad today.

*I am not knowing Spanish very well.

*The pizza is being stale.

*The kids are not liking it.

Revise the sentences to make them grammatical. When you compare the
two versions, you should be able to figure out which of your internal grammar rules has been broken.

The four sentences with *walked* in the list of pairs illustrate how arbi-
trary, or unsystematic, some of our rules are. There is something in our
lexicon that restricts us from using the preposition *to* with *home,* although
we do, of course, say "to town." The second pair with *walked* demonstrates
the arbitrariness of determiners in some common situations. *City* takes
the determiner; *town* does not. And although we do say, "I have *a* cold,"
we don't say, "I have *a* flu." Some of the rules for using determiners are
different for British speakers. The British go "to hospital" and "to university," and they "look out of window." Americans go "to college" and "to

school" but "to *the* university" and "to *the* hospital"; and we "look out of *the* window."

The grammar rules illustrated here are obviously not the kind that you studied in your grammar classes; chances are, you were not even aware that you follow rules like these when you speak and write. And certainly you don't want to worry about such rules—or even try to remember them. You couldn't remember them all even if you wanted to; in fact, no one has ever described them all. With these few we have just scratched the surface. We are looking at these rules simply to illustrate the kinds of information that our internal lexicon includes and to help you recognize and appreciate that your way with words is truly remarkable.

It is obvious that for a native speaker the restrictions illustrated by these pairs of sentences have somehow become internalized. Linguists sometimes describe such features as a built-in hierarchy, much like the taxonomy that scientists use in classifying plants and animals. Each level—phylum, class, order, family, genus, and species—includes features that differentiate it from the other levels. The farther down the hierarchy, the more specific the details that distinguish the classes. The following scheme illustrates certain features of nouns:

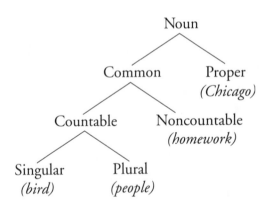

The restrictions built into the word determine its place in the hierarchy; each word carries with it only those features in the higher intersections (or nodes) that it is connected with: *Homework* is a noncountable, common noun; *bird* is a singular, countable, common noun. Determiners, too, have such built-in features: The indefinite article, *a* (or *an*), includes "singular" and "countable," so we are restricted from using it with *homework;* it signals only those nouns that fit in the lowest, left-hand branch, like *bird.* The **definite article,** *the,* is much more versatile as a determiner: It can signal nearly all nouns, even noncountables:

Have you finished <u>the</u> homework?

The happiness I felt at that moment is beyond description.

Many words in our lexicon can appear in both branches of a node, depending on their context. For example, some nouns can be both countable and noncountable:

I had a strange experience yesterday.
I've had experience working with animals.

I baked *a* pie today.
I'll have pie with ice cream, please.

Ron had two beers today already.
He drinks beer often.

The countable/noncountable feature applies also to certain signalers of nouns, such as *less/fewer, amount of/number of,* and *much/many.* The commercial that advertises a certain brand of soft drink as having "less calories" than another brand has failed to make the countable/noncountable distinction: *Calories* is a countable noun; the fact that it's plural tells us that. We generally reserve *less* for noncountables; the description of that soft drink should be "*fewer* calories." We would also talk about the "number of calories," not the "amount of calories," just as we would say "many calories," not "much calories." Such noncountables as *water* and *cotton* and *love* and *homework* pattern with "amount of" and "much"; *calories* does not.

FOR GROUP DISCUSSION

A careful writer would avoid writing sentences like these two:

*There have been less bicycle accidents in the county this year.
*I have also noticed an increase in the amount of bicycles on the roads.

But there's no problem with these:

There are fewer students enrolled in the advanced ceramics class this year.
There is an increase in the number of students enrolled in the beginning course.

Think about where in the noun hierarchy you would find *accidents, bicycles,* and *students.* How would a careful writer revise those first two sentences? If you were helping a nonnative speaker revise those sentences, how would you explain the changes?

Would that careful writer avoid any of these?

There were less than a dozen bicycle accidents in the county this year.

We had fewer accidents than last year.

We have less dollars than we need.

We have less money than we need.

We have less than ten dollars to last until payday.

You probably gave that nonnative speaker some advice about the use of *less/fewer* and *amount of/number of.* Should you revise your explanation? In what way?

PARTS OF SPEECH

The traditional grammar course commonly opens with the classification of words into "parts of speech." You perhaps remember your own language arts classes from junior high, where you began your study of grammar by defining *noun* and *verb* and *adjective* and *adverb* and such. As you learned in the discussion of the lexicon, our internalized grammar includes rules and restrictions that determine how we use our words. In a sense, those rules constitute definitions of a sort for our word classes; so in this study of the parts of speech we look at those internalized definitions.

We begin by classifying the words of our lexicon into two broad groups: **form classes** and **structure classes.** To understand the difference between the two groups, imagine an inexperienced speaker of English saying a sentence such as,

Stranger standing porch.

Even though it doesn't sound exactly like English, the sentence certainly communicates. Now imagine the same sentence spoken by an experienced speaker:

A stranger is standing on the porch.

or, perhaps,

That stranger is standing near the porch.

The added words make the message more explicit, of course, but the nouns and verb the first speaker used are adequate to get the gist of the message across. Those are the *form-class words;* the missing ones are the *structure-class words,* those that provide the grammatical connections.

In general, the form-class words—nouns, verbs, adjectives, and adverbs—provide the primary lexical content; the structure classes—determiners, auxiliaries, qualifiers, prepositions, conjunctions—explain the grammatical or structural relationships. Using a metaphor, we can think of form-class words as the bricks of the language and structure words as the mortar that holds them together.

Probably the most striking difference between the form classes and the structure classes is characterized by their numbers. Of the approximately half-million words in our language, the structure words number only in the hundreds. The form classes, however, are large, open classes; new nouns and verbs and adjectives and adverbs regularly enter the language as new technology and new ideas require them. They are sometimes abandoned, too, as the dictionary's "obsolete" and "archaic" labels testify. But with few exceptions, the structure classes remain constant—and limited. We have managed with the same small store of prepositions and conjunctions for generations, with few changes. It's true that we don't hear *whilst* and *betwixt* anymore, nor do we see them in modern prose and poetry, but most of our structure words are identical to those that Shakespeare and his contemporaries used.

In one way the contrast between the form and structure words is actually quite misleading. Even though the structure words number only a few hundred, they are by far the most frequently used words in the language. An amazing statistic was reported by G. H. McKnight in 1923: "[A] mere forty-three words account for half of the words actually uttered in English; and a mere nine account for fully a quarter of all spoken words."[1] The nine are *and, be, have, it, of, the, to, will,* and *you.* Assuming that *be* and *have* are included because of their role as auxiliaries, there are no form-class words in the list. Except for the pronouns *it* and *you,* they are all structure-class words.

A third class, the **pronouns,** straddles the line between the form and structure classes. Many pronouns are like the form classes, insofar as they have variations in form; and of course they function as nouns, as substitutes for nouns and noun phrases. But they also belong with the structure classes: The possessive and demonstrative pronouns constitute important subclasses of the determiners (*my* house, *that* boat). Also, like the structure classes, pronouns are a small, closed class, admitting no new members. (We take up pronouns in Chapter 12.)

---

[1]McKnight's research is reported by Cullen Murphy in "The Big Nine" (*Atlantic Monthly,* March 1988).

THE FORM CLASSES

Nouns, verbs, adjectives, and adverbs are called the form classes because each class has specific forms, a set of inflectional endings, or **inflections,** that distinguishes it from all other classes. The feature of form is very useful in defining the class. For example, instead of defining *noun* in its traditional way, as "the name of a person, place, or thing," you can define it according to its form: "A noun is a word that can be made plural and/or possessive." And instead of defining *verb* as a word that shows action, which isn't very accurate, you can use the criterion of form, which applies to every verb, without exception: "A verb is a word that has an *–s* and an *–ing* form." These are the definitions built into your internal grammar system.

Nouns

Nouns have an inflection for plural (*–s* or *–es*) and for **possessive case:**

Singular	Plural	Singular Possessive	Plural Possessive
cat	cats	cat's	cats'
treasure	treasures	treasure's	treasures'
fortress	fortresses	fortress's	fortresses'

Not every noun fits into the entire set, as we saw earlier in the case of noncountables such as *homework,* which has no plural. And some nouns have irregular plurals, an inflection other than *–s* or *–es: children, men, feet, mice, crises.* But certainly the vast majority of our nouns are inflected in this regular way, with *–s* (or *–es*) for those that have a plural form, with *– 's* for singular possessive and *–s'* or (*–es'*) for plural possessive.

It's easy to make mistakes in writing the plural and possessive of some nouns; read aloud the three inflected forms in the set of nouns—*cats, cat's, cats'*—and you'll understand why. They sound identical; in speech we make no distinction. The apostrophe is strictly an orthographic signal, a signal in the written language.

As you may know, the apostrophe is easy to misuse. It's not unusual to see it used mistakenly in plurals, especially if the plural looks a bit strange:

*Fishing license's sold here.

This sign was spotted in the window of a sporting goods store; clearly, someone goofed. And a poster announcing the schedule of a musical group that reads,

*Now playing Tuesday's at The Lounge.

is also wrong. We use the apostrophe with the *s* in the possessive case, not in the plural: *Joe's Bar & Grill, Tuesday's meeting.* The only exception to that rule occurs in the case of letters or numbers that would be unreadable without the apostrophe:

There are three *t's* in my name.

And sometimes it occurs with decades:

The 1960's were troubled times for many people.

In this latter case, however, it is even more common to see the decade referred to as "the 1960s"—without the apostrophe.

Probably the best rule of thumb to remember is that when you add an *s* sound, you add the letter *s*—in both plural and possessive: *cat, cat's, cats, cats'.* Words that end with an *s* (or an *s*-like sound), such as *fortress* or *church* or *dish,* require a whole syllable for the plural, an *–es: fortress/fortresses, church/churches, dish/dishes.* But we write the singular possessive just as we do with words like *cat:* We simply add *'s: fortress's, church's, dish's.* For the plural possessive, we simply add the apostrophe to the plural, as we do with *cats': fortresses', churches', dishes'.*

With nouns that already have one or more *s* sounds, we don't always add another when we make it possessive. For example, the word *Texas* has two *s* sounds in the last syllable (the letter *x* is actually a combination of two sounds: those of *k* and *s*). In speech when we make *Texas* possessive, we don't normally add another *s,* so in writing we add only the apostrophe to form the possessive case: *Texas' laws.* We should note that neither the spelling nor the pronunciation of the possessive case of these words with multiple *s*-sounds is universally agreed upon. Allowing your own pronunciation to determine spelling is one way to resolve the issue.

Most names that end in a single *s* sound have a second *s* sound for the plural and possessive, just as the word *fortress* does: *Ross's cat; I know two Rosses; Mr. Jones's cat; The Joneses' house; Thomas's car.*

Plural-Only Forms.   Some nouns, even when singular in meaning, are plural in form. One such group refers to things that are in two parts—that are bifurcated, or branching: *scissors, shears, clippers, pliers, pants, trousers, slacks, shorts, glasses, spectacles.* As subjects of sentences, these nouns present no problems with **subject–verb agreement:** They take the same verb form as other plural subjects do. Interestingly, even though a pair of shorts is a single garment and a pair of pliers is a single tool, we generally use the plural pronoun in reference to them:

I bought a new pair of shorts today; <u>they're</u> navy blue.

I've lost my pliers; have you seen <u>them</u>?

A different situation arises with certain plural-in-form nouns that are some-times singular in meaning. Nouns such as *physics, mathematics,* and *linguis-tics,* when referring to an academic discipline or course, are treated as singular:

Physics <u>is</u> my favorite subject.
Linguistics <u>is</u> the scientific study of language.

But such nouns can also be used with plural meanings:

The mathematics involved in the experiment <u>are</u> very theoretical.
The statistics on poverty in this country <u>are</u> quite depressing.

Again, you can use your intuitive knowledge of pronouns to test these nouns:

<u>It</u> [mathematics] <u>is</u> my favorite subject.
<u>They</u> [the statistics on poverty] <u>are</u> quite depressing.

Collective Nouns.   Collective nouns such as *family, choir, team, major-ity, minority*—any noun that names a group of individual members—can be treated as either singular or plural, depending on context and meaning:

The <u>family have</u> all gone their separate ways. (<u>they</u>)

(It would sound strange to say "The family *has* gone *its* separate way.")

The whole <u>family is</u> celebrating Christmas at home this year. (<u>it</u>)
The <u>majority</u> of our city council members <u>are</u> Republicans. (<u>they</u>)
The <u>majority</u> always <u>rules</u>. (<u>it</u>)

Certain noncountable nouns and indefinite pronouns take their number from the modifier that follows the headword:

The remainder of the building <u>materials are</u> being donated to
    Habitat for Humanity.
The rest of the <u>books are</u> being donated to the library.

The headwords *remainder* and *rest* are noncountable nouns in this context; their plurality clearly derives from the modifier, which determines the form of the verb. A singular noun in the modifier would change the verb:

The remainder of the <u>wood is</u> being donated to Habitat for Humanity.

The rest of the <u>manuscript is</u> being donated to the library.

Some of our **indefinite pronouns,** among them *some, all,* and *enough,* work in the same way:

Some of the <u>maps were</u> missing.

All of the <u>cookies were</u> eaten.

Again, notice what happens to the verb in such sentences when the noun in the *of*-prepositional phrase is singular:

Some of the <u>water is</u> polluted.

All of the <u>cake was</u> eaten.

The pronoun to use in reference to these noun phrases depends on the meaning, and it is usually obvious:

<u>They</u> [some of the maps] <u>were</u> missing.

<u>It</u> [some of the water] <u>is</u> polluted.

One special problem occurs with the word *none,* which has its origin in the phrase *not one.* Because of that original meaning, many writers insist that *none* always be singular, as *not one* clearly is. However, a more accurate way to assess its meaning is to recognize *none* as the negative, or opposite, of *all* and to treat it in the same way, with its number determined by the number of the modifier:

All of the <u>guests want</u> to leave.

None of the <u>guests want</u> to leave.

All of the <u>cookies were</u> left.

All of the <u>cake was</u> left.

None of the <u>cookies were</u> left.

None of the <u>cake was</u> left.

These examples clearly suggest that in the case of noun phrases with collective nouns, certain noncountable nouns, and indefinite pronouns as headwords, the concept of number refers to the whole noun phrase, not just to the noun headword.

Proper Nouns. In contrast to **common nouns,** which refer to general things, places, attributes, and so on, **proper nouns** are those with a specific referent: *Empire State Building, Grand Canyon, William Shakespeare, London, The CBS Evening News, Aunt Mildred, November, Thanksgiving.* Proper nouns name people, geographic regions and locations, buildings, events, holidays, months, and days of the week; they usually begin with capital letters. Most proper nouns are singular; exceptions occur with the names of mountain ranges (*the Rocky Mountains, the Rockies, the Andes*) and island groups (*the Falklands*), which are plural.

EXERCISE 40

Problems of subject–verb agreement sometimes occur when modifiers follow the headword of the subject noun phrase:

*The <u>instructions</u> on the loan application <u>form was</u> very confusing.

*This <u>collection of poems</u> by several of my favorite romantic poets <u>were</u> published in 1910.

In these incorrect examples, the writer has forgotten that the headword determines the number of the noun phrase. To figure out the correct form of the verb, you can use the pronoun-substitution test:

The instructions [<u>they</u>] <u>were</u> very confusing.

This collection [<u>it</u>] <u>was</u> published in 1910.

Now test the following sentences to see if they are grammatical:

1. The statement on the income tax form about deductions for children and other dependents were simply not readable.

2. The type of career that many graduates are hoping to pursue pay high salaries and provide long vacations.

3. Apparently the use of robots in Japanese factories have been responsible for a great deal of worker dissatisfaction.

4. The problems associated with government deregulation have been responsible for the economic plight of several major airlines in recent years.

5. The government's deregulation policy regarding fares have also resulted in bargains for the consumer.

6. The inability to compete with those low airline fares are also responsible for the financial problems of the bus companies.

7. The impact of computers on our lives is comparable to the impact of the industrial revolution.

8. This new book of rules with its 100 ways to play solitaire really amaze me.

9. Carmen's collection of computer games and board games were really impressive.

10. The amount of money and time I spend on computer games is more than I can afford.

Verbs

Although traditional grammar books often describe **verbs** in ways that make them seem complicated, they are really quite simple and systematic, especially when compared with verbs in other languages. With one exception, English verbs have only five forms—the base, or present tense, and four inflected forms. The forms and uses of verbs are described in Chapter 7, pages 130–133.

Adjectives

A third open class of words is that of **adjectives,** which can sometimes be recognized by their comparative and superlative inflections, a semantic feature known as **degree:**

Positive	Comparative	Superlative
big	bigger	biggest
silly	sillier	silliest
intelligent	more intelligent	most intelligent

Note that *more* and *most* are variations of the inflections –*er* and –*est*.

   A number of adjectives do not fit this set. For example, we do not say "the mainest reason" or "a more principal reason." The adjectives that do not take the inflections of degree also do not fit into the "adjective test frame":

   The _____ NOUN is very _____.

The adjective test frame is useful in identifying adjectives: A word that fits into both slots is an adjective—and most adjectives do fit:

> The frisky kitten is very frisky.
>
> The comical clown is very comical.
>
> The tough assignment is very tough.

The formula illustrates the two main slots that adjectives fill; however, not all adjectives fit both slots:

> *The principal reason is very principal.
>
> *The afraid children are very afraid.
>
> *The medical advice was very medical.

The test frame, then, can positively identify adjectives: Only an adjective can fit both slots. But it cannot rule them out—that is, just because a word doesn't fit, that doesn't mean it's *not* an adjective.

Adverbs

Our most recognizable **adverbs**—and the most common—are those that are formed by adding –*ly* to the adjective: *slowly, deliberately, exclusively, perfectly.* These are called adverbs of **manner.** Some common adverbs have the same form as the adjective: *fast, far, near, hard, long, high, late.* These are sometimes called **flat adverbs.**

Like adjectives, the –*ly* adverbs and the flat adverbs have comparative and superlative forms:

Positive	Comparative	Superlative
slowly	more slowly	most slowly
fast	faster	fastest

The comparative form of -*ly* adverbs, usually formed by adding *more* rather than *er,* is fairly common. However, the superlative degree of the -*ly* adverbs—*most suddenly, most slowly, most favorably*—is rare enough in both speech and writing to have impact when used; these forms invariably call attention to themselves and in most cases will carry the main stress:

> The committee was most favorably disposed to accept the plan.
>
> The crime was planned most ingeniously.

There are a number of adverbs, in addition to the flat adverbs, that have no endings to distinguish them as adverbs, nor are they used with *more* or *most*. Instead we recognize them by the information they provide, by their position in the sentence, and often by their movability, as we saw in Chapter 8.

Time:	*now, today, nowadays, yesterday, then, already, soon*
Duration:	*always, still*
Frequency:	*often, seldom, never, sometimes, always*
Place:	*here, there, everywhere, somewhere, elsewhere, upstairs*
Direction:	*away*
Concession:	*yet, still*

There are also a number of words that can serve as either prepositions or adverbs: *above, around, behind, below, down, in, inside, out, outside, up.*

Derivational Affixes

Besides the inflectional endings that identify the form classes, we also have an extensive inventory of **derivational affixes,** suffixes and prefixes that provide great versatility to our lexicon by allowing us to shift words from one class to another and/or to alter their meanings. For example, the noun *beauty* becomes a verb with *–ify (beautify),* an adjective with *–ful (beautiful),* and an adverb with *–ly* added to the adjective *(beautifully).*

Some of our suffixes change the meaning rather than the class of the word: *boy/boyhood; citizen/citizenry; king/kingdom; terror/terrorism.* Prefixes, too, generally change the meaning of the word rather than the class: *un*deniable, *pro*-American, *inter*action, *intra*murals, *il*legal, *dis*enchanted. Some prefixes enable us to derive verbs from other classes: *en*chant, *en*courage, *en*able, *de*rail, *de*throne, *be*witch, *be*devil, *dis*able, *dis*member.

This remarkable ability to expand our lexicon with uncountable new forms provides yet more evidence (if we needed more) for the idea of the inherent language expertise that native speakers possess. With this system of word expansion it's easy to understand why no one has yet come up with a definitive number of words in English. And although we follow certain rules in shifting words from one class to another, there is no real system: We can take a noun like *system*, turn it into an adjective *(systematic),* then a verb *(systematize),* then a noun again *(systematization).* There's also the adverb *systematically* in that set; and the same base, *system,* produces *systemic* and *systemically.* But we can't distinguish between those adjectives that pattern with *–ize* to form verbs *(systematize, legalize, realize, publicize)* and those that pattern with *–ify (simplify, amplify, electrify)* or another affix *(validate, belittle).*

EXERCISE 41

Fill in the blanks with variations of the words shown on the chart, changing or adding derivational morphemes to change the word class. In some cases, you may think of more than one possibility.

	NOUN	VERB	ADJECTIVE	ADVERB
1.	grief			
2.		vary		
3.				ably
4.		defend		
5.				quickly
6.			pleasant	
7.	type			
8.		prohibit		
9.				critically
10.			valid	
11.		appreciate		
12.	danger			
13.		accept		
14.			pure	
15.		steal		

KEY TERMS

Abstract noun
Adjective
Adverb
Apostrophe
Collective noun
Common noun
Comparative degree
Countable noun

Definite article
Degree
Derivational affix
Determiner
Flat adverb
Form classes
Indefinite article
Indefinite pronoun

Inflection
Irregular verb
Lexical rule
Lexicon
Manner adverb
Mass noun
Noncountable noun
Noun

Parts of speech
Past participle
Past tense
Plural-only noun
Positive degree
Possessive case

Present participle
Pronoun
Proper noun
Regular verb
Stative verb
Structure classes

Subject–verb
  agreement
Superlative degree
Verb

RHETORICAL REMINDERS

Have I selected words with clear and precise meanings?

Have I considered the countable/noncountable features of nouns in using such modifiers as *less/fewer, amount of/number of,* and *much/many?*

Have I been careful to recognize the singular/plural aspect of the subject noun phrase, especially when tricky words like collective nouns, plural-only forms, and indefinite pronouns are involved?

PUNCTUATION REMINDER

Have I remembered that the apostrophe added to a noun turns it into the possessive case: *cat/cat's* (singular); *cats/cats'* (plural)?

CHAPTER 12

Pronouns

CHAPTER PREVIEW

One word that accurately describes the place of **pronouns** in English is the adjective *ubiquitous*—a word that may be new to your lexicon. It means "everywhere present, constantly encountered, widespread"—and that's what pronouns are. You will rarely encounter a passage of two or more sentences that doesn't contain several pronouns. In fact, the sentence you just finished reading contains three. (And this first paragraph contains ten!)

We looked briefly at pronouns in earlier chapters when we substituted them for noun phrases in order to demonstrate whether the subject of the sentence was singular or plural and to figure out where the subject ended and the predicate began:

Jenny's sister *[she]* graduated from nursing school.

The gymnasium *[it]* needs a new roof.

Those substitutions—*she* and *it*—are among the personal pronouns, the kind you probably recognize most readily. But there are many other classes of pronouns as well—reflexive, demonstrative, relative, indefinite, and others. In this chapter we look at all of the pronouns, concentrating especially on those members of various classes that sometimes cause problems for writers.

Don't make the mistake of thinking that this is a list for you to memorize. It's not that at all. The purpose of describing our inventory of pronouns is to raise your consciousness about this important category of the lexicon and to point out those areas that require some thought on the part of writers.

PERSONAL PRONOUNS

The easiest way to understand the system of **personal pronouns** is in terms of **person** and **number.** The forms in parentheses (possessive, objective) are variations in **case,** the choice of which is determined by the pronoun's function in the sentence.

PERSON	NUMBER	
	Singular	Plural
1st	I (my, me)	we (our, us)
2nd	you (your, you)	you (your, you)
3rd	he (his, him) she (her, her) it (its, it)	they (their, them)

Number, of course, refers to the singular/plural distinction. *Person* is related to point of view, the relationship of the writer to the reader. The reference of the first person includes the writer; second person refers to the person addressed; third person refers to "third parties," someone or something other than the writer or the person addressed. (*Note:* The second-person pronoun, *you,* sometimes has a more general meaning, as you read in Chapter 6—much more like third person point of view. See pages 125–126.)

The Missing Pronoun

This set of personal pronouns may look complete—and, unfortunately, it does include all we have. But, in fact, it has a gap, one that is responsible for a great deal of the **sexism** in our language. The gap occurs in the third-person singular slot, the slot that already includes three pronouns representing masculine *(he),* feminine *(she),* and neuter *(it).* You'd think that those three would be up to the task of covering all the contingencies, but they're not. For third-person singular we have no choice that is sex-neutral. When we need a pronoun to refer to an unidentified person, such as "the writer" or "a student" or just "someone," our long-standing tradition has been to use the masculine:

> The writer of this news story should have kept <u>his</u> personal opinion out of it.
>
> Someone left <u>his</u> book on the table.

But that usage is no longer automatically accepted. Times and attitudes change, and we have come to recognize the power of language in shaping those attitudes. So an important step in reshaping society's view of women has been to eliminate the automatic use of *he* and *his* and *him* when the sex of someone referred to could just as easily be female.

In a paragraph we looked at in Chapter 5 in connection with sentence rhythm, the writer has made an effort to avoid sexism with the generic *salesperson,* a title that has all but replaced the masculine *salesman.* But notice the pronoun in the last sentence:

> Never invest in something you don't understand or in the dream of an artful salesperson. Be a buyer, not a sellee. Figure out what you want (be it life insurance, mutual funds or a vacuum cleaner) and then shop for a good buy. Don't let someone else tell you what you need—at least not if he happens to be selling it.
>
> —Andrew Tobias

In speech we commonly use *they* for both singular and plural:

> Don't let someone else tell you what you need—at least not if <u>they</u> happen to be selling it.

Eventually, perhaps, the plural pronoun will take over for the singular; in the second person *(you/your/you),* we make no distinction between singular and plural, so it's not unreasonable to do the same in the third person. But such changes come slowly. What should we do in the meantime?

One common, but not necessarily effective, way to solve the problem of the pronoun gap is with *he or she:*

> ...at least not if <u>he or she</u> happens to be selling it.

An occasional *he or she* works in most situations like this one, but more than one in a paragraph will change the rhythm of the prose, slow the reader down, and call attention to itself when such attention is simply uncalled for.

The awkwardness of *he or she* in a passage becomes even more obvious when the possessive and objective case pronouns are also required. Avoiding sexist language by using *his or her* and *him or her* as well as *he or she* quickly renders the solution worse than the problem. Here, for example, is a passage from a 1981 issue of *Newsweek:*

> To the average American, the energy problem is mainly his monthly fuel bill and the cost of filling up his gas tank. He may also remember that in 1979, and way back in 1974, he

had to wait in long lines at gasoline stations. For all of this, he blames the "Arabs" or the oil companies or the government, or perhaps all three. Much of the information that he gets from the media, as well as his own past experience, tells him that energy prices will continue to go up sharply and that gas lines are going to come back whenever a conflict flares up in the Middle East.

—Fred Singer ("Hope for the Energy Shortage")

Now imagine a version in which the problem of sexism has been solved with *he or she:*

To the average American, the energy problem is mainly his or her monthly fuel bill and the cost of filling up his or her gas tank. He or she may also remember that in 1979, and way back in 1974, he or she had to wait in long lines at gasoline stations. For all of this, he or she blames the "Arabs" or the oil companies or the government, or perhaps all three. Much of the information that he or she gets from the media, as well as from his or her own past experience, tells him or her that energy prices will continue.... *Enough!*

That's only one short paragraph. Imagine reading a whole essay. Clearly, there are better solutions to the problem.

Because we do have a sex-neutral pronoun in the plural, often that singular noun can be changed to plural. In the *Newsweek* article, for example, the writer could have started out by discussing "average Americans":

To average Americans, the energy problem is mainly their monthly fuel bills and the cost of filling up their gas tanks.

That revision, of course, has changed the relationship of the writer to the reader: The writer is no longer addressing the reader as an individual—a change the writer may not want. Often, however, the plural is an easy and obvious solution. For example, in the following passages from books about language, the change to plural does not affect the overall meaning or intent:

Of all the developments in the history of m̶a̶n̶ the human race, surely the most remarkable was language, for with i̶t̶ ̶h̶e̶ our ancestors were was able to pass on their h̶i̶s̶ cultural heritage to succeeding generations who then did not have to rediscover how to make fire, where to hunt, or how

to build another wheel.

—Charles B. Martin and Curt M. Rulon

It has been said that whenever a person speaks he is either mim-

icking or analogizing.

above "a person": people
above "he is": they are

—Charles Hockett

We should emphasize that these quoted examples of sexist language were written several decades ago, when the masculine pronoun was the norm. Chances are, none of them would have been written in this way today. All of us who are involved with words, who are sensitive to the power of language, have gone through a consciousness raising in the matter of pronoun selection.

Here, then, are some of the ways in which you can make up for the pronoun gap when you write and/or revise your own sentences:

1. USE THE PLURAL:

Every writer should be aware of the power of language when <u>he</u> chooses <u>his</u> pronouns.
Revision: Writers should be aware of the power of language when <u>they</u> choose <u>their</u> pronouns.

2. USE *HE OR SHE* IF YOU CAN USE IT ONLY ONCE:

Revision: Every writer should be aware of the power of language when <u>he or she</u> chooses pronouns.

3. AVOID *HIS* AS A DETERMINER, EITHER BY SUBSTITUTING ANOTHER ONE OR, IN SOME CASES, DELETING THE DETERMINER:

The writer of the news story should have kept <u>his</u> opinion out of it.
Revision: The writer of the news story should have kept (<u>all</u>) opinion out of it.

4. TURN THE FULL CLAUSE INTO AN ELLIPTICAL CLAUSE OR A VERB PHRASE, THUS ELIMINATING THE PROBLEM SUBJECT:

Revision: Every writer should be aware of the power of language when <u>choosing pronouns.</u>

This fourth method of revision is often a good possibility because the offending pronoun nearly always shows up in the second clause of a passage, often as part of the same sentence. In our example, we have turned the complete subordinate clause into an elliptical clause—that is, a clause with something missing. In this case what's missing is the subject. (The elliptical clause, which may have hidden pitfalls, is discussed in Chapter 8.)

5. REWRITE THE ADVERBIAL CLAUSE AS A RELATIVE *(WHO)* CLAUSE:

When <u>a person</u> buys a house, he should shop carefully for the lowest interest rate.
Revision: <u>A person who</u> buys a house should shop carefully for the lowest interest rate.

The relative clause, with its neutral *who,* eliminates the necessity of a personal pronoun to rename *a person.*

6. CHANGE THE POINT OF VIEW:

Second person: As a writer <u>you</u> should be aware of the power of language when you choose <u>(your)</u> pronouns. When you buy a house, <u>you</u> should. . . .
First person: As writers, <u>we</u> should be aware of the power of language when we choose <u>(our)</u> pronouns.

See also the section called "The *Everyone/Their* Issue" on pages 265–267.

EXERCISE 42

1. Rewrite the *Newsweek* passage using the second person. (*Note:* You might begin with "If you are an average American …".)

2. The following passage was written in 1944, at a time when the masculine pronoun was accepted as the generic singular. Revise it to reflect today's concerns about sexism in language.

Of all born creatures, man is the only one that cannot live by bread alone. He lives as much by symbols as by sense report, in a realm compounded of tangible things and virtual images, of actual events and ominous portents,

always between fact and fiction. For he sees not only
actualities but meanings. He has, indeed, all the impulses
and interests of animal nature; he eats, sleeps, mates,
seeks comfort and safety, flees pain, falls sick and dies,
just as cats and bears and fishes and butterflies do. But he
has something more in his repertoire, too—he has laws
and religions, theories and dogmas, because he lives not
only through sense but through symbols. That is the special asset of his mind, which makes him the master of
earth and all its progeny.

—Susanne K. Langer ("The Prince of Creation," *Fortune*)

We *and* Us *as Determiners*

The possessive case of pronouns is the form we generally use as determiners, the signalers of nouns: *my* house, *our* friends, *their* new car. In
some circumstances, however, with the first person plural pronoun *(we,
us, our)*, the subjective and objective cases act as determiners. They
aren't very common in this function, so writers are sometimes unsure
of the form:

> We students got together and demonstrated against the proposed
> tuition increase.

> The boss requires us waiters to share our tips with the busing staff.

The form of the pronoun is determined by the function of the noun being
signaled: When it's a subject, as with *students,* the form is *we;* when it's an
object, as with *waiters,* the form is *us.*

An alternative interpretation of this pronoun + noun structure is that of
headword + appositive—the headword being the pronoun and the noun
the appositive that renames it. The important point to recognize is that the
case of the pronoun is determined by the function of the two-word structure, the slot in the sentence that it fills.

PERSONAL PRONOUN ERRORS
Case

Among the most common pronoun errors that writers make are the errors
of **case.** As you'll recall, case refers to the change that pronouns undergo
on the basis of their function in the sentence. Following are the various
forms for the three cases:

Subjective:	I	we	you	he	she	it	they
Possessive:	my	our	your	his	her	its	their
	(mine)	(ours)	(yours)	(his)	(hers)	(its)	(theirs)
Objective:	me	us	you	him	her	it	them

(You'll recall too that the relative pronoun *who* also has different endings for the possessive *[whose]* and objective *[whom]* cases, also determined by its function in the relative clause.)

The subject slot of the sentence, of course, takes the **subjective case**. The subjective case is also traditionally used in the subject complement slot following *be* as the main verb. For example, when a phone caller says,

"May I speak with Ann?"

Ann will reply,

"This is she,"

unless she wants to be informal, in which case she might reply,

"Speaking."

At any rate, she would not sound grammatical if she said,

"This is her."

On the other hand, the formal "It is I" is often replaced with the less formal "It's me," and nobody gets upset. In many writing situations, however, the informal "It's me" would be inappropriate. The writer who thinks that "It is I" is too formal (and sometimes it does sound stuffy) can probably find a way around it without being nonstandard.

In Chapter 1 the transitive verbs were defined as those with direct objects. When a pronoun fills that object slot, we use the **objective case:**

My roommate helped me with my biology assignment.

You'll recall that the Pattern 6 sentence has a second object slot: the indirect object. It, too, takes the objective case when it's filled by a pronoun:

Marie gave him a gift.

The other object slot we've been seeing in our sentences is that of object of the preposition. It's another that takes the objective case:

Marie gave a gift to him.
I walked to town with him.
I walked to town with Joe and him.

Joe walked to town <u>with him and me.</u>

Marie walked <u>between Joe and me.</u>

Pronouns in the **possessive case** function as determiners, or noun signalers. The alternative forms of the possessive case, shown on the chart in parentheses, are used when the headword of the noun phrase, the noun, is deleted:

This is <u>my bicycle.</u> ➤ This bicycle is <u>mine.</u>

This is <u>her bicycle.</u> ➤ This is <u>hers.</u>

We should note that nouns in the possessive case function in the same way:

This is <u>Pete's bicycle.</u> ➤ This is <u>Pete's.</u>

Most errors of case that writers make occur with the subjective and objective cases. And most of them probably occur as the result of hyper-correction:

*There's no rivalry between <u>my brother and I.</u>

*The supervisor told <u>Jenny and I</u> that we might get a raise next week.

In both cases, the noun/pronoun compound is functioning as an object, so the correct pronoun choice is *me,* not *I.* This is a common error, however, possibly because people remember being corrected by their parents or teachers when they said such sentences as

Me and Bill are going for a bike ride. ("No, dear. Bill and *I.*")

Bill and me are going to be late. ("No, dear. Bill and *I.*")

As a consequence of those early lessons, some people simply find it hard to say "my brother and me" or "Jenny and me," no matter what function the pronoun has in the sentence. The correct version of those sentences is,

There's no rivalry <u>between my brother and me.</u>

The supervisor told <u>Jenny and me</u> that we might get a raise next week.

If we substituted a pronoun for the complete noun phrase the sentence would be:

There's no rivalry <u>between us.</u>

The supervisor told <u>us</u> that we might get a raise next week.

We wouldn't consider for a moment using *we.*

The Unwanted Apostrophe

Perhaps the most common writing error of all—and not just among students—occurs with the pronoun *it:*

   *The cat caught it's tail in the door.

Here's the rule that's been broken with the word *it's:*

Personal pronouns have no apostrophes in the possessive case.

If you check the chart showing the case of the personal pronouns on page 257, you'll see that there are no apostrophes. Notice that the rule also applies to the alternative forms of the possessive—*hers* and *his* and *yours* and *theirs*—those that are used when the headword of the noun phrase is deleted. They have no apostrophes either. (For these pronouns, the rule is more logical because *their* and *his* and *her* and *your* are already in the possessive case.)

   This is their bicycle./This is theirs.
   This is her bicycle./This is hers.
   Where is your bicycle?/Where is yours?

   When we say that *it's* can mean only "it is" or "it has," we are actually stating an exception to the general apostrophe rule. In every other use of the *apostrophe+s*—that is, when we add *'s* to nouns and indefinite pronouns—there are three possible meanings. In the first two examples below the apostrophe signals a **contraction,** where part of a word—in fact, a whole syllable—has been deleted; the third example illustrates the possessive case:

   1. John's coming./Someone's coming. = *is coming*
   2. John's been here./Someone's been here. = *has been*
   3. John's hat is on the table./Someone's hat is on the table. = possessive case

It's certainly understandable for writers to treat *it* in the same way, to assume that the possessive case of *it* is formed by using the apostrophe with the *s,* as in the case with nouns and indefinite pronouns—in other words, that the word *it's* has the same three possible meanings that *John's* or *someone's* does. But it doesn't.

   The error probably occurs so easily because *it* is the only personal pronoun that gets that added *s,* as nouns do. The other personal pronouns actually have new forms for the possessive case, as the chart on page 257 shows: *I* becomes *my* in the possessive; *he* becomes *his; she* becomes *her; you* becomes *your; we* becomes *our;* and *they* becomes *their. It* is unique in that it retains its same form, with an added *s.*

Here's what you have to remember—and check for: When you add *'s* to *it,* you're actually writing "it is" or "it has"; the possessive case has no apostrophe. Because *it* is such a common word, and because the unwanted apostrophe is such an easy error to slip in, you should probably make a point of double-checking all instances of *its* and *it's* during your final proofreading.

The Ambiguous Antecedent

Another error that turns up with personal pronouns is the ambiguous **antecedent**—the pronoun that has more than one possible referent:

> When Bob accidentally backed the car into the toolshed, <u>it</u> was wrecked beyond repair.

Here we can't be sure if the pronoun *it* refers to the car or to the toolshed.

> Just before they were scheduled to leave, Shelley told Ann that <u>she</u> couldn't go after all.

Here we may suspect that *she* refers to Shelley—but we can't be sure. And the careful writer wouldn't make us guess.

> When the first-night audience was invited backstage to meet the cast, <u>they</u> had a wonderful time.

Here we assume that it's the audience that had a wonderful time; but the reader has every right to assume that a pronoun will refer to the last-mentioned possibility—in this case, *the cast.*

> Uncle Dick and Aunt Teresa took the kids to <u>their</u> favorite restaurant for lunch.

Whose favorite restaurant?

The ambiguous antecedent often gets resolved by the context; within a sentence or two the reader will very likely understand the writer's intention. But not always. And, of course, the reader shouldn't have to wait.

The Vague Antecedent

Our use of pronouns is dictated by our internal rules. In Chapter 1, in connection with the sentence slots, you saw how automatically you use pronouns when you substituted them for noun phrases:

The old gymnasium needs a new roof.

It   needs a new roof.

Here's a similar one:

My sister's boyfriend works for a meat-packing company.

He   works for a meat-packing company.

As you can clearly see, the pronoun stands in for the entire noun phrase, not just for the headword—and certainly not for a modifier of the headword. Now look at the following sentences with that principle in mind:

The neighbor's front porch is covered with trash, but *he* refuses to clean it up.

The neighbor's dog gets into my garbage every week, but *he* refuses to do anything about it.

My sister's boyfriend works for a meat-packing plant. *She's* a vegetarian.

It's hard to keep track of the administration's stand on immigration. *They* say something different every week.

Last summer I didn't get to a single baseball game, even though *it's* my favorite sport.

Notice what has happened. The subject of the second clause in each case is a pronoun. But its antecedent is not a complete noun phrase; it's only a noun modifier. The problem is not with communication: The reader will understand these sentences. And in a conversation we might not even notice anything amiss. But there is a problem of fuzziness that could easily cause a blip in the reader's comprehension. As writers we have the obligation to consider the reader's expectations, to get rid of the fuzziness caused by vague antecedents.

See also the discussion of broad references in the section headed Demonstrative Pronouns.

REFLEXIVE PRONOUNS

Reflexive pronouns are those formed by adding *–self* or *–selves* to a form of the personal pronoun: *myself, ourselves, yourself, yourselves, himself, herself, itself, themselves.* The standard rule for using the reflexive is straightforward. We use it as an object in a clause when its antecedent is the subject:

John cut himself.

I glanced at myself in the mirror.

Jack cooked an omelet for Barbara and himself.

I cooked breakfast for Kelly and myself.

The tendency toward hypercorrection occurs with the reflexives as well as with the personal pronouns. It's quite common to hear the reflexive where the standard rule calls for *me,* the straight objective case:

> *Tony cooked dinner for Carmen and <u>myself.</u>
>
> *The boss promised Pam and <u>myself</u> a year-end bonus.

Note that the antecedent of *myself* does not appear in either sentence. Another fairly common nonstandard usage occurs when speakers use *myself* in place of *I* as part of a compound subject:

> *Ted and <u>myself</u> decided to go out and celebrate.

These nonstandard ways of using the reflexive are probably related to emphasis as well as to hypercorrection. Somehow the two-syllable *myself* sounds more emphatic than either *me* or *I.*

The nonstandard use of the reflexive occurs only with the first-person pronoun, *myself,* not with *himself* or *herself.* In the case of third person, the personal pronoun and the reflexive produce different meanings:

> John cooked dinner for Jenny and <u>himself</u> (John).
>
> John cooked dinner for Jenny and <u>him</u> (someone else).

This second interpretation assumes that another person, a known "someone else," is part of the situation, otherwise, *him* refers to *John.*

Intensive Reflexive Pronouns

When we use the reflexive to add emphasis to a noun, we call it the **intensive reflexive pronoun.** It can appear in a number of positions:

> I <u>myself</u> prefer classical music.
>
> I prefer classical music <u>myself.</u>
>
> <u>Myself,</u> I prefer classical music.

Each of these versions produces a different rhythm pattern. In the first version, the main stress falls on *myself,* whereas in the second it probably falls on *classical.* In the third, added stress is given to *I.*

RECIPROCAL PRONOUNS

Each other and *one another* are known as the **reciprocal pronouns.** They serve either as determiners (in the possessive case) or as objects, referring to previously named nouns: *Each other* refers to two nouns; *one another* refers to three or more, a distinction that careful writers generally observe.

David and Ann help <u>each other.</u>

They even do <u>each other's</u> laundry.

All the students in my peer group help <u>one another</u> with their rough drafts.

DEMONSTRATIVE PRONOUNS

The demonstrative pronouns are used as determiners. They include the features of "number" and "proximity."

<u>PROXIMITY</u>	<u>NUMBER</u>	
	Singular	*Plural*
Near	this	these
Distant	that	those

<u>That</u> documentary we saw last night really made me think, but <u>this</u> one is a waste of time.

<u>Those</u> trees on the ridge were almost destroyed by the gypsy moths, but <u>these</u> seem perfectly healthy.

Like other determiner classes, the demonstrative pronoun can be a substitute for a noun phrase (or other nominal structure) as well as a signal for one:

<u>These old shoes and hats</u>   will be perfect for the costumes.

↓

<u>These</u>   will be perfect for the costumes.

To be effective, however, the demonstrative must replace or stand for a clearly stated antecedent. In the following example, which we saw in Chapter 9, *this* has no clear antecedent; there is no noun phrase in the first sentence that the demonstrative *this* stands for:

My roommate just told me she's planning to withdraw from school. <u>This</u> came as a surprise.

Here the subject of the second sentence, *this,* refers to the whole idea in the first sentence, not to a specific noun phrase, as pronouns usually do. Such sentences are not uncommon in speech, nor are they ungrammatical. But when a *this* or a *that* (or *it*) has this kind of **broad reference,** you can usually improve the sentence by providing a noun headword for the demonstrative pronoun—in other words, by turning the pronoun into a determiner, by using a complete noun phrase in place of the pronoun:

<u>This decision</u> came as a surprise.

or

<u>This news</u> came as a surprise.

When you don't provide that headword, you are making the reader do your work. If you have trouble pinning down the precise noun, you might be tempted to leave it out. But if you, the writer, have trouble, think of the problem the reader will have in trying to interpret your fuzzy pronoun.

EXERCISE 43

Edit the following passages, paying special attention to the pronoun problems.

1. Claire has always been interested in children and plans to make that her profession when she graduates. Both Claire and myself are majoring in early childhood education.

2. The goal of animal-rights activists is not just to prevent animal cruelty, as they advocated in earlier times, but also to promote the idea that they have intrinsic value, that they have a right to live. As a result of their efforts, the Public Health Service has revised their policy regarding the treatment of laboratory animals.

3. When my sister Beth asked me to go to Salem with her to visit our grandmother, I had no idea that she was sick. We were almost there before she told me she had had stomach cramps since early morning. Our grandmother took one look at her and called the doctor, then drove her to the hospital, which turned out to be a good decision. It turned out to be appendicitis.

INDEFINITE PRONOUNS

The **indefinite pronouns** include a number of words that we use as determiners:

> **Quantifiers**   *enough, few, fewer, less, little, many, much, several, more, most*
>
> **Universals:**   *all, both, every, each*
>
> **Partitives:**   *any, either, neither, none, some*

One is also commonly used as a pronoun (as are the other cardinal numbers—two, three, etc.) along with its negative, *none*. As a pronoun, *one* (or *ones*) often replaces only the headword, rather than the entire noun phrase:

The blue shoes that I bought yesterday will be perfect for the trip.
The blue ones that I bought yesterday will be perfect for the trip.

The personal pronoun, on the other hand, would replace the entire noun phrase:

They will be perfect for the trip.

The universal *every* and the partitives *any, no,* and *some* can be expanded with *–body, –thing,* and *–one:*

$$
\text{some}\begin{cases}\text{body}\\\text{thing}\\\text{one}\end{cases} \quad \text{every}\begin{cases}\text{body}\\\text{thing}\\\text{one}\end{cases} \quad \text{any}\begin{cases}\text{body}\\\text{thing}\\\text{one}\end{cases} \quad \text{no}\begin{cases}\text{body}\\\text{thing}\\\text{one (two words)}\end{cases}
$$

These pronouns can take modifiers in the form of clauses:

Anyone *who wants extra credit in psych class* can volunteer for tonight's experiment.

They can also be modified by participles or participial phrases:

Everyone *reporting late for practice* will take fifteen laps.

And by prepositional phrases:

Nothing *on the front page* interests me anymore.

And, unlike most nouns, they can be modified by adjectives that follow the headword:

I don't care for anything *sweet.*
I think that something *strange* is going on here.

Notice the strong stress that you put on the postnoun adjective.

The Everyone/Their *Issue*

The question of number—that is, whether a word is singular or plural—often comes up in reference to the indefinite pronouns *everyone* and *everybody.* In form they are singular, so as subjects they take the *–s* form of the verb or auxiliary in the present tense:

Everyone is leaving the room at once.

An illustration of the scene described by this sentence, however, would show more than one person—more than two or three, probably—leaving the room, even though the form of *everyone* is singular. In spite of this anomaly, the issue of subject–verb agreement is not a problem.

But often such a sentence calls for the possessive pronoun. And when it does, the traditional choice has been the singular masculine:

Everyone picked up <u>his</u> books and left the room.

But that makes no sense—even if the *everyone* refers to men only. And it certainly makes no sense if the group of people includes women. The only reasonable solution is the plural, in spite of the singular form of *everyone:*

Everyone picked up <u>their</u> books and left the room.

Unfortunately, even though the solution may be reasonable, your teacher is likely to mark *their* an error of pronoun/antecedent agreement.

It is interesting to discover that the problem arises only with the possessive pronoun. No one disputes the correctness of the subjective case, <u>they</u>:

The teacher asked everyone to leave, and <u>they</u> did.

Certainly *he* would make no sense at all. The objective case, too, requires the plural:

Everyone in the class cheered when the teacher told <u>them</u> the test had been canceled.

There is simply no logic in insisting on the singular for the possessive case when both logic and good grammar call for the plural in every other situation.

It's true that in form *everyone* is singular; this is also true of collective nouns, such as *crowd* or *group*. But these nouns call for plural pronouns when the members of the collection are seen as individuals:

The crowd began to raise <u>their</u> voices.

Everyone in the group began to raise <u>their</u> voices.

No matter how logical it may be to use the plural pronoun in reference to these indefinite pronouns, to do so contradicts the advice in most handbooks, most of which take the traditional view that *everyone* and *everybody* are singular and cannot be replaced by *they.* If you feel uneasy about using the plural because your reader—your composition teacher, perhaps, or your boss—may take the traditional view, you can always avoid the problem by substituting a different subject:

<u>All of the people</u> began to raise their voices.

<u>All of the students</u> picked up their books and left the room.

English is such a versatile language that we nearly always have alternatives.

EXERCISE 44

Edit the following passages, paying particular attention to the nonstandard use of pronouns and to those with unclear referents.

1. I recall with great pleasure the good times that us children had at our annual family reunions when I was young. Our cousins and ourselves, along with some younger aunts and uncles, played volleyball and softball until dark. They were a lot of fun.

2. Aunt Yvonne and Uncle Bob always brought enough homemade ice cream for them and everyone else as well. There was great rivalry, I remember, between my brother and I over who could eat the most. Nearly everyone made a pig of himself.

3. It seemed to my cousin Terry and I that the grownups were different people at those family reunions. That may be true of family reunions everywhere.

4. Nowadays my father seems to forget about them good days and concentrates on the sad ones instead. He often tells my brother and myself about his boyhood during the Great Depression. He remembers the long years of unemployment for he and his whole family with very little pleasure. That doesn't really surprise me, because they were hard times.

FOR GROUP DISCUSSION

The following paragraph includes twelve pronouns from four subclasses: personal, relative, demonstrative, and indefinite. The pronoun *it* accounts for six of the twelve, the first two in reference to *pyramid,* the other four to *management.*

Management as a practice is very old. The most successful executive in all history was surely that Egyptian who, 4,500 years or more ago, first conceived the pyramid, without any precedent, designed it, and built it, and did so in an astonishingly short time. That first pyramid still stands. But as a discipline, management is barely fifty years old. It was first dimly perceived around the time of the First World War. It did not emerge until the Second World War, and then did so primarily in the United States. Since then it has been the fastest-growing new function, and the study of it the fastest-growing new discipline. No function in history has emerged as quickly as has management in the past fifty or sixty years, and surely none has had such worldwide sweep in such a short period.

—Peter F. Drucker *(The Atlantic Monthly)*

Examine the sentences that include the four instances of *it* in reference to *management*. Consider ways of revising them that would cut down that number. One thing to think about is the place and frequency of the antecedent word, *management*.

In addition to the twelve pronouns, the paragraph also includes two instances of the word *so* in its role as a "pro-form." What does *so* stand in for?

KEY TERMS

Ambiguity	Indefinite pronoun	Pronoun
Antecedent	Intensive reflexive	Reciprocal pronoun
Broad reference	pronoun	Referent
Case	Number	Reflexive pronoun
Demonstrative	Objective case	Sexism
pronoun	Person	Subjective case
Determiner	Personal pronoun	
Everyone/their issue	Possessive case	

RHETORICAL REMINDERS

Sexism

Have I avoided sexism in my choice of pronouns?

Have I avoided the awkward *he/she* and *his/her*?

Case

Have I used the objective case *(me, him, her)* for object slots in the sentence?

Have I avoided "between _____ and I"?

Have I kept apostrophes out of possessive pronouns *(its, hers, theirs)?*

Antecedents

Have I avoided ambiguous antecedents? Does my reader understand the referent of every *he, his, him, she, they,* and so on?

Reflexives

Have I used the reflexive pronoun *(-self, -selves)* only in object positions and only when its referent precedes it in the sentence?

Broad Reference

Have I avoided the fuzzy use of the broad-reference *this* and *that?*

PUNCTUATION REMINDER

Have I remembered that personal pronouns—including *it*—do not take an apostrophe in the possessive case?

Punctuation:
Its Purposes, Its Hierarchy,
and Its Rhetorical Effects

CHAPTER PREVIEW

In the preceding chapters, you learned about the structure of sentences: their basic slots and the options we have for expanding and combining them. An important consideration throughout the book has been the effect of those options on the reader—hence the word *rhetorical* in the title. Those rhetorical effects extend also to punctuation, so in addition to the possibilities for constructing sentences, you have learned about both the required and the optional punctuation rules that apply.

As you might expect, the conventions of punctuation have changed through the centuries, just as language itself has changed. Early punctuation practices, designed to assist in the oral reading of medieval manuscripts, eventually evolved into our modern system, based more on structural boundaries than on the oral reader's needs. By the eighteenth and nineteenth centuries, the system we know today was generally in place. However, even though our punctuation rules are well established, they still include a great deal of flexibility. They are open to changing styles. Today we tend toward an "open" or "light" style, omitting commas where they are optional, where the boundaries are apparent without them. For example, modern writers often omit the comma with *and* in a series (known as the *serial comma*), as well as the comma following certain introductory adverbial phrases:

At the grocery store I bought milk, eggs and cheese.

If both optional commas were included, the sentence would have a "heavy," overpunctuated appearance:

At the grocery store, I bought milk, eggs, and cheese.

It's not unusual for writers to sometimes make punctuation decisions in this way, based on aesthetic grounds, on the look of the sentence.

(The writer who prefers both of those commas on principle but wants to avoid the heavy look they create can revise the sentence by putting the opening phrase in closing position. There it will not be set off: "I bought milk, eggs, and cheese at the grocery store.")

In this chapter we look more closely at the punctuation decisions that writers make. First we focus on the underlying purposes of punctuation rules; then we will examine punctuation as a hierarchy, a description that can sometimes help you make those decisions; finally, we review the rhetorical effect of your punctuation decisions. At the end of the chapter you will find a brief glossary of the punctuation rules that have been described in the earlier chapters, covering commas, colons, dashes, semicolons, and parentheses, along with a few other issues that writers must deal with in connection with these and other punctuation marks. This section will serve as a handy reference tool.

THE PURPOSES OF PUNCTUATION MARKS

In his book *A Linguistic Study of American Punctuation,* Charles F. Meyer classifies the purposes of punctuation into three categories: syntactic, prosodic, and semantic. Although you may not recognize these three words, they do in fact describe the punctuation principles you have been studying in the preceding chapters.

> *Syntax* refers to the structure of sentences—the main subject matter of this book. When you learned about the parts of the sentence and their relationships and their expansions, you were learning about syntax.
>
> *Prosody* is the study of rhythm and intonation, which you remember especially from Chapter 5.
>
> *Semantics* is the study of meaning.

Syntax

Linguists generally agree that the purpose underlying most of our punctuation rules is syntactic: In other words, the structure of the sentence determines the punctuation marks it will contain. A good example of a syntactically based punctuation rule is the one you learned in connection with the sentence patterns in Chapter 1: "Do not mark slot boundaries with punctuation." This rule is clearly based on syntax, on sentence structure. In fact, syntax overrides all considerations of rhythm. Even though the reader may have to stop for breath between slots, that pause is not marked by a comma. Here's an example from Chapter 1 of a fairly long sentence, one that requires an extra breath—but has no boundaries that take punctuation:

> The images and information sent back by *Voyager 2* have given space scientists here on Earth enough information about four of our distant planets to keep them busy for years to come.

The predicate contains an indirect object and a direct object with two post-noun modifiers, but not one of those boundaries calls for punctuation.

Prosody

We often revise a sentence in order to change the way that the reader will read it—to change its rhythm pattern. For example, the intonation pattern of the sentence you just read would change if the first two words were reversed:

> Often we revise a sentence...

With this word order the reader will probably put more stress on *often*. To guarantee that emphasis, we can follow *often* with a comma. You'll recall from the discussion of sentence rhythm in Chapter 5 that the visual signal of a comma causes the reader to give added length and stress to the preceding word.

> Often, we revise a sentence...

This, then, is an example where the purpose of the punctuation mark can be attributed to prosody. There's simply no other reason for that comma.

In Chapter 10 we saw another example of prosody in the discussion of the coordinate series, when we compared the rhythm patterns of two punctuation styles:

1. You have your own style of writing, just as you have your own style of walking and whistling and wearing your hair.
2. You have your own style of writing, just as you have your own style of walking, whistling, wearing your hair.

It is the rhythm of (2) that changes the message: It has an open-ended quality, as if to suggest, "I could go on and on with the list." Again, the purpose of the punctuation is to produce that rhythm. In this case, however, we would have to say that semantics is also involved: The punctuation affects both the rhythm and the meaning.

Semantics

One situation in which semantics, or meaning, determines the need for punctuation is that of the nonrestrictive phrase or clause, as we saw in the discussion of noun modifiers in Chapter 9. Syntax, of course, determines the boundaries of that modifier, but semantic considerations dictate the presence or absence of the commas: Does the modifier define the noun or simply comment on it?

This pair of sentences illustrates the distinction:

1. The man sitting by the window is talking to himself.
2. My mother, sitting by the window, is talking to herself.

We can assume in (1) that the scene includes at least one other man and that the purpose of the participial phrase is to identify the referent of the subject noun phrase, *the man.* That kind of identification is unnecessary in (2), where the subject noun phrase, *my mother,* has only one possible referent—no matter how many other women are present. Here the participial phrase merely comments.

The purpose of the punctuation is perhaps even more obviously a semantic one for the writer who has to decide between the following:

1. My sister Mary is coming for a visit.
2. My sister, Mary, is coming for a visit.

The sentence without commas implies that the writer has more than one sister. Clearly, it's the meaning that dictates the use of the comma.

The following pair also makes clear that the purpose of punctuation is sometimes semantic:

1. Call the boss Henry.
2. Call the boss, Henry.

These two are different sentence patterns: In (1) *Henry* is an object complement; in (2) *Henry* is a noun of direct address, known as a **vocative.**

Meyer cites the following pair of sentences to illustrate another situation where the comma changes the meaning:

1. Earlier negotiations were planned.
2. Earlier, negotiations were planned.

Here the punctuation has actually changed the class of the word *earlier.* In (1) it is an adjective, a modifier of the noun; in (2) it is an adverb, modifying the whole sentence.

In both of these last two examples, where the comma changes the meaning, it also alters the structure, the syntax, of the sentence. And it changes the rhythm. So these are probably good examples to illustrate the combination of all three punctuation purposes: syntactic, prosodic, and semantic.

THE HIERARCHY OF PUNCTUATION

If you were asked to place the parts of the sentence into a hierarchy, starting with "word," the result would look like this:

> word
>
> phrase
>
> clause
>
> sentence

The hierarchy of punctuation works in much the same way, usually in reverse order, with "sentence" at the top.

In the study of punctuation cited earlier, Meyer describes the hierarchy, the levels of punctuation, according to the kinds of boundaries that a particular punctuation mark encloses. For example, occupying the top level are the period, the question mark, and the exclamation point, all of which define sentence boundaries—and only sentence boundaries.

At the next level are the colon, the dash, and parentheses, all of which can define sentence boundaries, but also define the boundaries of clauses and phrases and words.

The semicolon occupies the next level. It also defines sentence boundaries, but in a much more limited way than the other three; and it has only one other role, that of the coordinate series.

At the bottom level of the hierarchy is the comma, which can define word and phrase and clause boundaries, but not sentence boundaries.[1]

Here then is the hierarchy of punctuation marks:

> period, question mark, exclamation point
>
> colon, dash, parentheses
>
> semicolon
>
> comma

The hierarchy is obviously not a measure of importance or of frequency. In fact, the comma, although it occupies the lowest level, is our most fre-

---

[1]When a comma does define the sentence boundary, it is called a comma splice—usually considered an error but sometimes used for special effect. See pages 46–49.

quent punctuation mark; and the exclamation point, one of three marks at the highest level, is the least frequent. The purpose of this scheme, rather, is to recognize the level of the functions that these marks can perform. For example, in Chapter 9 we looked at the following sentence in connection with appositives:

> Three committees—program, finance, and local arrangements— were set up to plan the convention.

The word boundaries here, marked by commas, are subordinate to those of the phrase boundaries; in order to distinguish the two levels, then, we use two different punctuation marks. The dashes mark the higher, or super-ordinate, level. To use commas for both levels of punctuation would make the sentence difficult to read. In the following version of the sentence, where the word boundaries are taken care of by conjunctions rather than commas, we have used commas for the phrase boundaries:

> Three committees, program and finance and local arrangements, were set up to plan the convention.

However, we could have retained the dashes in this revision, even though the phrase has no internal commas. Dashes would make the series stand out more strongly.

Because commas play so many roles in the sentence—providing boundaries for words and phrases and clauses—a sentence, especially a long one, can sometimes become heavy with commas:

> During the second two-year stretch of a president's term in office, he may find himself on the defensive, even with his own party, and, when, as frequently happens, his party loses a number of Senate and House seats in the midterm election, that second stretch can become even more defensive.

This sentence contains many levels of punctuation, with its coordinate independent clauses. The first clause contains opening and closing adverbial phrases, both of which are set off by commas. The other independent clause includes a subordinate *as*-clause embedded in a subordinate *when*-clause. Yet the only internal punctuation mark used for all of these levels is the comma.

One way to improve the sentence, to make it clearer for the reader, is to consider other punctuation marks that perform at some of these levels. One obvious boundary where we can use different punctuation is at the clause level—that is, to mark the two independent clauses—in place of the comma following *party*. We know that colons, dashes, and semicolons can all mark clause boundaries. In this case the best choice is the semi-colon, because of its "and" meaning. (You'll recall that the colon generally connects two sentences with a "namely" or "here it comes" meaning—rather than "and.") Another choice is to begin a new sentence here. The semicolon, however, makes clear the close connection of the two inde-pendent clauses.

Next we should look at the comma following *and:* What is its function? It works with a partner, the comma after *election,* to set off the subordinate *when*-clause. Is there any other mark that can do that job? In this position, the answer is probably "no." (On some occasions, dashes or parentheses can enclose subordinate clauses, as we shall see later.) But now that we've substi-tuted a semicolon, it is possible to eliminate *and.* After all, the reason for the *and* was the comma, which we've deleted. (You'll recall the rule about con-necting two independent clauses with a comma: It requires a conjunction.)

Already our sentence looks better—and reads much more easily:

> During the second two-year stretch of a president's term in office, he may find himself on the defensive, even with his own party; when, as frequently happens, his party loses a number of Senate and House seats in the midterm election, that second stretch can become even more defensive.

We're also using a comma here to set off the opening prepositional phrase. There's nothing else that can do that job, so that one has to stay. And we're using commas to set off the *as*-clause within the *when*-clause. Have we any other choice? Well, yes. We could mark that boundary with dashes—if we think it deserves the extra attention that dashes provide:

> During the second two-year stretch of a president's term in office, he may find himself on the defensive, even with his own party; when—as frequently happens—his party loses a number of Sen-ate and House seats in the midterm election, that second stretch can become even more defensive.

You may have noticed another place where a dash would fit: in the first clause after *defensive,* to set off the adverbial *even*-phrase—in this case, only one dash, not a pair. But we probably don't want dashes in both places: They lose their special quality when they're used too often. And twice in one sentence is probably too often. We'll want to try it out in that earlier spot, just to see the difference. But chances are we'll leave the dashes where we have them now, where they replace two commas.

Now compare the two versions of that sentence—the original and the last revision. They're both punctuated "correctly." But certainly the difference makes clear how important it is for the writer to understand the various boundaries that require punctuation, to know how the tools of punctuation work.

THE RHETORICAL EFFECTS OF PUNCTUATION

The important word in the subtitle of this book—*Grammatical Choices, Rhetorical Effects*—is the word *Choices*. In fact, *Choices* could almost serve as the book's complete title. A theme that runs throughout the chapters is the importance of understanding consciously the language structures you use subconsciously so that you can choose the structures that will achieve your desired rhetorical effects. When you understand how those structures work, they become effective tools in your hands. Those grammatical choices, of course, include punctuation choices.

In Chapter 3 you studied a variety of ways to combine the clauses into a compound sentence with the comma, the semicolon, and the colon. These five variations offer as many choices as you will ever need in this situation for effecting appropriate responses in your reader:

1. I loved the book, but I hated the movie.
2. I loved the book; but I hated the movie.
3. I loved the book; I hated the movie.
4. I loved the book; however, I hated the movie.
5. I loved the book: I hated the movie.

The first one we might think of as the basic compound-sentence rule, the comma-plus-conjunction, which puts fairly equal emphasis on the two clauses. The next three, with the greater pause the semicolon gives the reader, put more emphasis on the second clause. But there are differences among them too. Seeing the bare semicolon of (3), the reader will sense a kind of tight finality—no argument, no concessions; the addition of *however* in (4) adds a note of deliberation, a degree of thoughtfulness in coming to a decision about the movie. The colon in (5) commands special attention: The reader will pause and give even more stress to the word of contrast, *hated*, than in the other four versions.

How about using just the comma—in other words, a comma splice? The sentences are certainly short and closely connected:

I loved the book, I hated the movie.

Yes, that choice could work. (After all, it's not always an error—at least, not when famous writers use it.) The comma splice gives both clauses a kind of flatness—especially the second one. As in the version with the bare semicolon, the reader will sense that same "no argument" tone. However— and this "however" is important—that comma splice will work best if you're one of those famous writers. Then the reader will recognize your choice as deliberate, not as an error: The reader will know that you know the rule. But in an essay for your English class, the teacher will probably mark the comma splice as an error and ask you to review the rule. On the job, your supervisor will probably fix the splice before handing your report on to the next level—and be on the lookout in your next report. And a prospective employer who spots a comma splice in your letter of application might see it as an error—and remain prospective.

In a survey of 3,000 college essays that had been marked by English teachers, researchers found that the comma splice was the second most commonly marked punctuation error.[2] So you see, teachers do take it seriously. As you read earlier, those five rules offer as many choices in that punctuation situation as you will ever need for effecting the response you are looking for.

The most commonly marked punctuation error in that survey was the omitted comma following an introductory element. This situation is covered in several of the highlighted rules you read in previous chapters: Where that introductory element is a verb phrase or contains a verb phrase and where the introductory element is a subordinate (adverbial) clause, the comma is required. Here are some examples:

To understand the punctuation of compound sentences, you have to recognize independent clauses.

After examining the marked errors in 3,000 papers, the researchers published their findings.

When the researchers examined those papers, they discovered the most common error of all: the misspelled word.

Writers rarely deviate from this punctuation. However, when that opening structure is a prepositional phrase, you have a choice. If you want the reader to pause, to put strong stress on the opening element, particularly on its last word, then go ahead and use the comma:

In that survey, the third most commonly marked punctuation error was the lack of a possessive apostrophe.

You might recall that the comma is recommended for the opening prepositional phrase if it exceeds five or six words. That recommendation is related to readability. If the comma would help the reader, you'll want to include it, no matter how many words in the opener.

---

[2]See the article by Connors and Lunsford listed in the Bibliography.

The highlighted boxes throughout the book are reserved for those rules that constitute agreed-upon conventions. They are rules that you should know thoroughly. And while it's true that writers do deviate from them on occasion, you will want to consider the effect on your reader before doing so. Chances are, the reader will have more confidence in your ideas when you demonstrate your expertise of the standard punctuation conventions—even those situations where deviations from the standard may be common.

Not all of the punctuation rules in the first eleven chapters are highlighted. For example, there is no hard and fast rule about the serial comma (page 42). And certainly the use of conjunctions in the series rather than commas will produce quite different rhetorical effects. Another discussion that emphasizes variation describes the choices we have with dashes and colons for special emphasis (page 202). With these two punctuation marks, you achieve different levels of formality. And using them well can affect the reader's judgment of your ability as a writer—and very likely the reader's judgment of your ideas.

If you had the notion, before studying *Rhetorical Grammar,* that punctuation is nothing more than a final, added-on step in the writing process, I hope you have learned otherwise. Many of the punctuation choices you make are determined by the rhetorical situation; those choices are an integral part of the composing and revision stages in all of your writing tasks.

Remember, punctuation can do in writing what your voice does in speech—not as well in many cases, but even better in some. Punctuation helps the reader hear your voice and understand your message.

FOR GROUP DISCUSSION

1. One of Robert Frost's most famous poems is "Stopping by Woods on a Snowy Evening." In some printed versions the last stanza begins like this:

   The woods are lovely, dark, and deep,
   But I have promises to keep

   In others, the punctuation of the first line follows the poet's original:

   The woods are lovely, dark and deep,

   Given what you know about the punctuation of the series and of the appositive, do you think that these two versions mean the same thing? If they do, why would anyone object to that extra comma?

2. In the discussion of the serial comma in Chapter 3, we looked at a sentence without the comma before *and:*

> Individuals are acquiring more control over their lives, their minds and their bodies, even their genes, thanks to the transformations in medicine, communications, transportation and industry.

Is it possible that the group of three noun phrases—*their lives, their minds, their bodies*—is not intended to be a group, a series? What other function might "their minds and their bodies" have? Show how we might punctuate it without ambiguity in two different ways, depending on its meaning.

EXERCISE 45

The following paragraphs are reproduced exactly as they were published— with one exception: *All internal punctuation has been removed; only the sentence-end marks have been retained.* Your job is to put the punctuation marks back into the sentences. (Don't forget hyphens and apostrophes!) As you know, punctuation rules are not carved in stone; consequently, in some places your version may differ from the original—and still be correct. You can check your versions against those of the authors in the Answers to the Exercises section.

> Management is still taught in most business schools as a bundle of techniques such as budgeting and personnel relations. To be sure management like any other work has its own tools and its own techniques. But just as the essence of medicine is not urinalysis important though that is the essence of management is not techniques and procedures. The essence of management is to make knowledge productive. Management in other words is a social function. And in its practice management is truly a liberal art.
>
> The old communities family village parish and so on have all but disappeared in the knowledge society. Their place has largely been taken by the new unit of social integration the organization. Where community was fate organization is voluntary membership. Where community claimed the entire person organization is a means to a person's ends a tool. For 200 years a hot debate has been raging especially in the West are communities organic or are they simply extensions of the peo-

ple of which they are made? Nobody would claim that the new organization is organic. It is clearly an artifact a creation of man a social technology.

—Peter F. Drucker *(The Atlantic Monthly)*

The charter school movement is not yet big. Just 11 states beginning with Minnesota in 1991 have passed laws permitting the creation of autonomous public schools like Northland a dozen more have similar laws in the works. Most states have restricted the number of these schools 100 in California 25 in Massachusetts in an attempt to appease teachers unions and other opponents. Nevertheless the charter movement is being heralded as the latest and best hope for a public education system that has failed to deliver for too many children and cannot compete internationally.

A handful of other places notably Baltimore Maryland and Hartford Connecticut are experimenting with a far more radical way to circumvent bureaucracy hiring a for profit company to run the schools.

—Claudia Wallis *(Time)*

KEY TERMS

Colon	Prosody	Semantics
Comma	Punctuation	Semicolon
Dash	Punctuation	Syntax
Exclamation point	hierarchy	Vocative
Parentheses	Question mark	

Glossary of Punctuation

Apostrophe

1. Possessive Case

A. For Singular Nouns

To show the possessive case, add *'s* to singular nouns, both common and proper:

Bob's friend   the ocean's blue color

The rule also applies to indefinite pronouns:

someone's book   everyone's vote

Note. The one exception to this rule applies to the pronoun *it,* which we turn into possessive without an apostrophe—only the *s:*

The car lost its brakes.

(All other personal pronouns have a separate form for the possessive: I/ *my;* she/ *her;* he/ *his;* you/ *your;* we/ *our;* they/ *their.*)

This exception for the pronoun *it* causes endless errors. It's hard to remember that *it's* always means "it is" or "it has," whereas in the case of all other nouns and the indefinite pronouns, the *'s* has three possibilities:

John's here. = John *is* here.
John's been here. = John *has* been here.
John's book is here. = John owns the book (possessive)

When a singular noun ends in *s,* the rule gets a bit fuzzy. A good rule of thumb is related to pronunciation: When you add the sound of *s* in forming the possessive case (Ross's friend), add the letter *s* with the apostrophe; however, if you pronounce the possessive *without* adding an *s* sound, do *not* add the letter: Jesus' followers, Texas' laws.

B. For Plural Nouns

To make a regular plural noun possessive, add only the apostrophe:

the cats' tails   the students' complaints

For irregular plurals (those formed without adding *s*), add *'s:*

the women's movement   children's books

2. **Plurals of Initials and Words Other Than Nouns**
In making initials and non-nouns plural, when the addition of *s* alone would be misleading, include an apostrophe:

A's and B's (but ABCs)   p's and q's
do's and don't's

3. **Contractions**
In writing contractions, use an apostrophe to replace the missing syllable or letter(s):

don't = do not   he'll = he will
it's = it is, it has   can't = cannot
Pat's = Pat is, Pat has

Brackets

1. **Within Parentheses**
Use brackets for parenthetical material that is already within parentheses:

> The anthropologist who lived with the Iks in northern Uganda (reported by Lewis Thomas in *The Lives of a Cell* [1974]) apparently detested the tribe he was studying.

2. **In Quoted Material**
Use brackets for interpolations or explanations within quoted material—to show that it is not part of the quotation:

> "Everyone close to the king surmised that she [Mrs. Simpson] would be nothing but trouble for the realm."

Colon

1. **Appositives**
Use the colon to introduce an appositive or a list of appositives:

> The board appointed three committees to plan the convention: finance, program, and local arrangements.

Often such a list is introduced by "as follows" or "the following":

> The three committees are as follows: finance, program, and local arrangements.
> The board appointed the following committees: finance, program, and local arrangements.

Remember that a complete sentence precedes the colon; what follows the colon is an appositive. *Do not* put a colon between a linking verb and the subject complement:

> *The committees that were appointed are: finance, program, and local arrangements.

2. **Conjunction of Sentences**
Use a colon to join the two independent clauses of a compound sentence, where the second completes the idea, or the promise, of the first. The connection often means "namely" or "that is":

> To the rest of the nation, the baseball strike and hockey lockout share one characteristic: they both seem downright stupid.
>
> *—Time*

Only one obstacle lay between us and success: We had to come up with
the money.

Note. The convention of capitalizing the first word of a complete sentence following the colon is on the fence: Some publishers always capitalize; others capitalize only when what follows is a direct quotation; others capitalize questions
and direct quotations. Whichever method you follow, as with any optional convention, be sure to follow it consistently.

Comma

1. **Compound Sentences**
   Use a comma along with a coordinating conjunction between the clauses in a
   compound sentence:

   > I didn't believe a word Phil said, and I told him so.

   Remember that the comma alone produces a comma splice.

2. **Series**
   Use commas when listing a series of three or more sentence elements:

   > We gossiped, laughed, and sang the old songs at our class reunion.
   > We hunted in the basement, in the attic, and through all the storage
   > rooms, to no avail.

   The serial comma, the one before *and,* is optional; however, usage—either with
   or without it—must be consistent.

3. **Introductory Subordinate Clauses**
   Use a comma to set off an introductory subordinate clause:

   > When the riot started, the police fired tear gas into the crowd.
   > Because the 1993 flood was so devastating, some farmers in the Mid-
   > west decided to relocate.

4. **Sentence–ending Clauses**
   Use a comma to set off a subordinate clause following the main clause if the
   subordinate clause has no effect on the outcome of the main clause:

   > Some people refused to leave their homes, even though the hurricane
   > winds had started.

   Note that in the following sentences the idea in the main clause will not be realized without the subordinate clause; therefore, we use no comma:

   > I'll pack up and leave if you tell me to.
   > We left the area because we were afraid to stay.

   In general, *if* and *because* clauses are not set off; those introduced by *although* and
   even though are. If you are in doubt about the punctuation of the clause in post-
   sentence position, you can shift it to the beginning of the sentence; there it will
   always be set off.

   You should also be aware that the rules regarding subordinate clauses are
   among the least standardized of our punctuation conventions.

5. **Introductory Verb Phrases**
   Use a comma to set off any introductory phrase that contains a verb:

   > After studying all weekend, I felt absolutely prepared for the midterm exam.

Having worked at McDonald's for the past four summers, Maxie felt
confident when he applied for the job of assistant manager.

To get in shape for ski season, my roommate has begun working out on
the NordicTrack.

Note. In most cases the subject of the sentence must also be the subject of the
verb in that introductory phrase; otherwise, the verb phrase dangles. Exceptions
occur with set phrases:

Speaking of the weather, let's have a picnic.

To tell the truth, I have never read *Silas Marner.*

6. **Introductory Prepositional Phrases**
Use a comma to set off adverbial prepositional phrases of approximately six or
more words:

Toward the end of the semester, everyone in my dorm starts to study
seriously.

It is perfectly acceptable to set off shorter prepositional phrases, especially if you
think the reader should pause. For example, information of specific dates is
sometimes set off:

In 1994, the Republicans gained strength in the midterm election.

In making the decision about such commas, consider the punctuation in the
rest of the sentence: Don't overload the sentence with commas.
Set off any prepositional phrase that might cause a misreading:

During the summer, vacation plans are our main topic of conversation.

See the next section for prepositional phrases that are parenthetical.

7. **Other Sentence Modifiers**
Set off words and phrases that modify the whole sentence or that have a parenthetical meaning—at both the beginning and the end of the sentence:

A. Adverbs

Luckily, we escaped without a scratch.
We escaped without a scratch, luckily.
Meanwhile, there was nothing to do but wait.

B. *Yes* and *no:*

Yes, he's the culprit.
No, I can't go out tonight.

C. Prepositional phrases

In fact, there was nothing I could do about her problem.
In the meantime, I listened to her sad tale.

These parenthetical words and phrases often provide a transitional tie to
the previous sentence, which the comma emphasizes. They are also used
to slow the reader down or to shift the point of sentence stress.

D. Absolute phrases

The rain having stopped, Doug and Deborah decided to go
ahead with the picnic.

Eben and Paula relaxed in front of the fire, their feet propped on the coffee table.

8. **Nonrestrictive Modifiers**

Use commas to set off commenting (nonrestrictive) modifiers in the noun phrase. Remember that an adjectival is nonrestrictive when the referent of the noun it modifies is already clear to the reader or if the noun has only one possible referent:

My oldest brother, a senior history major, spends every night in the library.

9. **Coordinate Adjectives**

Use commas in the noun phrase between coordinate adjectives in preheadword position. Coordinate refers to adjectives of the same class—for example, subjective qualities:

a tender, delightful love story
a challenging, educational experience
a tall young man
a huge red ball

A good rule of thumb for making a decision about commas between these prenoun modifiers is this: If you could insert *and* or *but,* use a comma:

A tender and delightful love story

Notice that the two phrases without commas contain adjectives from different classes (height, age, size, color)—so they will not be separated:

*a tall and young man
*a huge and red ball

10. **Nouns of Direct Address**

Use a comma to set off nouns of direct address in both opening and closing position:

Students, your time is up.
Put your pencils down, everyone.
Help me, dear.

11. **Direct Quotations**

Use commas to set off direct quotations that fill the direct object slot after verbs such as *say* and *reply:*

The waiter said, "Good evening. My name is Pierre."
Harold replied, "I'm Harold, and this is Joyce."

Note. This is actually an exception to the punctuation rule you learned in Chapter 1: "Do not mark the boundaries of the basic sentence slots with commas." When the direct object is a direct quotation, we do mark the boundary.

Direct quotations can also be introduced by colons:

Harold replied: "I'm Harold, and this is Joyce."

12. **State and Year**

Use commas to set off the name of a state when it follows the name of a city:

I was surprised to learn that Cheyenne, Wyoming, isn't a larger city.

Also set off the year in a complete date:

> I remember where I was on November 22, 1963, when I heard the news reports of President Kennedy's assassination.

Notice that we include commas both before and after the state name and the year.

Dash

1. **Interruptions within a Sentence**
   Use a dash (or pair of dashes) to set off any interrupting structure within the sentence or at the end:

   > Tim decided to quit his job—a brave decision, in my opinion—and to look for something new.
   > Tim decided to quit his job and look for another—a brave decision.

   When the interrupter is a complete sentence, it is punctuated as a phrase would be:

   > Tim quit his job—he was always a rash young man—to follow Horace Greeley's advice and go West.

2. **Appositives**
   Use dashes to call attention to an appositive:

   > The microorganisms that seem to have it in for us in the worst way—the ones that really appear to wish us ill—turn out on close examination to be rather more like bystanders, strays, strangers in from the cold.
   >   —Lewis Thomas

   Use a pair of dashes to set off a list of appositives that are themselves separated by commas:

   > All of the committees—finance, program, and local arrangements— went to work with real enthusiasm.

   The list of appositives set off by a dash can also come at the beginning of the sentence when the subject is a pronoun referring to the list:

   > The faculty, the students, the staff—all were opposed to the provost's decision to reinstate the old dormitory regulations.

   Namely and *that is,* both of which are signalers of appositives, can be preceded by either a dash or a comma; the dash gives the appositive more emphasis:

   > Some mammals have no hair—namely, the whales.
   > The provost's decision brought out over 1,500 student protesters, that is, a third of the student body.

Ellipsis Points

1. Three periods, each preceded and followed by a space, are used to indicate the omission of one or more words within a quoted sentence. An omission at the end of a sentence is indicated by a period (preceded by no space) followed by three spaced periods. Here is an original sentence and the cut versions that illustrate these two styles:

   > A group of the West Oxfordshire local squires and the wealthier farmers, just like their opposite numbers in countless other towns

and villages up and down the country, had decided to have the local fields apportioned privately, and farmed efficiently. A surveyor was needed, and Webb was brought over from Stow-on-the-Wold, ten miles away.

—Simon Winchester *(The Map That Changed the World)*

A group of the West Oxfordshire local squires and the wealthier farmers...had decided to have the local fields apportioned privately, and farmed efficiently. A surveyor was needed....

2. Four periods are also used for the omission of a complete sentence or more, even a complete paragraph. In poetry the omission of a line is indicated by a complete line of periods.

Exclamation Point

1. Exclamatory Sentence

The exclamation point is the terminal punctuation for the exclamatory sentence, a transformation that changes the emphasis of a declarative sentence, usually with a *what* or *how:*

We have a hard-working committee.
What a hard-working committee we have!
It's a gorgeous day.
What a gorgeous day it is!

The exclamation point is actually optional—and in some cases would be inappropriate:

How calm the ocean is today.
What a sweet child you have.

2. Emphasis

The exclamation point is used in sentences that call for added emotions; however, it should be used sparingly. It is rarely used in formal prose.

"Get out!" he shouted. "I never want to see you again!"
The history exam held a real surprise for me: I had studied the wrong chapters!

Hyphen

1. Compound Words or Phrases

The hyphen expresses a compound word or phrase in prenoun position as a unit:

a two-inch board
a silver-plated teapot
a well-designed running shoe
an out-of-work carpenter

Note that when they are not in prenoun position the hyphens are not needed in most cases:

The board is two inches wide.
The shoe was well designed.
The carpenter is out of work.

When the modifier in prenoun position is an *–ly* adverb, the hyphen is not used:

a nicely designed running shoe
a clearly phrased message

Parentheses

1. Interruptions

Parentheses, in many cases, function just as dashes and commas do—to set off explanatory information or, in some cases, the writer's digressions:

I stopped her and put a five-sou piece (a little more than a farthing) into her hand.

—George Orwell

It is hard to remember, when reading the Notebooks, that Camus was a man who had a very interesting life, a life (unlike that of many writers) interesting not only in an interior but also in an outward sense.

—Susan Sontag

Unlike dashes, which call attention to a passage, the parentheses generally add the information as an aside: They say, "By the way," whereas the dash says, "Hey, listen to this!"

2. Technical Information

Parentheses are also used for including technical information within a text:

English poet William Cowper described the experience of tithing in "The Yearly Distress, or Tithing Time at Stock, in Essex" (circa 1780).

For years I never missed an issue of *Astounding* (now published as *Analog*).

Punctuation Notes

A. A complete sentence added parenthetically within another sentence has neither an opening capital letter nor end punctuation:

The long winters in North Dakota (newcomers quickly learn that March is a winter month) make spring a time of great joy.

B. When a complete sentence is enclosed in parentheses—one that is not embedded in another sentence—the terminal punctuation is within the parentheses:

I look forward to every month of the year. (February, I will admit, is short on saving graces, but at least it's short.) April is probably my favorite, with its clean spring air and promise of good times to come.

Period

1. Sentence End

The period marks the end of a declarative or imperative sentence:

It's raining. Close the window.

The period is omitted at the end of a sentence that is included within another sentence:

> Tim quit his job (he was always a rash young man) to follow Horace Greeley's advice and go West.

Note that the first word of the enclosed sentence is not capitalized.

2. Abbreviations

Abbreviations with internal periods have no space after the internal period.

> U.S.   S.Dak.   A.M.

Initials of personal names, however, retain the space:

> J. F. Kennedy   H. L. Mencken

The period is omitted after an abbreviation at the end of a sentence that has a period of its own:

> My publisher is part of Pearson Education, Inc.

The abbreviating period is retained before other end punctuation:

> Did you remember to bring the pillows, blankets, towels, etc.?

Question Marks

1. Terminal Punctuation

Use the question mark as terminal punctuation in all direct questions:

> Do you have anything to add?
> What can you tell me?
> He said what?

However, polite requests in the form of questions are often punctuated with the period:

> Would you mind opening the window.

2. Quotations

In punctuating quoted questions, include the question mark within the quotation marks:

> John asked, "Do you have anything to add?"

When a quoted statement is embedded at the end of a question, the question mark is outside the quotation marks:

> Who said, "Give me liberty or give me death"?

Note that the period is omitted from the quoted sentence.

When a quoted question is embedded in another question, only one question mark is used—and that one is inside the quotation marks:

> Did he ask you straight out, "Are you a shoplifter?"

Quotation Marks

1. For Direct Quotations

Use double quotation marks to indicate another person's exact words, both spoken and written:

> In 1943 Churchill told Stalin, "In war-time, truth is so precious that she should always be attended by a bodyguard of lies."

Notice that the quotation marks are outside the period. This system applies even when the quotation marks enclose a single word, such as a title:

> My father's favorite poem is Rudyard Kipling's "If."

However, quotation marks are placed inside semicolons and colons:

> She said, "Come to the party"; I had to turn her down.

2. Within Direct Quotations

Use single quotation marks when the quoted material is within a quoted passage:

> Describing the degeneracy of the nation in a letter to Joshua F. Speed, Lincoln wrote that "as a nation we began by declaring that 'all men are created equal.' We now practically read it 'all men are created equal except Negroes.'"

Notice that both the single and the double quotation marks are outside the period.

For quotation marks with questions, see the preceding section under "Question Marks."

3. For Special Terms

Single quotation marks are sometimes used to set off special terms. At the end of the sentence the closing mark is placed within the period:

> In Chapter 1 you learned the definition of 'categorical proposition'.

Semicolon

1. As a Conjunction

Use a semicolon to connect independent clauses in a compound sentence. You can think of the semicolon as having the connective force of the comma-plus-conjunction:

> The use of the semicolon indicates a close relationship between clauses; it gives the sentence a tight, separate-but-equal bond.

The semicolon can also be used with the conjunction:

> Great indeed is Fear; but it is not, as our military enthusiasts believe and try to make us believe, the only stimulus known for awakening the higher ranges of men's spiritual energy.
>
> —William James

2. In the Separation of a Series

Use semicolons to separate a series of structures that have internal punctuation:

> In this chapter we looked at three purposes underlying our punctuation system: syntactic, related to structure; prosodic, related to sentence rhythm; and semantic, related to meaning.

Glossary of Terms

For further explanation of the terms listed here, check the index for page references.

Absolute adjective. An adjective with a meaning that is generally not capable of being intensified or compared, such as *unique* or *perfect* or *square*. Careful writers avoid such usages as *very perfect* or *more unique*.

Absolute phrase. A noun phrase that includes a postnoun modifier and is related to the sentence as a whole, providing a detail or point of focus: "She sat quietly, *her hands folded in her lap.*"

Abstract noun. A noun that refers to a quality, such as peace or happiness, rather than a material, concrete object.

Active voice. A feature of transitive verb sentences in which the subject is generally the agent and the direct object is the goal or objective of the action. *Voice* refers to the relationship of the subject to the verb. See also *Passive voice.*

Adjectival. Any structure, no matter what its form, that functions as a modifier of a noun—that is, that functions as an adjective normally functions. See Chapter 9.

Adjective. One of the four form classes, whose members act as modifiers of nouns; most adjectives can be inflected for comparative and superlative degree *(big, bigger, biggest)*; they can be qualified or intensified *(rather big, very big)*; they have characteristic derivational affixes such as *–ous (famous), –ish (childish), –ful (graceful),* and *–ary (complementary).*

Adjective phrase. An adjective that includes a modifier: *very nice, afraid to fly.*

Adverb. One of the four form classes, whose members act as modifiers of verbs, contributing information of time, place, reason, manner, and the like. Like adjectives, certain adverbs can be qualified *(very quickly, rather fast)*; some can be inflected for comparative and superlative degree *(more quickly, fastest)*; they have characteristic derivational endings such as *–ly (quickly), –wise (lengthwise), –ward (backward).*

Adverbial. Any structure, no matter what its form, that functions as a modifier of a verb—that is, that functions as an adverb normally functions. See Chapter 8.

Agency. The relationship of the subject and verb. See also *Agent.*

Agent. The initiator of the action in the sentence—the "doer" or "perpetrator" of the action. Usually the agent is the subject in an active sentence: "*John* groomed the dog"; "*The committee* elected Pam." In a passive sentence the agent, if mentioned, will be the object of a preposition: "Pam was elected by *the committee.*"

Agreement. (1) Subject–verb. A third-person singular subject in the present tense takes the -*s* form of the verb: "*The dog barks* all night"; "*He bothers* the neighbors." A plural takes the base form: "*The dogs bark*"; "*They bother* the neighbors." (2) Pronoun–antecedent. The number of the pronoun (whether singular or plural) agrees with the number of its antecedent. "*The boys* did *their* chores"; "The *man who* works for us is on vacation." (Note that both *man* and *who* take the –*s* form of their verbs.)

Ambiguity. A condition in which a structure has more than one possible meaning. The source may be lexical ("She is *blue*") or structural ("*Visiting relatives* can be boring") or both ("The detective looked *hard*").

Anaphora. A figure of speech describing repetition at the beginning of successive sentences: "*Mad* world! *Mad* kings! *Mad* composition!" [Shakespeare]

Anastrophe. A figure of speech describing a reversal of the normal order of a sentence: *The rest of the story you know.*

Antecedent. The noun or nominal that a pronoun stands for.

Antithesis. The juxtaposition of contrasting ideas: "I come to bury Caesar, not to praise him."

Appositive. A structure, usually a noun phrase, that renames a nominal structure, that shares a nominal slot: "My neighbor, *a butcher at Weis Market,* recently lost his job."

Article. One of the determiner classes, including the indefinite *a,* or *an,* which signals only countable nouns, and the definite *the,* which can signal all classes of nouns.

Asyndeton. A figure of speech describing the omission of a conjunction: "*I came, I saw, I conquered.*"

Auxiliary verb. One of the structure-class words, a marker of verbs. Auxiliaries include forms of *have* and *be,* as well as the modals, such as *will, shall,* and *must.* See also Do-*support.*

Backgrounding. The process of placing known information, or perhaps less important information, in a subordinate role in the sentence rather than in a position of main focus. See also *Foregrounding.*

Broad reference. A pronoun that refers to a complete sentence rather than to a specific noun or nominal. The broad-reference clause is introduced by *which.* "Judd told jokes all evening, *which drove us crazy.*" The demonstrative pronouns *this* and *that* and the personal pronoun *it* are also sometimes used with broad reference: "Judd told jokes again last night; *that* really drives me crazy." Those sentences with demonstratives can be improved if the pronoun is turned into a determiner: "*That silly behavior of his* drives me crazy."

Case. A feature of nouns and certain pronouns that denotes their function in the sentence. Pronouns have three case distinctions: subjective (*I, they, who,* etc.), possessive (*my, their, whose,* etc.), and objective (*me, them, whom,* etc.). Nouns have only one case inflection, the possessive *(John's, the cat's).* The case of nouns other than the possessive is sometimes referred to as common case.

Categorical proposition. A proposition in which the predicate makes an assertion about the subject. It commonly takes the form of "X is Y" or "X is not Y": "Smoking is harmful to your health"; "Smoking is not harmful."

Clause. A structure with a subject and a predicate. The sentence patterns are clause patterns.

Cleft sentence. A sentence variation using an *it*-clause or *what*-clause to shift the sentence focus: "A careless bicyclist caused the accident" $\longrightarrow$ "It was a careless bicyclist who caused the accident"; "What caused the accident was a careless bicyclist."

Cliché. A worn-out word or phrase: "hard as nails"; "cute as a bug's ear."

Climax. The arrangement of a series of words, phrases, or clauses in order of importance.

Cohesion. The connections between sentences. Cohesive ties are furnished by pronouns that have antecedents in previous sentences, by adverbial connections, by known information, and by knowledge shared by the reader.

Collective noun. A noun that refers to a collection of individuals: *group, team, family.* Collective nouns can be replaced by either singular or plural pronouns, depending on the meaning.

Comma splice. The connection of two independent clauses in a compound sentence with a comma alone. Conventional punctuation requires a conjunction with the comma.

Command. See *Imperative sentence.*

Common noun. A noun with general, rather than unique, reference (in contrast to proper nouns). Common nouns may be countable *(house, book)* or noncountable *(water, oil)*; they may be concrete *(house, water)* or abstract *(justice, indifference).*

Comparative degree. See *Degree.*

Complement. A structure that "completes" the sentence. The term includes those slots in the predicate that complete the verb: direct object, indirect object, subject complement, and object complement. Certain adjectives also have complements—clauses and phrases that pattern with them: "I was *certain that he would come*"; "I was *afraid to go.*"

Complex sentence. A sentence that includes a dependent clause.

Compound-complex sentence. A sentence with two or more independent clauses and at least one dependent clause.

Compound sentence. A sentence with two or more independent clauses.

Conditional mood. The attitude of probability designated by the modal auxiliaries *could, may, might, would,* and *should.*

Conjunction. One of the structure classes, which includes connectors that coordinate structures of many forms (e.g., *and, or*), subordinate sentences (e.g., *if, because, when*), and coordinate sentences with an adverbial emphasis (e.g., *however, therefore*).

Conjunctive adverb. A conjunction that connects two independent clauses with an adverbial emphasis, such as *however, therefore, moreover,* and *nevertheless.*

Contraction. A combination of two words written or spoken as one, in which letters or sounds are omitted. In writing, the omission is marked by an apostrophe: *isn't, they're.*

Coordinating conjunction. A conjunction that connects two or more sentences or structures within a sentence as equals: *and, but, or, nor, for,* and *yet.*

Coordination. A way of expanding sentences in which two or more structures of the same form function as a unit. All the sentence slots and modifiers in the slots, as well as the sentence itself, can be coordinated.

Correlative conjunction. A two-part conjunction that expresses a relationship between the coordinated structures: *either–or, neither–nor, both–and, not only–but also.*

Countable noun. A noun whose referent can be identified as a separate entity; the countable noun can be signaled by the indefinite article, *a,* and by numbers: *a house; an experience; two eggs; three problems.* See also *Noncountable noun.*

Dangling modifier. A verb phrase placed so that it has no clear relationship to its subject, which is the word it should modify. The dangling participle occurs when the sentence subject is not also the subject of the sentence-opening or -closing participle: "*Wearing her new outfit,* everyone looked admiringly at Mary." Revised: "Wearing her new outfit, Mary was the center of attention."

Declarative sentence. A sentence in the form of a statement (in contrast to a command, a question, or an exclamation).

Definite article. The determiner *the,* which generally marks a specific or previously mentioned noun: "*the* man on *the* corner"; "*the* blue coat I want for Christmas."

Degree. The variations in adjectives and some adverbs that indicate the simple quality of a noun, or positive degree ("Bill is a *big* boy"); its comparison to another, the comparative degree ("Bill is *bigger* than Tom"); or its comparison to two or more, the superlative degree ("Bill is the *biggest* person in the whole class"). In most adjectives of two or more syllables, the comparative and superlative degrees are marked by *more* and *most,* respectively.

Demonstrative pronoun. The pronouns *this* (plural *these*) and *that* (plural *those*), which function as nominal substitutes and as determiners. They include the feature of proximity: near *(this, these)* and distant *(that, those).*

Dependent clause. A clause that functions as an adverbial, adjectival, or nominal (in contrast to an independent clause).

Derivational affix. A suffix or prefix that is added to a form-class word, either to change its class *(fame–famous; act–action)* or to change its meaning *(legal–illegal; boy–boyhood).*

Determiner. One of the structure-class words, a signaler of nouns. Determiners include articles *(a, the),* possessive nouns and pronouns (e.g., *Chuck's, his, my*), demonstrative pronouns *(this, that, these, those),* indefinite pronouns (e.g., *many, each, every*), and numbers.

Diction. The selection of words, usually referred to in connection with the correct choice of words in terms of their meaning and the appropriate choice in terms of the audience and purpose.

Direct address. A noun or noun phrase addressing a person or group: "*Ladies and gentlemen,* may I have your attention"; "Tell me, *dear,* what you're thinking." In traditional grammar, this noun is called a vocative.

Direct object. A nominal slot in the predicate of the transitive sentence patterns. The direct object names the objective or goal or the receiver of the verb's action: "We ate *the peanuts*"; "The boy hit *the ball*"; "I enjoy *playing chess.*"

***Do*-support.** The addition of the auxiliary *do* to a verb string that has no other auxiliary. The question, the negative, and the emphatic transformations all require an auxiliary. *Do* also substitutes for a repeated verb phrase in compound sentences: "Bryan liked the movie, and I *did* too."

Ellipsis. See *Elliptical clause.*

Elliptical clause. A clause in which a part has been left out but is "understood": "Chester is older *than I (am old)*"; "Bev can jog farther *than Otis (can jog)*"; "*When (you are) planning your essay,* be sure to consider the audience." Ellipsis can be an effective stylistic device.

End focus. The common rhythm pattern in which the prominent peak of stress falls on or near the final sentence slot.

Expletive. A word that enables the writer or speaker to shift the stress in a sentence or to embed one sentence in another: "A fly is in my soup" ⟶ "*There* is a fly in my soup"; "I know *that* he loves me." The expletive is sometimes called an "empty word" because it plays a structural rather than a lexical role in the sentence.

Figurative language. Language that expresses meaning in nonliteral terms, characterized by figures of speech, such as metaphors, similes, analogies, and personification.

Figure of speech. Stylistic variations, also called figurative language, including comparisons (metaphor, similes, analogy, personification) that help the reader understand the writer's message, along with structural variations, including repetition, parallelism, and antithesis.

Flat adverb. A class of adverb that is the same in form as its corresponding adjective: *fast, high, early, late, hard, long,* and so on.

Foregrounding. The placement of important information in the position of prominent focus. See also *Backgrounding.*

Form classes. The large, open classes of words that provide the lexical content of the language: nouns, verbs, adjectives, and adverbs. Each has characteristic derivational and inflectional affixes that distinguish its forms.

Fragment. A phrase or clause that is punctuated as a full sentence. Some are simply punctuation errors; others are used deliberately for special effects.

Free modifier. A modifying phrase or clause that opens or closes the sentence, generally expanding on the main idea. Participial phrases, absolute phrases, and resumptive modifiers are among common free modifiers.

Gerund. An *-ing* verb functioning as a nominal: "I enjoy *jogging*"; "*Running* is good exercise"; "After *getting* my pilot's license, I hope to fly to Lake Tahoe."

Headword. The word that fills the noun slot in the noun phrase: "the little *boy* across the street"; the verb that heads the verb phrase.

Hedging. One of the metadiscourse signals in which the writer expresses uncertainty or a qualification: *may, perhaps, under certain circumstances.*

Helping verb. See *Auxiliary verb.*

Idiom. A combination of words whose meaning cannot be predicted from the meaning of the individual words. Many phrasal verbs are idioms: *look up* [a word]; *put up with; back down; give in.*

Imperative sentence. The sentence in the form of a command. The imperative sentence includes the base form of the verb and usually an understood subject *(you):* "*Eat* your spinach"; "*Finish* your report as soon as possible"; "You *go* on without me."

Indefinite article. The determiner *a,* which marks an unspecified countable noun. See also *Definite article.*

Indefinite pronoun. A large category that includes quantifiers (e.g., *enough, several, many, much*), universals *(all, both, every, each),* and partitives (e.g., *any, anyone, anybody, either, neither, no, nobody, some, someone*). Many of the indefinite pronouns can function as determiners.

Independent clause. The main clause of the sentence; a compound sentence has more than one independent clause.

Indirect object. The nominal slot following verbs like *give.* The indirect object is the recipient; the direct object is the thing given: "We gave *our friends* a ride home."

Infinitive. The base form of the verb (present tense), usually expressed with *to,* which is called the "sign of the infinitive." The infinitive can function adverbially ("I stayed up all night *to study* for the exam"); adjectivally ("That is no way *to study*"); and nominally ("*To stay up* all night is foolish"). The only verb with an infinitive form separate from the present tense is *be.*

Infinitive phrase. A verb phrase headed by the infinitive that functions as an adjectival, adverbial, or nominal.

Inflections. Suffixes that are added to the form classes (nouns, verbs, adjectives, and adverbs) to change their grammatical role in some way. Nouns have two inflectional suffixes (*–s* plural and *'s* possessive); verbs have four (*–s, –ing, –ed,* and *–en*); adjectives and some adverbs have two (*–er* and *–est*). Pronouns also have inflectional endings.

Intensive reflexive pronoun. The function of the reflexive pronoun when it serves as an appositive to emphasize a noun or pronoun: "I *myself* prefer chocolate." See also *Reflexive pronoun.*

Intonation. The rhythmic pattern of a spoken sentence, affected by its stress and pitch and pauses.

Intransitive verb. A verb that requires no complement to be complete.

Irregular verb. Any verb in which the *–ed* and *–en* forms are not that of a regular verb; in other words, a verb in which the *–ed* and *–en* forms are not simply the addition of *–d, –ed,* or *–t* to the base form.

Isocolon. A figure of speech describing the repetition of grammatical forms: "government *of the people, by the people, and for the people."*

It-cleft. See *Cleft sentence.*

Known–new contract. The common feature of sentences in which old, or known, information (information that is repeated from an earlier sentence or paragraph to provide cohesion, often in the form of a pronoun or related word) will appear in the subject slot, with the new information in the predicate.

Levels of generality. A method of paragraph analysis based on the relationship of each sentence to its predecessor, as coordinate, subordinate, or superordinate.

Lexical cohesion. The continuity of text created by the use of related words, including pronouns, and the repetition of key words. Parallel structures are important components of lexical cohesion.

Lexical rule. The rules built into our lexicon, features of words that govern their ability to combine with other words; for example, only countable nouns can be signaled by the indefinite article, *a,* or by numbers.

Lexicon. The store of words—the internalized dictionary—that every speaker of the language has.

Linking verb. A verb that requires a subjective complement to be complete. *Be* is commonly used as a linking verb: "She *is* a freshman"; "She *seems* nice."

Main clause. See *Independent clause.*

Manner adverb. An adverb that answers the question of "how" or "in what manner" about the verb. Most manner adverbs are derived from adjectives with the addition of *–ly: quickly, merrily, candidly.*

Mass noun. See *Noncountable noun.*

Metadiscourse. Certain signals, such as connectors and hedges, that communicate and clarify the writer's attitude, the direction and purpose of the passage: *for example, in the first place, next.*

Metaphor. The nonliteral use of a word that allows the speaker or writer to attribute qualities of one thing to another for purposes of explanation or persuasion: the *war* on drugs, the *engine* of government, *sunset* legislation, *food* for thought.

Modal auxiliary. The auxiliaries *may/might, can/could, will/would, shall/should, must,* and *ought to.* The modals affect what is known as the mood of the verb, conveying probability, possibility, obligation, and the like. Other modallike verbs include *have to, be + going to,* and *dare.*

Nominal. Any structure that functions as a noun phrase normally functions—as subject, direct object, indirect object, object complement, subject complement, object of preposition, appositive.

Nominalization. The process of producing a noun by adding derivational affixes to another word class: *legalize–legalization; regulate–regulation; friendly–friendliness.* Often the sentence will be more effective when the verb is allowed to function as a verb rather than being turned into a noun.

Nominalized verb. See *Nominalization.*

Noncountable noun. A noun referring to what might be called an undifferentiated mass—such as *wood, water, sugar, glass*—or an abstraction—*justice, love, indifference.* Whether or not you can use the indefinite article, *a,* is probably the best test of countability: If you can, the noun is countable.

Nonrestrictive modifier. A modifier in the noun phrase that comments about the noun rather than defines it. Nonrestrictive modifiers following the noun are set off by commas. See also *Restrictive modifier.*

Noun. One of the four form classes, whose members fill the headword slot in the noun phrase. Most nouns can be inflected for plural and possessive *(boy, boys, boy's, boys').* Nouns have characteristic derivational endings, such as *–ion (action, compensation), –ment (contentment),* and *-ness (happiness).*

Noun phrase. The noun headword with all of its attendant pre- and postnoun modifiers. See Chapter 9.

Number. A feature of nouns and pronouns, referring to singular and plural.

Object complement. The slot following the direct object in Pattern 7 sentences, filled by an adjectival or a nominal. The object complement has two functions: (1) It completes the idea of the verb; and (2) it modifies (if an adjectival) or renames (if a nominal) the direct object: "I found the play *exciting*"; "We consider Pete *a good friend.*"

Object of preposition. The nominal slot—usually filled by a noun phrase—that follows the preposition to form a prepositional phrase.

Objective case. The role in the sentence of a noun phrase or pronoun when it functions as an object—direct object, indirect object, object complement, or object of a preposition. Although nouns do not have a special form for objective case, many of the pronouns do: Personal pronouns and the relative pronoun *who* have separate forms when they function as objects.

Parallelism. See *Parallel structure.*

Parallel structure. A coordinate structure in which all the coordinate parts are of the same grammatical form: "The stew *smells delicious* and *tastes even better*" (parallel verb phrases); "The entire cast gave *powerful* and *exciting* performances" (parallel adjectives); "I'll take either *a bus* or *a taxi*" (parallel noun phrases).

Participial phrase. An *–ing* or *–en* verb phrase functioning as an adjectival, the modifier of a noun.

Participle. The –*ing* (present participle) or –*en* (past participle) form of the verb. The term *participle* refers both to these forms of the verb and to their function as adjectivals.

Passive voice. A feature of transitive sentences in which the direct object (the objective or goal) is shifted to the subject position. The auxiliary *be* is used with the past participle form of the verb. The term *passive* refers to the relationship between the subject and the verb: "Ed ate the pizza" ⟶ "The pizza *was eaten* by Ed." See also *Active voice.*

Past participle. The –*en* form of the verb.

Past tense. The –*ed* form of the verb, usually denoting a specific past action.

Person. A feature of personal pronouns relating to point of view, the relationship of the writer or speaker to the reader or listener: It can refer to writer or speaker (first person), the person addressed (second person), and the person or thing spoken about (third person).

Personal pronoun. A pronoun referring to a specific person or thing: In the subjective case the personal pronouns are *I, you, he, she, we, you, they,* and *it.* The personal pronouns have different forms for objective and possessive case.

Personification. A figurative use of language in which a human attribute is applied to a nonhuman noun: *blind* justice, *friendly* rain.

Phrasal verb. A verb combined with a preposition-like word producing a meaning that cannot be predicted from the meaning of the separate parts: *look up, look up to, put up with, make up.*

Phrase. A word or combination of words that constitutes a unit of the sentence.

Plural-only noun. A noun that has no singular form: *shorts, trousers, slacks, scissors, clothes.*

Point of view. The relationship of the writer to the reader, as shown by the use of pronouns: first, second, and/or third person.

Polysyndeton. A figure of speech describing the addition of conjunctions in a series: I invited Harold *and* Joyce *and* Marv *and* Jean.

Positive degree. See *Degree.*

Possessive case. The inflected form of nouns *(John's, the dog's)* and pronouns *(my, his, your, her, their, whose, etc.),* usually indicating possession or ownership.

Power words. Words that have the power to make a difference in the emphasis and rhythm of a sentence, often affecting reader expectation as well.

Predicate. One of the two principal parts of the sentence, the comment made about the subject. The predicate includes the verb, together with its complements and modifiers.

Preposition. A structure-class word found in pre-position to—that is, preceding—a nominal. Prepositions can be classed according to their form as simple, or single-word (*above, at, in, with, of,* etc.), or phrasal (*according to, along with, instead of,* etc.).

Prepositional phrase. The combination of a preposition and its object. In form, the object of the preposition is usually a noun phrase ("After *my nap,* I'll clean the house"), but it can also be a verb phrase, a gerund ("After *cleaning the house,* I'll take a nap").

Present participle. The –*ing* form of the verb.

Present tense. The base form and the –*s* form of the verb: *help, helps.* The present tense denotes a present point in time ("I *understand* your position"), a habitual action ("I *jog* five miles a day"), or the "timeless" present ("Shakespeare *helps* us understand ourselves").

Pronoun. A word that substitutes for a noun—or, more accurately, for a nominal—in the sentence. See Chapter 12.

Proper noun. A noun with individual reference to a person, a geographic region or location, building, holiday, historical event, work of art or literature, and other such names. Proper nouns are capitalized.

Prosody. The study of the rhythm and intonation of language, which are determined by pitch, stress (loudness), and juncture (pauses).

Qualifier. A structure-class word that qualifies or intensifies an adjective or adverb: "We worked *rather* slowly"; "We worked *very* hard."

Reader expectation. An awareness by the writer of what the reader is expecting to read.

Reciprocal pronoun. The pronouns *each other* and *one another,* which refer to previously named nouns.

Redundancy. Unnecessary repetition.

Referent. The thing (or person, event, concept, action, etc.)—in other words, the reality—that a word stands for.

Reflexive pronoun. A pronoun formed by adding *–self* or *–selves* to a form of the personal pronoun, used as an object in the sentence to refer to a previously named noun or pronoun.

Regular verb. A verb in which the *–ed* form (the past tense) and the *–en* form (the past participle) are formed by adding *–ed* (or, in some cases, *–d* or *–t*) to the base. These two forms of a regular verb are always identical: "I *walked* home"; "I have *walked* home every day this week."

Relative adverb. The adverbs *where, when,* and *why,* which introduce adjectival (relative) clauses: "The town *where* I was born has only one traffic light."

Relative clause. A clause introduced by a relative pronoun *(who, which, that)* or a relative adverb *(when, where, why)* that modifies a noun: "The car *that Joe bought* is a lemon."

Relative pronoun. The pronouns *who (whose, whom), which,* and *that* in their role as introducers of relative (adjectival) clauses.

Repetition. A technique for strengthening the continuity of text with key words. Repetition is especially important in parallel structures.

Restrictive modifier. A modifier in the noun phrase whose function is to restrict, or define, the meaning of the noun. A modifier is restrictive when it is needed to identify the referent of the headword. The restrictive modifier is not set off by commas. See also *Nonrestrictive modifier.*

Resumptive modifier. A modifier at the end of the sentence that repeats and elaborates on a word from the main clause: "The IRS often intimidates people without cause, *intimidates and harasses them.*"

Rhythm. The intonation contour of valleys and peaks in the spoken language, characterized by variations in stress, pitch, and juncture (pauses).

Run-on sentence. A compound sentence without a proper connection between independent clauses. See *Comma splice.* The term is also used for sentences that go on too long, even though their punctuation may be correct.

Second person. See *Person.*

Semantics. The study of the meaning of words and sentences.

Sentence. A word or group of words based on one or more subject–predicate, or clause, patterns. The written sentence begins with a capital letter and ends with terminal punctuation—a period, a question mark, or an exclamation point.

Sentence fragment. A part of a sentence—often a noun phrase, verb phrase, or subordinate clause—punctuated as a complete sentence.

Sentence patterns. The simple skeletal sentences, made up of two or three or four required elements, that underlie our sentences, even the most complex among them. The seven patterns listed in Chapter 1 account for almost all of the possible sentences of English.

Sequence of tenses. The difference in verb tenses that appear in a sentence with more than one clause.

Serial comma. The comma that is used before the conjunction in a series: "On our fishing trip to Alaska, we caught salmon, halibut, *and* the elusive Arctic grayling." Some publications, as a matter of policy, omit the serial comma.

Series. Three or more words, phrases, or clauses that act as a unit.

Sexism. The long-standing tradition of the language, which is now undergoing change, in which the masculine pronoun is used in a general sense, to include the feminine; and the word *man* is used to mean "human being" or "people": "All *men* are created equal."

Simile. A comparison that uses *like* or *as:* "My love is *like a red, red rose*" (Robert Burns).

Stative. A quality of nouns, verbs, and adjectives that refers to a relatively permanent state, as opposed to a changing condition. A stative verb is not generally used in the *–ing* form: We would say, "I resemble my mother," not "I am resembling my mother." A stative noun would not be linked by an *–ing* verb: We would say, "He is a mechanic," not "He is being a mechanic."

Stress. See *Prosody.*

Structure classes. The small, closed classes of words that explain the grammatical or structural relationships of the form classes. The major ones are determiners, auxiliaries, qualifiers, prepositions, conjunctions, and expletives.

Style. A writer's manner of expression, influenced by word choice, sentence length and complexity, figurative language, tone, and other sentence features.

Subject. The opening slot in the sentence patterns, filled by a noun phrase or other nominal structure, that functions as the topic of the sentence.

Subject complement. The nominal or adjectival that follows a linking verb, renaming or describing the subject ("Pam is *the president*"). In the passive voice the transitive sentence with an object complement (Pattern 7) will have a subject complement: "We elected Pam president" ⟶ "Pam was elected *president.*"

Subject–verb agreement. See *Agreement.*

Subjective case. The role in the sentence of a noun phrase or a pronoun when it functions as the subject of the sentence. Personal pronouns have distinctive inflected forms for subjective case: *I, he, she, they,* and so on. And in the subject complement slot, a pronoun will be in the subjective case. The relative pronoun *who* is also subjective-case—*whose* (possessive), *whom* (objective).

Subjunctive mood. An expression of the verb in which the base form, rather than the inflected form, is used (1) in certain *that* clauses conveying strong suggestions or resolutions or commands ("We suggest that Mary *go* with us"; "I move that the meeting *be* adjourned"; "I demand that you *let* us in") and (2) in the expression of wishes or conditions contrary to fact ("If I *were* you, I'd be careful"; "I wish it *were* summer"). The subjunctive of the verb *be* is expressed by *were*, or *be*, even for subjects that normally take *is* or *was*.

Subordinate clause. A dependent clause introduced by a subordinating conjunction. It is also called an adverbial clause. "I was sad *when he left.*" (Note: In some descriptions of grammar, the term *subordinate clause* is synonymous with *dependent clause.*)

Subordinating conjunction. A conjunction that introduces an adverbial, or subordinate, clause expressing the relationship of the clause to the main clause. Among the most common are *after, although, as, as long as, as soon as, because, before, even though, if, provided that, since, so that, though, till, until, when, whenever, whereas, while.*

Subordinator. A conjunction that turns a sentence into a dependent clause. See *Subordinating conjunction.*

Summative modifier. A modifier—usually a noun phrase—at the end of the sentence that sums up the idea of the main clause: The teacher canceled class on the Friday before spring break, *a decision that was greeted with unanimous enthusiasm.*

Superlative degree. See *Degree.*

Syntax. The way in which the words of the language are put together to form the structural units, the phrases and clauses, of the sentence.

Tense. A grammatical feature of verbs and auxiliaries relating to time. Tense is designated by an inflectional change *(walked)*, by an auxiliary *(will walk)*, or both *(am walking, have walked)*.

***There*-transformation.** A variation of a basic sentence in which the expletive *there* is added at the beginning and the subject is shifted to a position following *be:* "A fly is in my soup" ⟶ *"There is a fly in my soup."*

Third person. See *Person.*

Tone. The writer's attitude toward the reader and the text: serious, formal, tongue-in-cheek, sarcastic, casual, and so on.

Transitive verb. The verbs of Patterns 5, 6, and 7, which require at least one complement, the direct object, to be complete. With only a few exceptions, transitive verbs are those that can be transformed into the passive voice.

Verb. One of the four form classes, traditionally thought of as the action word in the sentence. A better way to recognize the verb, however, is by its form. Every verb, without exception, has an *–s* and an *–ing* form; every verb also has an *–ed* and an *–en* form, although in the case of some irregular verbs these forms are not readily apparent. And every verb, without exception, can be marked by auxiliaries. Many verbs also have characteristic derivational forms, such as *–ify (typify)*, *–ize (criticize)*, and *–ate (activate)*. See Chapter 7.

Verb phrase. A verb together with its complements and modifiers; the predicate of the sentence is a verb phrase.

Vocative. See *Direct address.*

Voice. The relationship of the subject to the verb. See also *Active voice* and *Passive voice.*

***What*-cleft.** See *Cleft sentence.*

Bibliography

In the following books and articles, you can read further about some of the topics you have studied here.

Categorical Propositions
Jeanne Fahnestock and Marie Secor, *A Rhetoric of Argument,* 2nd ed. (New York: McGraw-Hill, 1990)

Cohesion
Jeanne Fahnestock, "Semantic and Lexical Coherence," *College Composition and Communication* 34 (1983): 400–416
M. A. K. Halliday and Ruqaiya Hasan, *Cohesion in English* (London: Longman, 1976)
William J. Vande Kopple, "Functional Sentence Perspective, Composition, and Reading," *College Composition and Communication* 33 (1982): 50–63

Comprehensive Grammar
Randolph Quirk, Sidney Greenbaum, Geoffrey Leech, Jan Svartvik, *A Comprehensive Grammar of the English Language* (New York: Longman, 1985)

Figures of Speech
Edward P. J. Corbett, *Classical Rhetoric for the Modern Student,* 2nd ed. (New York: Oxford University Press, 1971)
Arthur Quinn, *Figures of Speech: 60 Ways to Turn a Phrase* (Davis, CA: Hermagoras Press, 1993)

Grammar and Writing Instruction
Susan Hunter and Ray Wallace, eds., *The Place of Grammar in Writing Instruction: Past, Present, Future* (Portsmouth, NH: Boynton/Cook, 1995)
Rei Noguchi, *Grammar and the Teaching of Writing: Limits and Possibilities* (Urbana, IL: National Council of Teachers of English, 1991)
Constance Weaver, *Teaching Grammar in Context* (Portsmouth, NH: Boynton/Cook, 1996)
English Journal: Three grammar issues: May 2006, January 2003, and November 1996

Grammar Research
Noguchi (cited under "Grammar and Writing Instruction")
Pinker (cited under "Language Development")

Grammar Theory
George L. Dillon, *Constructing Texts* (Bloomington: Indiana University Press, 1981)

History of Grammar Rules
Brock Haussamen, *Revising the Rules: Traditional Grammar and Modern Linguistics,* 2nd ed. (Dubuque, IA: Kendall/Hunt, 1997)

Language Development
Jean Berko Gleason, *The Development of Language,* 4th ed. (Boston: Allyn and Bacon, 1997)
Steven Pinker, *The Language Instinct: How the Mind Creates Language* (New York: HarperCollins, 1994)

Levels of Generality
Francis Christensen, *Notes Toward a New Rhetoric: Six Essays for Teachers* (New York: Harper and Row, 1967)

Metadiscourse
Xiaoguang Cheng and Margaret S. Steffensen, "Metadiscourse: A Technique for Improving Student Writing," *Research in the Teaching of English* 30 (1996): 149–181
Avon Crismore, *Talking to Readers: Metadiscourse as Rhetorical Act* (New York: Peter Lang, 1989)
William Vande Kopple, "Some Exploratory Discourse on Metadiscourse," *College Composition and Communication* 36 (1985): 82–93

Modern Grammar
Martha Kolln and Robert Funk, *Understanding English Grammar,* 7th ed. (New York: Longman, 2006)

Punctuation
Christensen (cited under "Levels of Generality")
Robert J. Connors and Andrea A. Lunsford, "Frequency of Formal Errors in Current College Writing, or Ma and Pa Kettle Do Research," *College Composition and Communication* 39 (1988): 395–409
Charles F. Meyer, *A Linguistic Study of American Punctuation* (New York: Peter Lang, 1987)

Style
Corbett (cited under "Figures of Speech")
Keith Grant-Davie, "Functional Redundancy and Ellipsis as Strategies in Reading and Writing," *Journal of Advanced Composition* 15 (1995): 455–469

Answers to the Exercises

Chapter 1
Exercise 1, page 10
  1. teacher / is
  3. weasel / simply
  5. I / are
  7. Sojourner / was

Exercise 2, page 14
  1. The bus from Flagstaff / arrived/ at two o'clock (P 4)
  3. The…grill / smells / wonderful (P 3)
  5. AD / is / a…nature (P 2)
  7. Our…meeting / is / in the library (P 1)

Exercise 3, page 20
  1. Sometimes / a weasel / lives / in his den / for two days / without leaving
  3. Very soon / the issue / simply / disappeared / from…agenda
  5. [You] / wash / your hands / thoroughly / after…chemicals
  7. Jen / worked / steadily / in the lab / throughout the night / to finish her project before…deadline / before…deadline
  9. Everyone / smiles / in…language

Exercise 4, page 22
Active to Passive:
  1. The Memorial Arch in St. Louis was designed by Eero Saarinen.
  3. Our flight may be delayed by the storm.
  5. We could have been given clearer directions by the teacher.
Passive to Active:
  1. A falling tree damaged our garage roof.
  3. [We] must complete all of the lab experiments before the midterm exam.
  5. [People] have called outer space the last frontier.

Exercise 5, page 25
  1. In 1747 / a physician in the British Navy / conducted / an experiment / to discover a cure for scurvy. (P 5)

3. Dr. James Lind / fed / six groups of scurvy victims / six different remedies. (P 6)
5. Although ... findings, / it / finally / ordered / a daily dose of fresh lemon juice / for every British seaman. (P 6)
7. The British / called / lemons / "limes" / in the eighteenth century. (P 7)

Chapter 3
Exercise 7, page 41

1. Japanese blue-collar workers not only work more hours per day than American workers, they typically do so with more dedication and energy.
3. In the U.S. neither blue-collar workers nor students spend as much time at their respective jobs as do their Japanese counterparts.
5. Julie earned an A both in the final exam and in the course.
7. Not only did the chairman of the Planning Commission refuse to let the citizen's committee present their petition, he also refused to recognize them when they attempted to speak out at the meeting.
9. My history professor wouldn't let me take a make-up exam when I cut his class, nor would he accept my late paper.

Exercise 8, page 50

1. child, but
3. small, but
5. lounge, so empty; now (*or* empty. Now)
7. pianists; they've (*or* pianists. They've)
9. no punctuation

Exercise 9, page 57

1. dance, and / agile; but [or agile, but] / happy, so
3. habit, and, like ... habits, / acquired; however, it
5. smooth, but / right; it [or right. It]
7. equipment: the / paper; the / understand; and
9. legislators. They [or legislators; they]

Exercise 10, page 60

Here are some of the problems:

1. unparallel verb phrases: *to swim* and *jogging*
3. unparallel verb phrases: *enjoy flying* and *want to take*
5. unparallel ideas: One should be subordinated.
7. *Either* introduces a noun phrase, *or* a full sentence.

Chapter 4
Exercise 11, page 72

1. At the edge of the Mississippi River in St. Louis stands the Gateway Arch, the world's tallest monument. The stainless steel structure, designed by Eero Saarinen, commemorates the Westward Movement.
3. [No change in the first sentence.] It's not unusual for the temperature to reach 110° in Bakersfield, often the hottest spot in the valley. [Note that *summer* in the first sentence makes *June through September* redundant.]

5. Except for Boston's Fenway Park, Pittsburgh's new baseball stadium, PNC Park, is the smallest in the major leagues, with 38,127 seats. It was named by Pittsburgh-based PNC Bank Corporation. For the privilege of naming it, they will pay $1.5 million a year for twenty years. The opening date was April 9, 2001.

Exercise 12, page 76

1. The contractor for our house is obviously skeptical about solar energy, an attitude that doesn't surprise me. *or* It doesn't surprise me that the contractor ... energy. (Note: In this second rewrite, *obviously* would probably be omitted.)
3. Even though I know I should give up junk food to get in shape for summer, that kind of self-discipline isn't easy for me.
5. I would avoid a lot of frustration if I took time to study my computer manual.
7. My friend Abe ... Lake Erie. That scare, I assume, is the reason he became....

Exercise 13, page 84

Here's how you might begin the restaurant ad:

1. After all, people are different. Food preferences are different. Schedules are different. Some people have no time for lunch. Some have hours to spend. Some make mealtimes social occasions. Some gulp and get going. Some are vegetarians. Some require red meat....

Chapter 5

Exercise 14, page 92

There are, of course, no "right" and "wrong" answers for the question of main stress. The answers here are based on my readings of the passages—words that are likely candidates for strong stress:

1. Sentence 1. <u>understand</u> and <u>salesperson</u>; 2. <u>buyer, sellee</u>; 3. <u>want, vacuum, buy</u>; 4. <u>else, selling</u>
3. Sentence 1. <u>history, particularly, cancer</u>; 2. <u>fight, crusade, killer, victims</u>; 3. <u>culprit</u>; 4. <u>patient</u>; 5. <u>ill, ill, well</u>; 6. <u>disease, enemy, not, lethal, shameful</u>

Exercise 15, page 97

1. It's chocolate ice cream that Jody loves. / What Jody loves is chocolate ice cream.
3. It was our defense that won the Stanford game in the final three minutes with a crucial interception. / It was in the final three minutes that our defense won the Stanford game with a crucial interception. / It was in the Stanford game that the defense won with a crucial interception in the final three minutes. / There was a crucial interception in the final three minutes that won the Stanford game for us.
5. There was a month of unseasonably warm weather last winter that almost ruined the ski season. / It was last winter that a month of unseasonably warm weather almost ruined the ski season. / What almost ruined the ski season last winter was that month of unseasonably warm weather we had.
7. It was lightning that caused many of the forest fires. / What caused many of the forest fires was lightning. / There were many forest fires caused by the lightning.

Chapter 6

Exercise 16, page 110
Remember! You won't be using the word *snafu!*

Exercise 17, page 118
- A. Here are some possibilities for the first five in the list: turn down/reject; bring about/cause; bring on/induce; put up with/tolerate; stand for/represent, tolerate
- B. 1. suggest, offer, propose 3. replacing with, transforming into 5. establishes, creates, produces 7. consider 9. replaces/represents

Exercise 18, page 126
1. Yesterday I set out to catch the new season, and instead I found an old snakeskin. I was in the sunny February woods by the quarry; the snakeskin was lying in a heap of leaves right next to an aquarium someone had thrown away. I don't know why that someone hauled the aquarium deep into the woods to get rid of it; it had only one broken glass side. The snake found it handy, I imagine; snakes like to rub against something rigid to help them out of their skins, and the broken aquarium looked like the nearest likely object. Together the snakeskin and the aquarium made an interesting scene on the forest floor. It looked like an exhibit at a trial—circumstantial evidence—of a wild scene, as though a snake had burst through the broken side of the aquarium, burst … beauty.

   The snakeskin had unkeeled scales, so it belonged to a nonpoisonous snake. It was roughly five feet long by the yardstick, but I'm not sure because it was very wrinkled and dry, and every time I tried to stretch it flat it broke. I ended up with seven or eight pieces of….

Chapter 7

Exercise 20, page 137
Active to Passive:
1. The lead article in today's *Collegian* was written by my roommate.
3. The most expensive houses in town are built by my brother-in-law.
5. Every four years a new tax-collection system is tried out.
7. The Gulf Coast was devastated by Hurricane Katrina in 2005.

Passive to Active:
1. The cheerleading squad led the football team onto the field.
3. Someone burglarized Bill's apartment last weekend.
5. We will hold the election of student body officers on Tuesday.
7. The police are keeping the suspect in solitary confinement.

Either:
1. We elected John Kennedy president in 1960. (Passive to Active)
3. The next six chapters should be read before Monday. (A to P)
5. Manufacturing companies have moved thousands of jobs to Mexico. (P to A)

7. The courts have sent a number of executives from those companies to prison. (P to A)

9. A new vacation schedule is being tried out this year by our company. (A to P)

Exercise 22, page 143

1. Investors on Wall Street are concerned because the Japanese are buying so many American companies and so much real estate.

3. Analysts of the situation in China agree that opportunities for investment are growing.

5. When Julie applied for a work-study job, she was surprised to learn that her parents would have to submit a detailed financial statement.

7. The overuse of salt in the typical American diet obscures the natural taste of many foods. Nutritionists maintain that if people reduced their dependence on salt they would find their food tastier and more enjoyable.

Exercise 23, page 146

1. The small band of rebels *resisted* the army patrol for several hours, then *surrendered* just before dawn. News reports about the event did not *specify* how many troops were involved.

3. Several economists are saying that they *anticipate* an upturn…. Others, however, maintain that interest rates must *stabilize* if….

5. The chairman…*denounced* the practice…. He said that the new rules will *eliminate* all such questionable fund raising. To some observers, such practices *signify* [or *constitute*] bribery. Several senators have promised to *formulate* a new compromise plan.

Chapter 8

Exercise 26, page 160

(*Note:* You may have come up with even tighter versions using other kinds of modifiers.)

1. Even though the famous Gateway Arch is in St. Louis, it is Kansas City that claims the title "Gateway to the West."

3. Thomas Jefferson acquired the Ozark Mountains for the United States when he negotiated the Louisiana Purchase with Napoleon in 1803.

5. When the neighbors added a pit bull to their pet population, now numbering three unfriendly four-legged creatures, we decided to fence in our backyard.

7. Fad diets that severely restrict the intake of carbohydrates are not only ineffective, they are often dangerous, because carbohydrates are the body's prime source of energy.

Exercise 27, page 164

1. Sift the flour before mixing in the dry ingredients.

3. The police had no doubt about the suspect's guilt after finding his fingerprints at the scene of the crime.

5. If your term project is late, the grade will be lowered ten percent.

7. I was amazed by the generosity of strangers while collecting money for the hurricane victims.

9. When you revise and edit your papers, be sure to read the sentences aloud and listen to the stress patterns.

Exercise 28, page 167

1. *To save money* (infinitive/reason); *often* (adverb/frequency); *at my desk* (prep phr/place)
3. *After ... navy* (clause/time); *from the navy* (prep phr/place)
5. *As soon as the guests left* (clause/time); *in a heap* (prep phr/manner), *on the couch* (prep phr/place)
7. *When October came* (clause/time)
9. *slowly* (adverb/manner); *northward* (adverb/direction)
11. *home* (noun/place); *last night* (noun phr/time); *because of the snowstorm* (prep phr/reason)

Exercise 29, page 169

1. Ben was so *meticulous*....
3. The foreman gives his orders in a *brusque* manner.
5. It is usually *futile* to argue....
7. The basketball players looked *exhaused [fatigued]*....
9. The choir members were *thrilled [enthusiastic]*....

Chapter 9

Exercise 30, page 177

1. The administration's recent clean-air proposals have been criticized as inadequate, not only by ...
3. The stock market reached an all-time high last week and, if inflation can be kept in check, will probably keep going up.
5. A big yellow delivery truck is blocking the driveway, and its driver....
7. I found an expensive-looking copper-colored bracelet....
9. I have back-to-back exams on Wednesday.

Exercise 31, page 185

1. Having endured rain all week, we weren't surprised by the miserable weather on Saturday. [or "we weren't surprised when the weather turned miserable on Saturday."]
3. We were not at all surprised when the Republican county commisioner, known for her conservative views..., announced her candidacy....
5. After I spent nearly all day in the kitchen, everyone agreed....
7. Obviously intimidated by a long history of defeats in Morgantown, our basketball team just can't seem to beat the Virginia Mountaineers on their home court.

Exercise 32, page 190

1. Sentence 2: ... contract, expiring ...
3. ... husband, sitting ... platform, both.... Then the mayor, turning ...senator, shocked....

Exercise 33, page 190

1. Citizens in many parts of the country, mobilizing against crime and drugs, are driving drug dealers out of their neighborhoods.

   or

   ...are mobilizing to drive drug dealers out of their neighorhoods.

3. The computer has revolutionized the storage and retrieval of fingerprints, which have been used for criminal identification since 1891, when a police officer in Argentina introduced the method.

5. In 1997 an earthquake that struck the Assisi region of Italy destroyed many priceless fourteenth-century mosaics decorating the walls and ceiling of the Basilica of St. Francis.

   or

   In 1997 an earthquake struck the Assisi region of Italy, destroying many priceless mosaics from the fourteenth century, which decorated the walls and ceiling of the Basilica of St. Francis.

7. The amount of carbon dioxide in the air affects the rate of colon cancer because carbon dioxide absorbs ultraviolet light, which fuels the body's production of vitamin D.

9. We cannot build up our immunity to flu viruses because they mutate constantly, producing new varieties that spread from person to person and from place to place.

Exercise 34, page 193

1. My roommate's announcement that she is planning to withdraw from school came as a complete surprise.

   or

   When my roommate told me she is planning to withdraw from school, I was completely surprised.

3. Converting the central card catalog in the college library to a computer system took over four years.

5. Harriett was rather unhappy when Wendell didn't want to stay for the second half of the game.

7. When the president characterized the last two years as a period of "unprecedented prosperity" in his State of the Union message, one economist immediately labeled his statement "sheer hype and hyperbole."

Exercise 36, page 206

1. The cost of repairs to the nation's public transportation facilities—roads, bridges, and railroads—is an expenditure that cannot be delayed much longer if the system is to survive.

3. Since the early 1980s, a Chinese ban on the import of certain American goods, such as cotton, synthetic fibers, and soybeans, has had an adverse effect on the U.S. economy—especially on the farmers.

5. In recent years there have been documented sightings of one of our rarest birds, the ivory-billed woodpecker—North America's largest woodpecker.

Chapter 10

Exercise 38, page 215

Here are some examples:

1. My sister, who is one of the most conservative people I know, surprised everyone at the family reunion when she showed up in a 1920s-style dress trimmed with beads and feathers, her normally blonde hair dyed red.

3. At the far end of the diner's chrome and plastic counter sat a trucker, an old man with long grey hair, his leathery face a pattern of creases and scars, his fringed jacket worn nearly through at the elbows.

Chapter 11

Exercise 40, page 244

For those sentences that are ungrammatical, the corrected form is supplied.

1. The <u>statement</u> ... <u>was</u> ...

3. Apparently the <u>use</u> of robots ... <u>has</u> ...

5. The government's deregulation <u>policy</u> ... <u>has</u> ...

7. Correct

9. Carmen's <u>collection</u> ... <u>was</u> ...

Exercise 41, page 248

1. grief, grieve, grievous, grievously

3. ability, enable, able, ably

5. quickness, quicken, quick, quickly

7. type, typify, typical, typically

9. critic (criticism/critique), criticize (critique), critical, critically

11. appreciation, appreciate, appreciable, appreciably

13. acceptance (acceptability), accept, acceptable, acceptably

15. stealth, steal, stealthy, stealthily

Chapter 12

Exercise 42, page 255

1. If you are an average American, the energy problem is mainly your monthly fuel bill and the cost of filling up the gas tank. You may also remember that in 1979, and way back in 1974, you had to wait ... [etc.]

Exercise 43, page 264

1. Claire has always been interested in children and, when she graduates, plans to work with them. Both she and I are majoring in early childhood education.

3. When..., I had no idea Beth was sick.... Our grandmother took one look at her and called the doctor, then drove her to the hospital. That decision turned out to be a good one: Beth's cramps turned out to be appendicitis.

Exercise 44, page 267

1. I recall with great pleasure the good times that we had at our annual family reunions when I was young. With our cousins and younger aunts and uncles, we played volleyball and softball until dark. Those games were a lot of fun.

3. It seemed to my cousin Terry and me that the grownups were different people at those family reunions. Such memories of family reunions may be true for people everywhere.

Chapter 13
Exercise 45, page 280

1. Management is still taught in most business schools as a bundle of techniques, such as budgeting and personnel relations. To be sure, management, like any other work, has its own tools and its own techniques. But just as the essence of medicine is not urinalysis (important though that is), the essence of management is not techniques and procedures. The essence of management is to make knowledge productive. Management, in other words, is a social function. And in its practice management is truly a liberal art. [*Note:* If you put a comma after *practice* in the last sentence, you have improved on the original! A comma would make the sentence easier to read.]

   The old communities—family, village, parish, and so on—have all but disappeared in the knowledge society. Their place has largely been taken by the new unit of social integration, the organization. Where community was fate, organization is voluntary membership. Where community claimed the entire person, organization is a means to a person's ends, a tool. For 200 years a hot debate has been raging, especially in the West: are communities "organic" or are they simply extensions of the people of which they are made? Nobody would claim that the new organization is "organic." It is clearly an artifact, a creation of man, a social technology.

2. The charter school movement is not yet big. Just 11 states, beginning with Minnesota in 1991, have passed laws permitting the creation of autonomous public schools like Northland; a dozen more have similar laws in the works. Most states have restricted the number of these schools—100 in California, 25 in Massachusetts—in an attempt to appease teachers' unions and other opponents. Nevertheless, the charter movement is being heralded as the latest and best hope for a public education system that has failed to deliver for too many children and cannot compete internationally.

   A handful, of other places—notably Baltimore, Maryland, and Hartford, Connecticut—are experimenting with a far more radical way to circumvent bureaucracy: hiring a for-profit company to run the schools.

Index